A Knife
in the
Heart

A Knife
in the
Heart

MICHAEL
BENSON

PINNACLE BOOKS
Kensington Publishing Corp.
http://www.kensingtonbooks.com

PINNACLE BOOKS are published by

Kensington Publishing Corp.
119 West 40th Street
New York, NY 10018

All Kensington Titles, Imprints, and Distributed Lines are available at special quantity discounts for bulk purchases for sales promotions, premiums, fund-raising, and educational or institutional use. Special book excerpts or customized printings can also be created to fit specific needs. For details, write or phone the office of the Kensington special sales manager: Kensington Publishing Corp., 119 West 40th Street, New York, NY 10018, attn: Special Sales Department, Phone: 1-800-221-2647.

Pinnacle and the P logo Reg. U.S. Pat. & TM Off.

ISBN-13: 978-0-7860-2760-6
ISBN-10: 0-7860-2760-6

First Printing: March 2012

10 9 8 7 6 5 4 3 2 1

Printed in the United States of America

ACKNOWLEDGMENTS

Many of my sources for this book have asked to remain anonymous, and so I can only thank them privately. The others I would like to acknowledge here, for without them the writing of this book would have been impossible: Cecilia Barreda, spokesperson for the Pinellas County Sheriff's Office (PCSO); Connie Y. Brookes, legal assistant with the Hebert Law Group; the eagle-eyed production editor Robin Cook; Lane DeGregory, at the *St. Petersburg Times;* Stephanie Finnegan; Laura Forti, at Turner Broadcasting; Lisa Lafrance; Detective/Corporal Michael Lynch, of the Pinellas Park Police Department (PPPD); counselor/therapist Kathy A. Morelli; Jamie Severino; Erin Slothower; and Jan Zagorski, senior administrative clerk, Pinellas Park Police; and Rachel Wade. Thanks to Anne Darrigan for the emergency (and marathon) use of her computer.

Also, special thanks to my agent, Jake Elwell, at Harold Ober Associates, to my super editor and "Man of Ideas," Gary Goldstein, and as always to my wife, Lisa Grasso.

AUTHOR'S NOTE

Although this is a true story, some names will be changed to protect the privacy of the innocent. Pseudonyms will be noted upon their first usage. When possible, the spoken word has been quoted verbatim. However, when that is not possible, conversations have been reconstructed as closely as possible to reality, based on the recollections of those who spoke and heard the words. In places, there has been a slight editing of spoken words, but only to improve readability. The denotations and connotations of the words remain unaltered. In some cases, witnesses are credited with verbal quotes that in reality only occurred in written form.

FOREWORD

This is youth's sub-rosa culture, an MTV world of shallow who-did-whom lives, a tinderbox world—one spark: senseless violence. Pinellas Park, Florida, had long stopped being a Norman Rockwell world, replaced by a new generation of tender savages, unsupervised, enflamed by sex and drugs, running wild in the streets.

Regarding a teenaged girl's violent death, a writer asked an early investigator: "Was this a love triangle?"

"More like a love hexagon," the overworked peace officer replied. Promiscuity-plus. Made you feel like you had to spit the bad taste from your mouth. How did it turn so tragic?

It all boiled down to Rachel Marie Wade. She was the catalyst. It wasn't her lust, although there was plenty of that. Under any analysis, the driving force wasn't the diminutive blonde's humming libido as much as her nineteen-year-old mind, her *feverish* mind, stuck in self-centered overdrive.

She'd known many boys, and it always ended *bad.* Ex-boyfriends had been known to piss on her mom and dad's front door!

Now there was Joshua Camacho, who was not just her boyfriend again, but *hers,* her possession. If other girls didn't get that, if they wouldn't listen to the *truth,* drastic measures would need to be taken.

There was a spot between Rachel's eyes that went supernova when she thought of her rival: eighteen-year-old Sarah Ludemann, who was decidedly *not diminutive,* who thought she was *all that* when she was with Joshua.

All that! Ha!

Sarah was nothing, Rachel thought: she was less than zero, just an opening act, a fat body to warm up Rachel's man so Rachel could get the real loving.

Sarah had to use her parents' car. Rachel had her own car.

Sarah still lived at home. Rachel had her own place.

Sarah had a curfew. Rachel could give her man what he wanted at *any hour*. She could offer him anything, any day of the week, 24/7—just as long as she wasn't waitressing at Applebee's.

After months of trying to talk sense, Rachel was through talking. Finally the two were going to have it out. Leaning tough-girl-style against the snout of her car, Rachel heard the racing minivan before she saw it. A 2000 green-over-gold Villager, it tore around the corner, almost on two wheels, like in that movie *Tokyo Drift*. It screeched to a halt only a few feet in front of her.

The moment was upon her. This was for Joshua, so good at making her feel special, so good at mind games. Um, when he screwed with a little girl's mind, it stayed *sca-rewed.*

Rachel tried to act cool, but everyone knew the number Joshua had done on Rachel. She said he'd held a gun to her head. "You'll never leave me. You'll never leave me," he'd said, repeating it like a mantra. She got the picture: Joshua gave the orders. Rachel obeyed. In the bedroom. Outside the bedroom. Wherever.

Some of Rachel's girlfriends had told her to get away from Joshua. They said that the slave master hold he had on her wasn't healthy, and he wasn't worth it.

Rachel didn't listen. Those girls, Rachel thought, didn't

know what they were talking about; they had never been *alone with Joshua.* They hadn't felt his complete and utter tautness. They didn't know how he could make Rachel feel. He made her melt down like a nuclear reactor.

Rachel said he'd told her: "If you love me enough, you'll fight for me." Well, bring it on—Rachel was ready. Rachel Wade did not make idle threats, and Rachel Wade did not back down. In her sweaty right hand, she tightly gripped the handle of a kitchen knife. . . .

Sarah Ludemann's world consisted of home, with her mom and dad, three big people in a little house, doing stuff with Joshua Camacho, and the halls of Pinellas Park High School (PPHS), where Sarah was a recent transfer student and a senior.

She had almost finished a veterinary program at another high school, but she dropped it and transferred to Pinellas Park High so she could be with Joshua. Her family and friends asked her, how could Sarah have switched schools over a boy? Wasn't there part of her that realized what a loser move that was?

As an only child, Sarah Ludemann had been a daddy's girl. She and her father did nearly everything together. She took karate lessons, loved to sing and dance. Then she met Joshua—a bad egg, Dad thought—and, snap, just like that, she wasn't her daddy's girl anymore.

Like many late bloomers, Sarah lengthened her stride in an effort to catch up. Maybe she'd moved too fast. Most of the time these days, she was nursing a bruise from getting hit or in tears over what an asshole Joshua could be.

She knew Joshua was seeing other girls, at least two. She'd already fought Erin, the mother of Joshua's baby. Now it was big mouth Rachel's turn. Sarah would prove she was Joshua's number one. Sarah hit the minivan's brakes and opened the driver's door in one fluid motion. . . .

It happened so fast, five seconds tops, silence brittle to the crackling curses of angry young women, a residential street now a stage, a stormy sea of hair and flailing arms—then a glint of metal, and a razor-sharp flash of violence tearing open the peaceful night, tearing open Sarah Ludemann's heart while breaking the hearts of those who loved her.

At twelve forty-five, on a warm spring night in Pinellas Park, Florida, in front of a home on Fifty-second Street North, under a clear sky and a bright quarter moon, Sarah Rose Ludemann was stabbed twice in the chest with a kitchen knife.

Sarah summoned up her will as things started swirling pretty fast. She found her way to the driver's seat of her vehicle and she called Joshua. By the time he answered, all she could say was "It hurts." She fell out of the vehicle to the pavement, where she lay motionless.

Chaos erupted, and young people continued to shout and push and shove. Rachel was beaten, dragged by her hair across a sandy lawn. Fearing the bloody knife could be used against her, Rachel managed to break free momentarily and hurl it into the distance.

Paramedics from the fire department appeared and worked urgently over the fallen Sarah; squad cars from the Pinellas Park Police Department (PPPD) came immediately behind.

First responders noted blood on the minivan's driver's seat, floor, and interior wall panel.

The victim's parents arrived on the scene. Her father, a big man on tortured knees, arrived first and saw all; he saw

Sarah, supine in the street, perpendicular to the minivan, her life slipping away.

"Lying in a puddle of blood" was how he remembered it.

Charlie Ludemann could tell by the sharp and urgent exchanges between paramedic firefighters that she was still alive—but it didn't look good.

Joshua Camacho arrived and went berserk, screaming that "somebody stab Sarah, somebody gonna get stabbed."

Police actively had to keep concerned witnesses back, so they couldn't interfere with the paramedics. A noisy ambulance, with SUNSTAR painted on the side, arrived.

Sarah—gray, limp, motionless—was placed on a gurney, loaded into the vehicle, and the ambulance pulled away, with siren screaming like a blues guitar. The ambulance was escorted by police officer John Coleman in his squad car.

The ambulance took the victim to Northside Hospital and Heart Institute, a little more than a mile away to the south; Sarah's parents were right behind.

Back at the crime scene, it took some time to calm everyone down and figure out who was who. Loud and unruly eyewitnesses were separated; first to halt hostilities, then to keep them from comparing notes.

The girl who'd had the knife was Rachel Marie Wade—thin, with big, sad eyes—now in possession of no knife. She complained of injuries to her head and face, but none were visible.

An hour after her arrival at the hospital, just before 2:00 A.M., Sarah Ludemann was pronounced dead.

One girl killing another wasn't common in Pinellas Park, or anywhere else. Ninety-six percent of all homicides involved a male victim and/or killer. Males usually killed during the commission of other crimes, such as robberies and drug deals gone bad. Female violence, as a rule, was emotional and involved matters of the heart. Girls fought over relationships: parents, siblings, and boyfriends. Girls were possessive about relationships. Intrusion and disrespect easily led to violence, sometimes pernicious violence, but almost never fatal violence. That was what made this one special.

The homicide investigation immediately dug into the emotional relationships between the players, revealing that Rachel Wade had a history of fiery and sometimes short-lived romances. Sarah Ludemann did not. Camacho was Sarah's first and only.

Now, as the rotating lights of cop cars still pulsed over the scene, the culprit sat quietly on a bench. All of her personal belongings had been confiscated as possible evidence, and she looked as dangerous as a sullen cheerleader.

"Can I have a cigarette?" she asked a cop.

PART ONE

The Tender Savages

Chapter 1

UNTHINKABLE CARNAGE

Pinellas Park, Florida, was a working-class town, between Tampa Bay and the Gulf of Mexico. In 1911, the town started out as one huge housing development when a Philadelphia publisher named F. A. Davis purchased almost thirteen thousand acres of undeveloped land and ordered a city to be built.

In the modern era, it became an industrial city, home to major corporations, such as UPS and FedEx, which utilized Pinellas Park as a hub for their distribution, working out of large warehouses. Most folks had blue-collar jobs.

In addition to industry, Pinellas Park had a large, close-knit residential community made up of people who were born and raised there, and chose to stay.

The major highways into Tampa went through Pinellas Park. At night the population was approximately fifty thousand residents, but hundreds of thousands passed through the city during daytime hours.

It was the third largest city in Pinellas County, behind Clearwater and St. Petersburg, and—perhaps revealingly—the county's only landlocked town.

There had been a time, a half century before, when the city was predominantly white, and its citizens liked it that way. Back then, prejudice ruled. But over the years, integration came and progressive thought pushed its way in.

Of course, old-fashioned beliefs had not left completely, but groups of young people were far more inclined to be comprised of races mixing together than were those of their elders.

Because there was no waterfront, there wasn't a lot of money in Pinellas Park. Rich folks, for the most part, chose to live near the shore where ocean breezes provided nature's air conditioning, where there were marinas for yachts and private boats. Instead, in Pinellas Park there were quite a few trailer parks and God-fearing people who worked hard and had kids.

The springtime was the best season in Pinellas Park. The hard rains of winter were over, and the oppressive heat of summer had yet to come. On the third Saturday of March, after the Florida State Fair and the Florida Strawberry Festival, the city hosted an annual event called "Country in the Park." There was a free daylong concert in the band shell behind City Hall, amusement park rides, NASCAR displays, and a firefighter chili cook-off.

Like anywhere, there was a segment of the local youth that had antisocial difficulties. These kids lacked upward mobility and hope. Regardless of race, they were apt to be caught up in the prevalent "gangsta" culture.

Pinellas Park High School—whose notable alumni included major-league baseball player Nick Masset, *Play-*

boy Playmate Pamela Stein, and former New York Jets quarterback Browning Nagle—was known for tragic and scandalous events. The school, in fact, had an uncomfortable history of violence, a Columbine-like legacy.

On February 11, 1988, the school was thrust into the headlines when two students—Jason Harless and Jason McCoy—brought stolen guns to school with them and shot three members of the faculty and administration, killing one. Harless was sentenced to seventeen years in prison, but he served only eight. McCoy was sentenced to six years in prison, but he only served fourteen months in a juvie facility.

In 2005, the school again earned unwanted publicity when police were called to break up a fight and used a Taser three times on one unruly student. That same year, a teacher was busted after he enticed several female students to e-mail him nude photos of themselves.

In mid-April 2009, a time when the young people of Pinellas Park should have had their minds on upcoming proms, graduation, how many teens could fit into a limo, and other celebrations of youth, teenaged Sarah Ludemann was battling the Joshua blues. Simultaneously, news came to her attention of unspeakable carnage.

On Friday night, April 10, four students had died, and another was seriously injured, when a 2005 Lexus, speeding south on Eighty-sixth Avenue in Seminole, was passing a 1993 Lumina on the left side, when the Lumina made a left turn. The cars came together, sending the Lexus into a large tree, where it caught fire. Three teens were pronounced dead at the scene, and a fourth passed away on his way to the hospital.

A car crash with multiple fatalities!

Knowing their school's problematic history, students worried.

Who would be next? Who would be the next kid to have something *horrible* happen?

Chapter 2

THE BUILDUP

Media efforts to tell this story in shorthand have framed Sarah Ludemann and Rachel Wade as two girls with a lot in common. But was that really the case? Sure, both had once dreamed of being a veterinarian. Beyond that, though, they came from very different places.

Sarah's mom, Gay, was a surgical nurse. Her dad, Charlie, drove a cab. They were from New York but migrated southward to be "warm and safe." They'd been married sixteen years when they had their only child, tomboy Sarah. Sarah lived her whole life in the same house, a single-level lime-colored stucco home.

She liked to hang out with her dad, riding beside him sometimes in his taxi, blasting the radio and singing Keith Urban songs. According to Sarah's friend since preschool, Danielle Eyermann, "Sarah loved to sing and dance." The friends would work out their own Britney Spears–style choreography. Sarah attended John Hopkins Middle School in St. Petersburg. Danielle said that when other girls her age already had real boyfriends, Sarah was still crushing on country singers and Tampa Bay Rays baseball players.

Sarah started high school at Tarpon Springs because it had a veterinary medicine program. But the school was more than an hour bus ride away, and she had to get up when it was still dark.

In tenth grade, Sarah and friend Amber Malinchock hung out a lot and ate at Chick-fil-A. It was there that Sarah met Joshua Camacho, who used to come out and talk to the girls when he was on break.

Joshua told them he was starting his senior year at Pinellas Park High School. Amber remembered he always reeked of French fries. One time he winked at Sarah, and that was that. She was giddy in love; her face was frozen into a dreamy smile.

Sarah decided soon thereafter to replace one dream with another. She didn't want to be a veterinarian anymore. She wanted to get close to Joshua Camacho—so she disregarded just about everybody's advice and transferred to Pinellas Park High.

Sarah was upset that fall when she showed up at her new school and Joshua gave her the cold shoulder. She had to prove her love for him before he would pay attention to her.

As Sarah's friend Amber later put it, "Most people have their first love when they're younger. She loved him. She really, really loved him."

They say that opposites attract. That was certainly the case here. The good girl was attracted to a bad boy. He sent her photos on her cell phone: flexing, smoking fat doobs, brandishing his CAMACHO tattoo in large letters across his back.

But he wasn't just a gangsta. He could sweet-talk, too. Sarah's mother didn't like it, but she understood the appeal. Was he good? Was he bad?

Sarah had been yanked off the straight and narrow, and Gay Ludemann wondered if she'd ever get back on track. Her friends said it was stupid to be attracted to a boy like that; it was like climbing out on the ledge and wondering what it would feel like to fall.

As Charlie put it, they did everything to get Sarah to "see the light." They warned her that she'd never been with a boy before. She didn't know what she was doing. She didn't know about the pitfalls of relationships. But it didn't matter what they said. Parents were so yesterday. Joshua was now.

Everything would be fine, if only it weren't for that thorn in Sarah's side—the little firecracker called Rachel Wade. Something was going to have to give with her.

It had been months of insults back and forth, stalking, harassment, and domestic violence. Dealing with Rachel was nerve-racking. For friends and foe alike. Rachel came off sometimes as, well, not quite stable. Her history demonstrated that. . . .

Rachel didn't come from a visibly broken home. Rachel's mom, Janet, was an assistant teacher at an elementary school. Her dad, Barry, was a food-distributor truck driver.

Her seemingly normal upbringing occurred in a suburban home, painted brown, with an aboveground pool in the backyard. The youngest of two children, she'd been a happy little girl, reading about, drawing, and pretending to be a Disney princess. She had so many friends and loved attention.

Rachel's friend Egle Nakaite said, "People sometimes thought she was prissy, but she wasn't, once you got to know her." Rachel was still in elementary school when she met Joshua Camacho, whose family—parents, six brothers, and a sister—had just moved to Florida from the Dominican Republic.

By high school, Rachel had no desire to be one of the goody-goody girls. She saw life as one big party. Studying was cutting into her fun time. By the time she was sixteen, she was a rebel, defying her parents' attempts to keep her home.

"I don't need your rules," she hissed, eyes squinted.

"I kept telling her that nothing good ever happens after midnight," her father, Barry, sadly recalled.

On March 9, 2005, less than two weeks after her fifteenth birthday, Rachel started a long and painful habit of running away from home. The first time, it scared her parents half to death. She had been punished, grounded. But instead of coming home after school and staying inside as she was supposed to, she didn't come home at all. Rachel's parents called her friends, who agreed that they'd seen Rachel at school, but not since. She didn't go home, but she did go to school the next day, and that was where cops nabbed her, taking her right out of class and into the Juvenile Assessment Center.

Rachel pulled a switcheroo on May 27, 2005. She called 911 on her parents.

Ha! That would show them.

When the dispatcher asked what her emergency was, Rachel said her parents wouldn't let her go out at night with her boyfriend and her friends. It was about ten o'clock when Officer John Coleman pulled up in front of the Wade household. Rachel complained to him that her parents didn't like the guy she was dating. They thought he was too old for her, and that she wasn't allowed to see him anymore. They said that she had to stay in her room. She was frustrated that her parents couldn't communicate with her.

After finishing with Rachel, Officer Coleman spoke with her dad. Barry Wade said that earlier in the day, he'd gone to one of Rachel's friends' houses to pick her up, and he saw her walking down the street with an older boy whom they didn't like.

Coleman tried to calm the situation down. He suggested family counseling, and recommended that another family member mediate the next time Barry and Rachel spoke.

Rachel's parents were away and her grandmother was babysitting on July 1, 2005, when Rachel snuck out her bedroom window. Her grandma called the police, suggesting they look for her at a guy named Jake's house. Rachel came home before she could be listed as missing; and when police spoke to Jake, he said he had not seen or heard from Rachel.

On October 12, Rachel fought with her mom and left the house. Janet called the police, who arrived to find Rachel had only gotten as far as the next block, where she'd stopped and cried. The cop took her home.

On November 17, 2005, a woman named Gail Kish called Detective Adam Geissenberger. Kish was the secretary of the freshman department at Pinellas Park High School, and Geissenberger was the PPPD investigator who normally worked the PPHS beat. Kish said there was a problem regarding a student there named Rachel Wade.

Geissenberger said he was familiar with Ms. Wade and would be right over. On the way, he recalled that he had seen Rachel just that morning in the parking lot outside school. She was with an older male, whom he recognized as Rachel's boyfriend, Jose Hernandez (pseudonym). It had been almost nine o'clock, and school had started at 7:05 A.M., but he took no action because the couple was walking toward the school rather than away from it, and perhaps they were just late.

At Kish's office, Geissenberger learned that Rachel had been in school but left when Hernandez called her from outside. Hernandez did not have permission to take her out of school, and she did not have permission to leave.

Kish was particularly wary about this situation because she knew Rachel's parents and knew that a few days earlier they had caught Rachel in Hernandez's car engaging in sexual activity. Since he was nineteen—although still a student at PPHS—and she was fifteen, they were very worried about the situation and threatened to have the young man prosecuted if it didn't stop. She would say she was going to walk the dog, but then she'd disappear. This morning's movements near the high school led Kish to believe that Jose and Rachel hadn't stopped having sex.

Geissenberger called the Wades, reported the new information, and asked if they still wanted Hernandez prosecuted. They said they did. The officer had an office in the high school and went there. He summoned Rachel Wade, who reported to him, appearing somewhat sheepish.

He explained that he was there because of her ongoing, inappropriate, and illegal relationship with Hernandez, and he was going to have to ask her a series of pretty personal questions.

Rachel was quiet for a few moments and then asked Geissenberger how much he already knew. He told her, and then asked her how long she'd been seeing Hernandez. She said it started right at the beginning of the school year, which that year had been August 3.

"You have been seeing him the whole time since the beginning of school?" the cop asked.

"No, our relationship has been off and on," Rachel replied.

"Are you sexually active with him?"

"Yes."

"How many times have you had sex with him?"

Pause. "Two or three," she said. All of the sex had been vaginal intercourse; all of it was consensual.

"Oral sex?"

"No."

"Why did you have sex with him, Rachel?"

"He pressured me to do it with him," she said. She held out for a while, but they kept getting closer and closer to doing it; then one day "it just happened."

Geissenberger asked about contraception. Rachel said they had used protection every time. Condoms at first, but she eventually went to the health department and got birth control pills, without telling her parents. Rachel said she and Hernandez had not had sex since they were caught. They'd only done it three times—once in his car and twice at his house.

He asked her about that morning. She said she hadn't been feeling good; and besides, she wanted to talk to Jose, so she left school, met him, and they drove around for an hour or so. Then she came back, and that was when Geissenberger saw her.

The officer put Rachel in a separate office with the door shut. He didn't want Rachel socializing and potentially interfering with the investigation.

Geissenberger found out which classroom Hernandez was in and pulled him out of class personally. In the cop's office, Geissenberger advised Hernandez that he was conducting a criminal investigation and read him his Miranda rights.

"This is about Rachel Wade, isn't it?" Hernandez asked.

"Why do you say that?"

"It's because she's a minor, right?"

"What do you mean by that?"

"You want to talk to me because I'm having sex with a minor, right?"

Geissenberger said that was precisely right. "I'm going

to ask you very direct questions about your relationship, and it would be in your best interests to tell me the whole and absolute truth."

"I understand. I'll tell the truth."

His answers jibed with Rachel's, at first. They'd had sex only two or three times. Always consensual. Always vaginal. Then his answers diverged from hers.

"Have you ever performed oral sex on one another?" the detective asked.

"Yes."

"Who does it to who?"

"In most cases, I do it to her, but she has done it to me as well, yes."

Hernandez told the cop about that morning. He said it was he, rather than she, who hadn't felt okay. Rachel came out of school and got in his car. They drove to his house, but they just talked there. No sex.

"You know, I've already talked to Rachel, and I think you are lying," Geissenberger bluffed.

Hernandez bit, and fessed up that he and Rachel had had vaginal intercourse that morning. He had also performed oral sex on her.

"Tell me again how many times you and Rachel have had sex?"

"Um, about twenty or thirty times," Hernandez said, although he maintained that it was always consensual, and usually took place either at his house or in his car.

Hernandez interrupted the interview and asked if he could call his boss at work and tell him that he was running late. The cop would not allow him to use his cell phone, but said it was okay to use the office phone.

He then asked if he could get his lunch from the cafeteria, and again Geissenberger said that was okay. The detective waited, and Hernandez returned with his lunch and ate as he answered further questions. The detective gave him a form to fill out, and then he went to talk to Rachel again.

"You lied to me about the number of times you had sex with Jose," he said.

"Sorry."

"And you lied about oral sex, too."

"It's embarrassing to talk about that stuff. I wanted to tell you the truth, but I've never been able to talk about that with anyone," she said.

"You have performed oral sex on Jose?"

"Yes."

"And he has performed oral sex on you?"

"Yes."

"And you and he had sex this morning, right?"

"Yes."

"And you have had sex between twenty and thirty times with him?"

"No!"

"How often?"

"Maybe fifteen times."

Rachel got a ride home from Ms. Kish. Hernandez was arrested by Detective Geissenberger and charged with lewd and lascivious battery in connection with unlawful sexual activity with a child.

Rachel was home only a matter of minutes when her mother called the police. Rachel came home spitting mad that her parents had told her school that she'd been caught having sex. It was humiliating beyond words. An officer came to the house and stayed long enough to make sure everyone had calmed down; then the cop left.

On November 20, 2005, Rachel's mom called the police. Detective Geissenberger responded. Janet said Rachel was out again with Jose Hernandez, the adult ephebophile who was illegally having relations with her daughter.

Police officers took all crime seriously, but some didn't feel Janet's plans to prosecute Jose were promising. The adult-having-sex-with-a-child thing seemed less perverted when one considered that Rachel and Jose attended the same school. Jose might have been an adult, technically, but he wasn't forty, either. The trick here, they suspected, was getting Rachel to keep her pants on. If it wasn't Jose, it was going to be someone else.

While the officer was questioning Rachel's mom, Rachel called, said it was no big deal, and she was on her way home.

"I still would appreciate it if you could fill out a report for me, anyway," Janet said. Paperwork was desirable because, in addition to the lewd and lascivious charges Hernandez was facing, Janet Wade was seeking an injunction against Hernandez.

The cop remained at the Wade house until Rachel did come home. Rachel explained that she'd been out with friends at a pool hall in Seminole.

With the cop still present, Janet noticed a red welt on Rachel's leg. She asked what had happened. Rachel said she got burned when she accidentally put her leg on a motorcycle's exhaust pipe.

Janet affirmed that she intended to do what she could to stop Jose. The officer reminded the Wades that the police were not in existence to play games with a fifteen-year-old girl every time she ran off. Then the officers said to be sure and call if there were future problems.

On November 22, 2005, Rachel and her mother argued anew. Janet told Rachel that from then on *every time* she left the house without permission, or failed to come home when she was supposed to, the cops would be called.

Rachel didn't like that. At first, Rachel punched inanimate things: the wall, a door. Then she fixed her hostility on her mom. The fight became physical. Rachel attacked her mother and threw objects at her.

Janet called 911.

"What objects did she throw?" the dispatch operator asked.

"Well, a hairbrush, for one thing. Hit me. Hit me in the lower thigh."

After that, Rachel, a little hellion now, ran into the kitchen and threw open cabinet doors. She found the place where the good knives were kept. She quickly chose one knife, which she liked; it was a knife sheathed in a white Pampered Chef knife carrier. Rachel slid the knife from its sheath and threw it at her mother, bouncing it off Janet's abdomen. Rachel scooped up the knife, quick like a cat, and locked herself in the bathroom.

Janet told 911 that Rachel had blades on her mind. There were "shaving razors" in that bathroom, and she didn't trust Rachel not to hurt herself.

Officer Shaun Grantham reported to the Wades' home and found Janet Wade waiting in front of the house. Grantham asked if Rachel was still around. Janet shook her head no.

Janet explained that right after she hung up with the operator, she screamed into the bathroom that Rachel better get out and give up the knife. Soon thereafter, Rachel exited the bathroom, put the knife back in its sheath and into its cabinet, hurriedly packed a bag of things, and stormed out the door, announcing that this time no one was ever going to find her! She disappeared into the night. Janet came outside, but she couldn't even tell which direction Rachel was headed.

The officer later noted that this was not his first time visiting the Wades' home, and a lot of fellow officers were familiar with the Wades and their problems as well. It had become a regular pattern for Rachel: run away from home in the evening, stay out all night, and return the following afternoon. For a while, she had been packing up her things and taking them with her at night, like she thought she was moving out on the sly.

Theft entered the mix. Janet caught Rachel in her purse, looking for something, probably money. When Janet tried to call 911, Rachel attacked and tried to wrestle the cell phone away from her mother. In the process, Rachel dug her nails into Janet's forearm.

"Has Rachel been suicidal before?" the cop asked.

"Yes," Janet Wade said, exhibiting long-suffering eyes.

Grantham checked out the bathroom, the one that Rachel had locked herself in, and found nothing suspicious, no evidence she had done anything to hurt herself.

He radioed in that he needed a search team, and a canine unit was assigned to the case. A police search dog named Dax was given a sniff of a piece of Rachel's unlaundered apparel. The dog was then sent out to find Rachel.

A photographer reported to the scene and took photos of the knife, its sheath, and the fingernail wounds on Janet Wade's forearm.

Grantham wanted to confiscate the hairbrush that Rachel threw at her mother, but the hairbrush could not be located.

The canine search was unsuccessful. It got off to a bad start when Officer M. Turner, the human half of the canine team, reported to the wrong address. Even after communications were repaired, conditions for tracking were less than desirable. There was a cool, strong wind from the northwest—and the search bore no fruit. Dax sniffed around the residential streets for eight minutes and gave up. Dax perked up for a time on one stretch of nearby street—then, nothing. Rachel might not have gone far on foot before she got into a car.

Rachel returned home at ten-thirty, the following night. Asked where she'd been, Rachel explained that she had been upset. She ended up sleeping on a chaise longue next to the Plantation Gardens Apartments pool. When she woke up in the morning, she just walked around before returning home.

On February 2, 2006, Barry Wade called cops to report his runaway daughter. The next day, Rachel was located at her friend Heather's house. Rachel said she spent the night with Heather, sitting outside the house and talking.

Ten days later, Barry called again, but this time the paperwork for a missing juvenile was still being filled out—"four earrings in right ear, five earrings in left ear, no tattoos"—when Rachel returned home.

On March 13, Barry called again, and Rachel came home on March 14, telling cops that she had spent the night with her friend Brittany. She didn't know her address, and didn't attend school that day because she feared she would be arrested for being a runaway.

Rachel left behind a note on March 23 when she split, wrote that she would be with friends and back in the morning. The cops were called, nonetheless. Barry Wade reiterated that his insistence on the documentation of each of Rachel's escapes was to create a paper trail in support of future court action that would, in turn, enable him to "help Rachel."

When Rachel returned, as she always did, she told her father and a cop that she'd been with her friend Sierra. She didn't know the last name. She went to St. Pete Beach, and slept in an unknown male's car.

* * *

Four days later, Rachel took off again. This time Rachel put on music in her room, just before sneaking out the window. It was mother Janet's turn to call police. Janet said that Rachel had no access to money. She didn't think Rachel's welfare was endangered, and she didn't think she had a substance abuse problem—but she did think Rachel was spending the night with a man.

On June 11, the police responded to reports of a fight at the Wades' place, Rachel and her father. She'd been away without leave, and to punish her, Barry took her cell phone away. Barry told the cop he was planning to seek the help of "mental-health physicians" for Rachel in the near future.

The next 911 call came in six days later, with Rachel returning right on schedule. A week after that, Rachel didn't come home from work. Barry verified that she'd been at work that day, but she just didn't come home afterward.

Rachel's attitude when answering grown-up questions grew increasingly belligerent. When Rachel came back now, she didn't care enough to make up a lie.

She told cops she didn't remember what she did or whom she was with.

One cop gave her a steady gaze and determined she was in good health. *Uninjured,* he wrote. More paperwork for Barry Wade's pile.

When they told her she should get a job and focus her attention on something constructive, she said she had a job. She had a telemarketing job at Vici Financial, located in the Winn-Dixie Shopping Mall.

Rachel was now in possession of her learner's permit to drive a car. Rachel's runaway problem intensified a notch during the weekend of July 22 and 23. She called home a few times to say she was with friends. She didn't have her cell phone with her and the Wades' caller ID failed to determine from which number she was calling.

"She must have done something to block the number," Barry said to the cop.

Then, disturbingly, Rachel did something she hadn't done before. She called and said she was on her way home—and then failed to show up. It was as if she wanted them to think something bad had happened to her—and who knew? Maybe it had. Rachel stayed away for the entire weekend before returning.

"Why do you keep running away?" a cop asked.

"Because I'm fed up with my parents," Rachel replied, scowling.

On August 6, now sporting a nose piercing in addition to her nine earrings, Rachel took off with her friend Natasha—no surname given—and didn't come back. When she returned the following day, she said she'd been at Natasha's house in St. Pete. No, she didn't know Natasha's last name. A week later, she was missing again, and the brevity of the resulting police reports demonstrated how routine it was getting to be. She did it again. Said it all.

Janet said next time she was going to have the cop take her straight to juvenile detention.

But she did take off again, on August 19, this time explaining that she went to the Countryside Mall in Clearwater with an unnamed friend. Rachel was not taken to juvie.

Rachel next disappeared on September 9, this time perhaps because she feared an upcoming court date from when she attacked her mother. Janet suggested cops pick her up at her telemarketing job in the Winn-Dixie Mall.

Police did go there, but they discovered Vici Financial had moved to another unknown location.

Police located her on September 10, at a party where alcohol was served. So in addition to being a runaway, Rachel was picked up for underage drinking. Barry came and got her, but she was upset and gone again the next day, calling home to tell her dad that she was in Tampa. Barry Wade told police that contrary to anything his wife might have said, he did not want his daughter taken to juvenile detention. She was to be brought home to him, and a report was to be filed.

The battery charge against Rachel for the fingernails to her mother's forearm was eventually dropped. Janet showed no inclination to help with her daughter's prosecution, which caused the state attorney's office to drop the matter.

Even when Rachel wasn't in trouble, she lingered in trouble's vicinity. Done with Jose and looking forward to bigger and better things, Rachel moved on with her life. On September 16, 2006, at ten o'clock at night, Pinellas Park police responded to a call that someone had been jumped in the street. By the time police arrived, the crowd of young people had dispersed, but four young pedestrians—two guys, two gals—in the area were stopped and questioned. One of them was Rachel Wade.

Why was Rachel in such a hurry to grow up? A lot of fifteen-year-old girls wanted to have boyfriends, but they understood that the security of living with parents outweighed the advantages of being without a safety net. No one could figure out what the unscratchable itch was. Was it just normal adolescent chemistry?

It was a proven scientific fact that a "normal" teenaged brain, with its still-developing frontal cortex and immature neural structure, came replete with impulsivity, social anxiety, and poor judgment.

Although it was true that adults also felt anxiety, teens and adults grew nervous over different things. The immature brain did not grow as anxious when encountering physical dangers (which is why teenagers tend to be reckless drivers) but became much more anxious over feelings of being left out and not being a part of things.

So maybe it was a simple matter of chemistry, making Rachel unwilling to be a normal teenager who had to (at least pretend to) obey her parents' rules.

Still, teens were responsible for their actions. Everyone's behavior wasn't influenced by social and environmental factors. Rachel's behavior should have been maturing.

On November 11, 2006, after a few months off, she ran away again. She dropped out of school as soon as she turned sixteen. She told friends her badass boyfriend was expelled, so she didn't want to go to school, either. Her parents tried taking her to counseling and got her a job at Paws of Paradise, a doggie day care business.

On January 26, 2007, Rachel took off, and Janet notified the authorities. Rachel returned, although not until January 28. A police officer spoke to Rachel to try to figure out what was up. Rachel was back to giving elaborate yet unhelpful explanations of her whereabouts. She said she didn't know what the big deal was. She'd left a note for her mother before leaving. Who was she with? Rachel said she was with a friend named Hiram. She didn't know his last name, and they'd gone together to Lakeland, Florida, to see a football game. She'd planned to come home the previous night, but Hiram had car trouble and they spent the night in the car "somewhere in Polk

County." She made it home on January 28, only after Hiram got gas.

Somewhere in this time frame, Rachel acquired a new beau, a guy named Nick Reynolds (pseudonym). He had his own place, a great place to hang out. There was a lot of sex and drugs going on.

On March 6, at 2:30 A.M., Rachel was a passenger in a car Nick was driving. According to their story, the car in front of them stopped abruptly, as if to purposefully cause an accident. Nick's car rear-ended the guy so hard that although they were not injured, Nick's car suffered extensive frontal damage, so bad he needed a tow. Nick and Rachel told police they'd gotten a pretty good look at the guy who'd done it to them: white male, sixteen to eighteen years old, with "bushy hair." They didn't know the make of the car. Police ended the investigation after it was discovered that surveillance cameras in the area had failed to capture the car accident.

On March 26, Officer John Lagasse responded to yet another call from Janet Wade. Rachel ran away again. This time Janet offered the authorities a key piece of intelligence. She gave Nick Reynolds's address to Officer Lagasse. Sure enough, Rachel was there, and the cop went and got her.

On April 14, Rachel told her mom on her way out the door that she would be home by early evening. Instead, she had not come home all night, and wasn't answering her cell phone. Rachel was again listed as a missing person. Lagasse found Rachel and spoke with her. Rachel said she had been out with friends, but she refused to give names.

"I was in East Lake, near Oldsmar. I didn't have phone

reception and no one would give me a ride home," Rachel explained.

Not that Rachel ever had a relationship with a boy that went smoothly, her relationship with Nick was particularly rocky. She still loved him and all, but . . . she no longer felt it was necessary to keep her blinkers on when it came to looking at other boys. Rachel liked to think of herself as an open person, a girl who always had her heart open for new romance.

Rachel ran into Joshua Camacho at a party. She hadn't talked to him in a long time and was instantly smitten.

On November 9, 2007, cops were called, responding to a domestic dispute at Nick's apartment. Nick and Rachel apologized for the noise, stated that they had been arguing about a relationship problem, but they were through, and the fight was not physical.

After fighting the good battle for many long months, after dealing with police on at least fourteen occasions when Rachel ran away, the Wades stopped calling.

Rachel had Nick, and the Wades understood that she was going to be there, with him, most of the time. You could see the defeat in their shoulders.

That didn't mean, however, that the PPPD was through with Rachel Wade—or her friends. Or her enemies.

It was also at about this time that one small subsection of the Pinellas Park population—young people who knew Rachel Wade—did its best to keep the PPPD busy all by themselves.

The instant Sarah Ludemann had received her driver's license, she demonstrated no fear of speed. Her father was a cabdriver, so it only made sense she'd drive like a pro, and that meant fast. She enjoyed playing road tag with her friends, weaving in and out of traffic, playing games of pursuit, playing chicken at high speeds.

At two in the afternoon on November 29, 2007, Sarah was burned by her own carelessness. She and three other drivers were allegedly using the roads as their personal playground. When the reckless parade of young people encountered a car accident on the road, the front car slowed down abruptly, starting a chain reaction that injured no one but caused medium to severe damage to all of the cars.

On December 6, 2007, cops were again called to Nick's apartment, and this time it was Rachel complaining. She explained her live-in boyfriend got pissed because she was babysitting for a friend instead of being with him. She wanted to move out and return to her parents' home. Nick threatened to throw all of her belongings in the lake. Rachel and Nick again agreed the argument was only verbal.

On December 21, with the holidays approaching, the kids of Pinellas Park were out in force. Officer Richard Bynum responded to a complaint of two cars full of kids fighting near the corner of 102nd Avenue and Sixty-third Lane. The incident involved many familiar names, as well as names that would later become recognizable. Jay and Joshua Camacho, Sarah Ludemann, and Ashley Lovelady were in one car. Erin Slothower and three of her girl-friends were in the other. Police questioned all eight of them, and everyone agreed no blows had been thrown. During the questioning, cops confiscated a set of brass knuckles from an unnamed occupant.

Rachel's on-again, off-again relationship with Nick was off again. During the evening of February 3, 2008,

Rachel's mom heard a commotion in front of the house. When she opened the front door, she saw a young man urinating on her lawn. Ten minutes later, Janet heard a noise again and went to investigate—now she found a young man urinating on her front door. The kid ran off and climbed into a waiting car, but Janet Wade got the license number.

"Ma'am, did you see genitals?"

"No."

"Neither time?"

"No genitals either time."

"Have any idea why young men are urinating on your property?"

"I'm pretty sure it has something to do with my daughter, Rachel."

Rachel broke up with Nick Reynolds a week before, and things had been going poorly. The officer talked to Rachel, who said that she'd gotten a call from one of Nick's friends, a guy named Eric, who said he'd been there earlier in the night, but he had nothing to do with any pissing. Sure enough, the license plate number belonged to Eric's car. While looking for Eric, the cop encountered Nick's dad, who explained that Nick was a friend of Eric's, and he was the ex-boyfriend of Rachel Wade. Nick's dad called Rachel's mom and apologized for his son's behavior. Janet Wade said she did not want to press any charges because there had been no property damage, but she did want a police report written up about it "in case they returned."

Jamie Severino was not Rachel's friend—heaven forbid—but she knew the Camacho family well. She was a hot chick and had dated Joshua's brother Jay—and had had his baby, a daughter named Alliana. Jamie was with

Jay when Erin was with Joshua, so the four of them hung out at the Camacho house.

Jay was older than the others, born in the spring of 1986. He wasn't a big man, but—at five-foot-seven, 165 pounds—he was bigger than Joshua. Jamie met him through her cousin when she was in middle school.

"Met him a long time ago, probably in like '04," Jamie said in 2011.

Jay was well inked, sporting eleven tattoos. On his back were prayer hands with the words ONLY GOD CAN JUDGE; on his left arm was M.O.B. JUANA, and on the left side of his chest was ASHLEY. He had LOVE on his left hand, and HATE on his right. On his left shoulder was a five-point star; on his neck was CLOWN NY. There were two clowns on his right arm, with GOOD TIMES, SAD TIMES and RAMON; and on his left leg was JC JAMIE S.

Jamie Severino knew Rachel because Rachel's ex, Nick, was Jay Camacho's best friend, and for a time Jay and Nick lived together. For a time Rachel lived with Nick as well, even though she was just a kid. All of Rachel's subsequent boyfriends would get to see Rachel's intimate NICK tattoo.

Predictably, Rachel's relationship with Jamie was stormy. The two had almost come to blows on several occasions. The first time came in high school when Jamie and Jay were first dating. Jamie heard from Rachel's ex-boyfriend Jose, the one Rachel's parents had arrested for having sex with Rachel when she was only fifteen, that Rachel was trying to "get with Jay." That led to altercations at the mall and in school, with insults hurled back and forth—but no violence. According to Jamie, Rachel started the hostilities, and the two didn't talk after that. Tensions eased somewhat when Rachel began dating Nick. Jamie felt that Nick was a bad influence on Jay.

Jamie said Nick was on pills at that time, and he got Jay

on them also—but despite that, there were times when Rachel and Nick and Jamie and Jay would hang out together.

The girls still weren't exactly best buddies, but they could be in the same room without a shouting match breaking out. Rachel was always careful that someone had her back if hostilities were about to erupt. When she was alone, she could be quiet—almost scared. But when she was with a guy or a group of girls—or on the computer— she'd get "all tough."

"She used to say that Nick hit her," Jamie recalled, searching for an explanation. "But every time I was around them, it was the other way around. I think she just did things to get attention."

In high school, Jamie claimed, Rachel was always the one who was doing something to stand out. She wanted— maybe needed—to be the center of attention.

Jamie had no idea what made Rachel so angry. There was a lot of anger around, and maybe Rachel fed off it. Maybe something *happened to her* to make her that way.

One night—the end of 2007, maybe the beginning of '08—Jamie, Jay, and Nick went out; Rachel stayed behind at Nick's house. While they were gone, Rachel was "blowing up the phone," trying to determine their location.

"We had just gone to the mall," Jamie recalled. "I guess she figured that Nick was hanging out with one of my girlfriends. That was *her* style, not mine."

Rachel would not be ignored. She texted Nick, saying she was going to kill herself. That brought the trio home. At Nick's house, they discovered Rachel lying, passed-out, on the floor. There was a bunch of pills next to her. They had to take her to the hospital and have her stomach pumped.

Later on, when the media was paying Rachel a lot of

attention, she would claim that she'd never done any drugs—but Jamie knew for a fact that that wasn't true.

When Rachel lived with Nick, she definitely did coke, pills as well: "Roxies." They were Roxicodone, a prescription painkiller containing codeine. In Pinellas Park, they were sometimes called "Blues."

The peacefulness between Jamie and Rachel only lasted until Jamie learned that Rachel was hooking her friends up with Jay. One day Jamie learned *for a fact* that Rachel's friend Lisa Lafrance had "been with" Jay.

Lisa wrote to Jamie on Myspace. The message went into graphic detail, explaining that Rachel had gotten them together and that Lisa and Jay had been "hanging out" every day.

Lisa remembered the incident well, although she didn't think it was fair to say that Rachel had put them together. Jay and Nick were friends. They hung out all of the time, and Rachel and Lisa hung out at Nick's. When Rachel was with Nick, Lisa was with Jay. Rachel had nothing to do with fixing them up. They had not needed fixing up.

When Jamie read what Lisa wrote on Myspace, she was pissed. Jamie and a seven-month-pregnant Erin Slothower were at the mall when they received a phone call, informing them that Lisa and Sarah wanted to fight them.

"There were maybe fifteen people hanging out, outside Nick's house," Jamie recalled.

According to Lisa, Jamie brought another friend with her: brass knuckles. "There was such animosity that I ended up fighting her, even though she had the brass knuckles on," Lisa recalled.

"Lisa and me had an actual physical fight," Jamie said. "And Rachel tried to jump in. Jay pulled her off. Afterward, Ashley and Sarah were like, 'We want to fight you.' And all this while Erin was, like, seven months pregnant.

There was a lot of fighting going on, leading up to what happened."

Jamie started in with Jay; and before long, Jay and Jamie were having a brawl, screaming and hitting each other. Rachel wanted part of this action.

Rachel went outside and screamed to Jamie: "Come on outside and I'm going to beat your ass. You're a psycho! Let's get away from the house and I'll beat your ass."

The cops were called. After being given a blow-by-blow description of events, Jay was arrested for abusing Jamie, his "underage girlfriend." According to the police report, Jay grabbed Jamie by the neck and forced her to the ground. The girl was treated at the scene for minor injuries, bruises on her arms and neck, and declined a trip to the hospital. The fight, Jamie claimed at the time, started when Jay swiped the girl's cell phone and her bottle of Roxies. When cops searched Jay, they found a pair of black brass knuckles in his back pocket.

Rachel Wade was eager to tell police how she saw the events. She expressed her opinion that the girl got what she deserved and had struck Jay before he retaliated.

A neutral passerby, who saw the incident, told police that it didn't look to her like Jay was beating Jamie as much as he was trying to "fend her off."

With Jay's permission, cops searched his room and found two bottles of prescription medication—methylphenidate (generic form of Ritalin) and acyclovir (a generic medication for herpes)—which were confiscated.

As Sarah Ludemann would later learn, when Rachel had an enemy on speed dial, Rachel could be relentless. After the fight at Nick's house, Jamie received phone call after phone call from Rachel, constantly challenging Jamie to a fight.

"If you come anywhere near me, I am going to beat your ass," Rachel would say.

The night of the fight outside of Nick's had historical importance because among the kids gathered, watching the action, was Sarah, who had come in support of Lisa with her best friend, Ashley Lovelady, and Joshua Camacho.

Why did Rachel react so strongly to the fight between Jay and Jamie? Jamie had a theory: "I think she was having sex with Jay when Nick wasn't home. I've long thought they had a relationship going on. If so, that's funny. I mean, that's pretty *nasty*! Having sex with Jay and then going out with Joshua? Seems pretty nasty to me."

After that, it was never a good thing when Jamie ran into Rachel. Jamie went to Applebee's with friends, and Rachel told Jamie right in front of everyone that Alliana wasn't Jay Camacho's baby. This was apparently a standard riff for Rachel, who also liked to tell Erin that her baby wasn't Joshua's.

When it came to harassment, Rachel was a tenacious master. If you were on her shit list, she could completely tie up your cell phone, calling every minute for hours, leaving voice mails and sending texts. After a while, friends and recipients both had to wonder why she didn't have something better to do. And the messages were disturbingly violent.

These young women lived in an "I'm gonna kick your ass" world, but Rachel kicked it up a notch:

I'm gonna slit your throat, she texted Jamie.
I'm going to kill you, she told Erin.

Sadly, Rachel's bloody threats had a desensitizing effect. She was a barker, not a biter—a mouthy bitch. When she started in with that crap with Sarah, nobody blinked. It was just Rachel being Rachel.

* * *

Jamie's opinion of Joshua had changed over the years. At first, she thought he was pretty cool. Quiet and shy. He was a guy who "didn't do nothing." He stayed inside.

The Camachos were a religious family. The parents were strict with their kids, who practically weren't even allowed out of the house until they turned eighteen. As soon as Joshua came of age and was let out, "he took after his brother and became a player."

But now, Jamie didn't think much of Joshua. He was a pint-sized mooch: "I don't think he is good-looking," she said of the bantamweight ladies' man.

What he did have, she conceded, was a seductive banter. Despite all of the evidence to the contrary, he had his women believing they were each his one and only.

Jamie did not believe that Joshua's list of girlfriends stopped at three. Sure, there was Sarah, Rachel, and Erin, but she believed the list was longer than that, and that he took gifts from all of them. Like a small-time gigolo, he lived off his "friends." They paid his bills and bought his clothes. That's why he didn't need to get a job.

"His brother used to do that to me," Jamie recalled. "He would be with the girl who had the most to give him."

For a busy guy like Joshua, the schedules of Sarah and Rachel were perfectly complementary. Sarah was available only during the early evening. She had a curfew and had to be home by eleven. Rachel was a waitress and worked at night, getting off work only after Sarah was back home.

People thought Joshua enjoyed the fact that "his friends" were fighting over him. "He was just like every dude," Jamie said. Well, not every dude, but *most* young guys. "He was a cheater. He cheated on girls. That was pretty much it."

And a beater. The brothers disciplined their women. Jay hit Jamie, and Jamie had seen Joshua hit Erin.

Janet Wade called police about her daughter one more time, on December 11, 2007. She and Rachel had gotten into a fight, and Rachel had stormed out and gotten into a car with friends. Officer Benjamin Simpkins, who would later testify at Rachel Wade's murder trial, answered the call. While he was talking to Janet, Rachel called her mom's cell phone; Janet put Officer Simpkins on the line. Janet and Rachel decided that Rachel should stay with friends for a "cooling-off period," after which they should try again to resolve their differences.

On February 21, 2008, Sarah and Joshua were leaving a Pinellas Park movie theater, located on U.S. 19, when Erin Slothower and Jamie Severino accosted them. There was screaming, and Erin pushed Joshua. Cops were called.

Years later, Erin remembered it this way: "I was up getting food at my job with Jamie. I was [eight months] pregnant and I saw them walking out of the movie theater and we started arguing because he said he was somewhere else. It was stupid."

Joshua was so upset about the way he'd been treated, he called the cops. He told Officer Scott Martin that his pregnant ex-girlfriend used "an open hand to push me backward." After he was attacked, Joshua said, Erin and Jamie got into their car and left. Joshua had no visible injuries. In a separate interview, Sarah told Officer Martin a story that matched Joshua's precisely. Joshua announced that he intended to get an injunction, preventing Erin from getting inside his personal space.

Martin had heard of more impressive assaults, but Joshua pressed the matter and the incident would eventually be referred to the state attorney's office.

After taking the statements from Joshua and Sarah, Martin visited Erin and promptly read her Miranda rights to her. Erin said she understood and wanted to talk.

"Joshua has been telling me that after the baby is born, he is going to take the baby away," Erin explained. That was the issue she was confronting him with in the parking lot that evening. He was *not* getting the baby. She wanted to make sure *that* was clear.

Lastly the cop interviewed Jamie Severino, who said that Erin really had no choice. Joshua was right in her face and screaming at her. She put her hand on his face and pushed him away. Joshua was lucky he didn't get punched in the face. It wasn't an attack at all, Severino explained. Erin was simply attempting to "create some space between the two of them."

Martin recommended that Erin be the one to file the injunction. He warned her to avoid contact with Joshua and to "refrain from future confrontations."

The state attorney's office gave this a glance and decided not to prosecute Erin Slothower for the assault on Joshua Camacho.

Erin didn't care if it was over. There was a bond between her and Joshua that could never be broken. She had a great reason to fight over Joshua, with Joshua, or whatever she wanted to do. She'd been Joshua's girlfriend since 1999, when the two went to elementary school together. He'd written her a note in class. It asked: *Do you like me?* She wrote yes. Now it was nine years later—and a difficult time for Erin. She was facing social ridicule.

"I was harassed constantly" was how she put it—because she was having *his* baby. Plus she knew that being a mother was going to be expensive; and even though it was hard, she continued to work during the final trimester of her pregnancy—indeed right up until her due date.

Predictably enough, life became even more complicated for Erin Slothower after Joshua's baby was born: "After I had Jeremiah, my schedule was very hard. I got up and went to school at seven and got out at eleven. Then I went to my first job till five, then to my second till nine. Then I got to go home to my little man and study and play with him."

On the rainy afternoon of March 14, 2008, Sarah Ludemann was out with Joshua in her mom's car on Forty-ninth Street in the southbound curb lane. Streets were wet and slippery, and they were rear-ended hard. It was Sarah's second car accident in four months.

The driver of the other car was David C. Tracy, who was cited by the responding officer with "careless driving." Both Joshua and Sarah were taken to Bayfront Medical Center, complaining of neck injuries. They were checked out and released.

On April 1, 2008, Officer Dean LoBianco, who would win that year's PPPD Officer of the Year Award, answered a complaint of domestic disturbance. A couple sounded like they were beating the crap out of one another on Sixty-third Lane.

It was early for this sort of call, only six-thirty in the evening. On his way to the address, Officer LoBianco was informed by dispatch that the woman involved, Rachel Wade, had left the residence on foot. The cop found her only a couple of blocks away, upset and crying, explaining that she and her off-and-on boyfriend, Nick, had just had a fight.

"Why did you go see Nick today?" LoBianco asked.

Rachel explained she wanted to discuss some ongoing difficulties that she and Nick were having with their relationship. They were in the bedroom when the argument started.

"What was the argument about?"

"Nick said he didn't like some of the people I'd been hanging out with." Rachel admitted that she was the first to get physical. She pushed him and hit him. He pushed her back.

Nick grabbed Rachel's cell phone and walked right out of the house with it. She followed, right outside and into the street, where she grabbed him by the back of his shirt and ripped it. Once the shirt started ripping, she couldn't stop ripping it, and she didn't stop until the shirt ripped off Nick's back.

"The only reason I even touched his shirt was to get my cell phone back!" Rachel said.

Nick called 911 and she split.

That brought LoBianco up to date. The officer took some pictures of Rachel's injuries.

Rachel waited in the cop car while the cop spoke to Nick, who gave the same story: Rachel struck first, and she tore his shirt. Since Rachel was the aggressor, the cop arrested Rachel and transported her to the Pinellas County Jail.

The case was promptly sent to the state attorney's office, which rapidly ruled that charges against Rachel be dropped because there was "no reasonable likelihood of a successful prosecution."

At seven-thirty in the evening, on June 13, 2008, Officer Shaun Grantham answered a call from Ashley Lovelady. Her car had been vandalized. Ashley said her best friend, Sarah Ludemann, had borrowed her car, a 1995 blue Honda Accord. Sarah needed the car to go to the Camacho house and talk with Joshua. While she was there, the side mirrors had been kicked off the Accord. Sarah said Jay Camacho did it—Jay being Ashley's ex-boyfriend.

Officer Grantham located and interviewed Sarah, who said she'd gone to visit Joshua because she needed to have a talk about their relationship. What she got was a visit with both Joshua and Jay on the front lawn. An argument ensued, and Jay was already feeling hostile when he noticed that it was Ashley's car parked in his driveway. He went over to the car to see if Ashley was in it. When he found it empty, he kicked off the mirrors, allowing them to hang.

"Who else saw this?" Officer Grantham asked.

"Joshua Camacho and his mother," Sarah replied.

The cop returned to Ashley Lovelady.

"What do you want to do about this?" he asked.

"I want to file charges and get my mirrors fixed," Ashley replied.

The cop handed Ashley a booklet entitled "Victims' Rights." He advised her to halt all contact with the brothers Camacho. She said she would.

Grantham's next stop was the Camacho house, where Joshua remained, but Jay had split. As a police photographer snapped images of the dangling mirrors, Grantham wanted to know where Jay was.

Joshua shrugged. "He moves from place to place," he said.

Grantham was a little persistent and Joshua admitted he'd seen Jay kick the mirrors.

Joshua explained that Jay was pissed at Ashley because she bitched about Jay doing other girls, like Ashley was his girlfriend, when "she wasn't nothing and had no right to complain about nothing."

Grantham handed Joshua a business card.

"Have Jay call me," the cop said.

Joshua said he would be sure to do that.

Even without Joshua's assistance, Jay was eventually located, but he escaped serious trouble when the state attorney's office, after its own investigation, concluded that the "facts and the circumstance as presented do not warrant prosecution."

By June 17, Rachel was again in a new phase of her life, taking a great step sideways in life, going from an on-and-off relationship with Nick Reynolds, to having a stormy on-and-off relationship with Joshua Camacho.

She wrote to Joshua on Myspace. In a blog entitled "Over You," she accused him again of hitting her, insulting her, cheating on her. Each time she caught him, he would say, "I'm sorry, I'll never do it again!" He lied, until it just got old; finally she looked at reality, and, well, reality said she deserved so much better! He was a boy. She needed a man! He had nothing to offer her. He was irresponsible, unreliable, unstable, immature, and nothing special to look at. And, most important, he didn't have the love and affection or the respect for her that she wanted! And since she left him, she saw that there were plenty of other guys who would offer her "at least 90 percent" of that!

So sorry buddy but you can take your bullshit somewhere else! she posted.

Sarah could do math. Ninety percent wasn't as good as 100 percent.

Sarah sat at the computer and attached a statement: And you think you found better?

* * *

At just past midnight, in the early morning of July 2, Officer Scott Galley answered a call from a female.

"I've been assaulted in a parking lot," reported the alleged victim.

When the cop arrived at the scene, he observed two vehicles in the parking lot. A young woman sat on the hood of a car, and two were sitting in a minivan.

Sarah Ludemann told Officer Galley, "I was parked in my parents' 2000 Mercury minivan, sitting in the northwest corner of a parking lot off U.S. Route 19. My window was rolled down." Erin Slothower was in the car with her.

"We were following my ex-boyfriend, Joshua Camacho, around because we're mad at him because he was sleeping with us both at the same time without us knowing about each other," Sarah explained.

Ludemann said they were arguing back and forth, and then Camacho reached in the window and punched the left side of her face. She was uninjured, however, and required no medical attention. She didn't want to press charges; but since she was a minor, that call wasn't hers.

"What did Joshua do after he punched you?" Galley inquired.

"He went to the other side of the van and started yelling at Erin." Erin, unafraid, got out of the van and the argument continued, face-to-face.

Galley talked to Erin next, whose baby was in an infant seat in the back of Sarah's minivan. Erin said she saw Joshua reach in the driver's window, but she didn't exactly see Sarah being punched. Still, the incident angered her, and she confronted Joshua. They argued but were not physical.

The officer located Joshua, read him his Miranda

rights, made sure he understood them, and asked for his version of the incident. Joshua said the girls didn't approve of his lifestyle, which involved as many women as possible, and they had been following him around. He'd been a passenger, at the time, in a car being driven by his friend Daniel McAndrews. Joshua admitted to hitting Sarah without being asked.

"I got so mad I hit her," he said.

His story jibed perfectly with Erin and Sarah's version—which didn't happen often in disputes of this nature. Joshua agreed that Erin had argued in Sarah's defense, but that he and Erin did not get physical.

Last, Galley spoke to Josh's friend McAndrews, who said he stayed in the car and didn't see anybody hit anybody. While Galley was still in the parking lot asking questions, Sarah's mom arrived.

Gay Ludemann said she did not want to press charges, but she wanted to know how to keep Joshua Camacho away from Ludemann. The cop gave her a copy of the "Victims' Rights" booklet and explained to her how to get an injunction for protection.

On Myspace there was a section called "About Me," in which the account holder described herself. That July, on her page, Rachel described herself as:

Independent Girl, pretty simple with the occasional complicated thought. It really didn't take much to make me smile.

She knew she sometimes came off as a bitch or intimidating, but the moment that folks started to get to know her, they could tell it was a "total misconception." She really wished her laziness wouldn't get the best of her, but it was something she was still trying to fight her way through. She had just recently noticed that she was a hopeless romantic and she dreamed of love like she saw in the chick flicks. A surefire way to win her over was to buy her Chinese food, Red Bull, or Starbucks. She liked to have a good time; and if it just happened to include a pocket filled with money and some alcohol, people shouldn't be surprised if she took advantage of it. She loved her life and everyone in it. She wrote how she was:

Always down to meet new people, so be my friend. I swear I'm nice most of the time. ☺ So go ahead and say hiiiyeee to me. Anything else, you can find out for yourself! ;)

During the evening of July 28, Sarah drove by Rachel's apartment on Belcher Road in Largo and shouted out, "Come fight me." For all of the fuss, Sarah and Rachel had still only met face-to-face once, and that was back when Rachel was still with Nick.

A few hours later, on July 29 at three thirty-six in the morning, Rachel called Sarah's phone and left a voice mail: "Why don't you act your age, Sarah? Seriously, answer your fucking phone and don't be a fucking pussy. You want to come through my fucking neighborhood and be a psycho bitch just like fucking Erin. Fuck with Josh's car, and you are fucking with me when you fuck with his shit. Seriously, I'm letting you know now you are either going to get fucked up or something of yours is, so watch the fuck out or answer your fucking phone and stop being a bitch."

The words were rapid-fire and almost sounded as if they were being read. The message lasted a mere twenty-two seconds.

Less than a day later, at 2:30 A.M., July 30, Rachel was driving through Pinellas Park with then-roommate Courtney Richards. During that drive, she called police, explaining they were in a white Chevy being chased and harassed by the occupants of a white Nissan. At that moment, they were in the vicinity of Seventy-eighth Avenue and Sixty-sixth Street. By the time police arrived, the two vehicles had moved four blocks up and two over. The Chevy stopped voluntarily. The Nissan was subjected to a traffic stop.

Responding to the call were Officers John Coleman and Scott Galley, along with Sergeant Anthony Motley. Coleman spoke first to Rachel, the person who had called. She said she was a passenger and her friend Courtney was driving. They were going home together after work at Applebee's. They stopped at Taco Bell, and a car pulled in aggressively and followed them out of the parking lot. Rachel didn't recognize the car, which followed them almost all of the way home. She did, however, recognize the driver, her archenemy Sarah Ludemann, with whom there was an ongoing dispute over a boy.

"I'm dating her ex-boyfriend," Rachel said.

The chase grew scarier. Sarah pulled alongside Courtney, and then in front of her, cutting her off so that Courtney had to swerve. It finally got to the point where Courtney had to pull off the road. It was too dangerous. And what did Sarah do? Rachel said Sarah rear-ended her. Six angry people piled out of Sarah's car. Rachel's car was attacked with Silly String. Rachel and Courtney tried to lock all doors and windows. Courtney didn't get the window closed fast enough. Two of the girls in the other car—Tiffany Mitchell and Danielle Larson—struck Courtney and kicked her car. They smashed an exterior passenger-side mirror, Rachel said.

Courtney repeated the story, but she left out the part

about being rear-ended. In fact, in Courtney's version, the cars pulled over to the side of the road together, and the Nissan was in front. She said she didn't know the girls who attacked; and no, she did not want to prosecute.

The police made a list of the six girls in the Nissan. In addition to Ludemann, Mitchell, and Larson, Ashley Lovelady, Magen [*sic*] Fitzgerald, and Autumn Seville were also along for the ride.

Interestingly, Sarah said that it was Courtney who had rear-ended her vehicle, not the other way around, and the contact had been made in the Taco Bell parking lot. That was why they were chasing: they'd been rammed.

The police closely inspected the front and rear of both vehicles, and neither showed any evidence of a crash.

Determining that there was a probable cause to search the cars, both vehicles were searched. One of the cars yielded two seeds and part of a stem that might have come from a marijuana plant. But since nothing else was found, the stem and seeds were disposed of without analysis.

Parents were called. The Nissan belonged to Fitzgerald's mom, and she admitted that she was using it without permission. In fact, Fitzgerald confessed, her parents thought she was home. She'd snuck out. Fitzgerald's father did not want to press charges for theft, and Ashley Lovelady's mother agreed to drive the Nissan back to the Fitzgerald house.

The next day, Sarah and Rachel formally accused each other of road rage. Rachel said she was chased. Sarah said she was rear-ended. Sarah told police that she chased the other car, only after it had bumped hers. Sarah said Rachel had once called her twenty times in two hours. Rachel said Sarah was sending her threatening e-mails.

* * *

During that summer, Sarah and Joshua were in New York City together for a few days. Joshua was visiting his relatives up there, and Sarah later joined him. Pictures of the two of them together were posted online, and—to make sure her rival saw them—Sarah sent Rachel taunting messages. Rachel looked at the photos and grabbed for her phone.

At 8:30 P.M., August 28, Pinellas Park police were called by Ramon Camacho—father of Jay and Joshua—complaining that his son Joshua's ex-girlfriend's new boyfriend, Javier Laboy, was harassing him and his family.

"Tonight, he threw an egg at my house," Mr. Camacho said. In addition, Laboy drove by the house repeatedly, before and after the egg, yelling things, disturbing Ramon and his neighbors. Police contacted Laboy and "encouraged a peaceful resolution."

At five o'clock on Friday evening, August 29, the players proved that they had shifting allegiances and could get into fights in any combination. Erin Slothower was the victim this time, and she was complaining about the tag team of Joshua Camacho and Sarah Ludemann. Erin was at her job as a server at American Pie Pizza. Trouble started when Joshua called Erin repeatedly and was insistent on starting an argument. Erin explained it wasn't a good time, since she was working. She had to hang up on Joshua.

Next, Sarah showed up at the pizza place in person. Sarah started to verbally abuse Erin in front of customers, and the restaurant's manager had to ask Sarah to leave. A police officer arrived, took statements, and made a short-lived attempt to get in touch with Joshua and Sarah. Since no battery was alleged, the matter was dropped.

A few hours later, still on August 29, Rachel called

Sarah and left this message: "Please tell me, Sarah, why you would be a dumb-ass cunt to fucking put a brand-new picture of you and Josh at the beach on your Myspace. Seriously, I told you to watch your fucking back and not to fucking chill with him. Now your ass is mine, and I'm guaranteeing you I'm going to fucking murder you. I'm letting you know that right now because you know what? Josh might have played me, but, bitch, I'm going to play your ass out, too, so watch. You are a fucking fat bitch and I'm going to fucking kill you, I swear on my life. Watch your fucking window when I get off of work tonight, you dumb bitch."

This recording was a tad less manic than the recorded call of July 29, and lasted for thirty-four seconds.

On Sunday, August 31, at 10:44 P.M., Rachel called Sarah again and left this voice mail: "It's so funny that you want to talk shit and you sit there and say that my man was over to your house. Well, tell me what he was wearing tonight, Sarah, because you are a dumb bitch for real, and if you're fuckin' lying, I'm going to find you and I'm going to beat your ass. And if you're not lying, I'm going to find you and beat your ass, okay? You can play your fucking games. You are a pathetic little bitch. You are a little fucking girl. Honestly, what do you have going for you that Josh wants you over me for? I've got a job, have my own place. What the fuck! Seriously? He can get anything he wants from me, any fuckin' thing, not to mention that I probably fuckin' look fuckin' ten times better than you. And you fuckin' run your mouth. You've still got your mommy and daddy's curfew, bitch. For God's sake, why the fuck do you run your fuckin' mouth, and why the fuck are you so pathetic? Please do leave the shirt under my face, because that's old news, just like you and him are. So keep talking shit, Sarah. You don't know when to stop. You haven't learned your lesson yet, and I'm the fuckin' teacher. I'm warning you now, keep fucking with me, Sarah, and you and Erin both are dumb psychotic bitches. I'm warning you now, I am going to show you psycho! So stop fucking with me. You are fucking with the wrong person, and you're fucking with the wrong thing that I care about. So keep it up, keep playing your motherfucking game and I am going to teach you how to grow up real motherfucking quick."

This one lasted one minute and fourteen seconds.

Forty-one minutes later, Rachel left another brief message: "Why don't you come outside now, Sarah? I'm outside your house. Come on out, I fucking dare you."

Rachel called again and again.

The annoyance pushed Sarah to the brink; at 11:15 P.M., she called the cops.

Officer Christopher Boyce located Rachel outside Joshua's home. Boyce said Rachel appeared "visibly upset," and complained that it was Sarah's fault. She started it by sending Rachel threatening e-mails.

Officer Boyce's report stated: *Ludemann advised that Wade was threatening her during some of the phone calls and just wanted Wade to stop calling her. Wade advised that she would stop calling Ludemann, but requested that I ask Ludemann to stop threatening her via e-mail. Camacho said that he does see Ludemann behind Wade's back and that* Ludemann was just trying to antagonize Wade into a fight. [Author's emphasis]

Sarah had to promise that she would neither call nor e-mail Rachel. She prophetically told police that she taped the messages because she "wanted it documented in case Wade followed through on her threats."

* * *

On September 12, Rachel wrote on her Myspace page:

I'm an independent chick! Yeah, I got a man. But I'm not one of those spoiled little girls who expects the world from her man. So y'all hoes can just stop hatin'.

On October 8, 2008, the Pinellas Park 911 operator received a call from Rachel Wade's phone. When police arrived at Rachel's apartment, she was there alone. She had gotten into an argument with Joshua, who had broken into the apartment.

"He pushed the door in and broke the dead bolt chain," Rachel complained.

Despite that, the fight had been verbal only. The responding officer looked for Joshua but couldn't find him.

"No further action," he concluded.

Two weeks later, Officer William Holmes answered a complaint from Joshua Camacho's baby mama, Erin Slothower, who said she'd been receiving threats from Rachel Wade that Wade intended to "slit her fucking throat and to do harmful things to her."

Officer Holmes added that both Erin Slothower and her friend Jamie Severino had expressed concerns that they were in fear that "Wade will do something to harm them."

Erin told police that although she had been the target of all the e-mails, some of them had been texted to her friend Jamie Severino's phone. Jamie had made it clear to Rachel that she and Erin wanted no more harassing messages, but Rachel didn't stop. Erin explained that Rachel was a girlfriend of her baby daddy, and Jamie had the baby of Joshua's brother Jay.

* * *

On Friday, November 7, 2008, a Pinellas Park grammar school teacher called police and said they had a kid, Isaiah, who complained that his parents had had a bad fight in the home.

The parents in question were Joshua and Jay's older sister, Janet Camacho, and her baby daddy Robert Williams (pseudonym). Officer Andrea Butson and Child Protection Investigation Division (CPID) investigator Jody Binge handled the complaint.

The allegation, made by their little boy, was that the verbal fight had grown until Janet Camacho grabbed a knife and threatened Robert Williams with it. She "attempted to cut" him. He was trying to take the knife away from her when she was cut. He then got a gun and pointed it at her. Although he "clicked" the gun, it didn't go off.

"That's ridiculous," Janet Camacho told the investigators. "There isn't even a real gun in my house. There is a BB gun, that's all." The BB gun belonged to her brother Joshua, who kept it locked up in his bedroom. The kids had never been allowed to touch it, and it had never been pointed at anyone. She admitted to having a fight with the father of her kids. They didn't live together anymore because they fought so much. The current conflict stemmed back two weeks earlier when Williams came to the Camacho residence to drop off the kids and there'd been a fight.

The investigators had a question: "You have a bandage on your hand. What happened there?"

"I cut myself on a piece of broken glass from a candle," she said.

Janet Camacho and Robert Williams's kids were interviewed separately. Destiny said she knew the difference between the truth and a lie, and she said her mother and father did not fight. It was determined that Isaiah was unable to tell the difference between a truth and a lie, so he was not considered a credible witness.

The kids were given the once-over and showed no signs of abuse.

Officer Butson spoke briefly to Joshua, who vouched for the fact that his BB gun was kept locked inside his bedroom closet. The allegations were untrue, he said.

On Wednesday, November 12, at 7:47 in the evening, Rachel affected a chummy tone at first: "Hey, Sarah, it's Rachel. I'm in my car and I'm sure you-all are walking because yours are broken or you don't have cars. You need the exercise. Maybe it'll thin you out a little bit. I don't know . . . I was just wondering where you are, because if you come to my job, you'll be arrested on the spot. And I'll spit in your food. I'm sure you won't mind because you're not even going to notice because you're going to scarf it down. You're like my fucking dog. You probably don't even chew your food. But do me a favor and meet me there, bitch. Bye."

Sarah did go to Applebee's, when she knew Rachel was working, and specifically asked to be seated in Rachel's section—the better to mess with her. She tripped Rachel while Rachel was carrying beer. She further harassed her rival by complaining to the manager that Rachel had spit in her food.

As the feud escalated, neither girl was having much fun. The only one having fun was Joshua. Friends of both Rachel and Sarah verified that Joshua was amused by the little war between his sex slaves.

One night in November, Rachel was angry with Joshua. She and her friend Lisa Lafrance put their heads together and came up with "the bright idea" to go to Janet's house, where Joshua's car was parked.

"We drove by and egged his car," Lisa said. "Only he didn't know it was us. At least we didn't think so, but I think he put two and two together."

Rachel and Lisa returned to Rachel's apartment. That same night, someone entered Rachel's building, ran up the stairs, pounded on her door, and then ran back down.

"They used to torment Rachel," Lisa observed. Later that night, a car stopped several times out in front of Rachel's building, honked the horn, and then left.

Lisa slept at Rachel's that night; and when she went out to drive home the following morning, November 12, she discovered three of her tires were slashed. Lisa called the cops and told Officer Lawrence Kolbicka that she didn't know for sure who did it, but the tires were still intact at ten o'clock the prior night.

She said her best guess was that the tires had something to do with the recent quarrel between Rachel Wade and Joshua Camacho. Joshua was angry because Rachel hung out with people of whom he did not approve.

Officer Kolbicka spoke to Joshua, who said he knew nothing about slashed tires. Joshua said the police "bothered him" and refused to answer further questions. Due to lack of evidence, the investigation ended there.

Two days later, a little after seven in the morning, police received a call from Charlie Ludemann. Officer Andrew S. Cappa answered the call. Charlie explained that earlier that morning his daughter Sarah and he had gotten into an argument as he was driving her to school. She was in a bad mood because she'd earlier had a fight with her boyfriend, Joshua Camacho. After arguing, Charlie took Sarah's cell phone from her as a disciplinary action. At the next traffic stop, Sarah got out of the car and walked. Charlie called the cops. The policeman retrieved Sarah, who had yet to reach school. He scolded her for her actions, explaining that until she was eighteen, her father had every right to take her cell phone away from her, especially since he was paying the bills for it. Cappa drove Sarah the rest of the way to school and advised both daughter and father to calm down.

On February 25, 2009, police were called when a gang of young people, maybe fifteen to twenty of them, were circled in the street, surrounding a fight that was about to happen. By the time the police arrived, the crowd was gone, but members were quickly located. They had split into two groups and were milling about, a few blocks apart. Asking questions, police learned that the dispute had been between Joshua Camacho and Javier Laboy.

Javier explained that Joshua was mad at him because he "played baby daddy for five months to his son." That is, Javier dated Erin Slothower. Joshua, Javier said, was packing a knife and brass knuckles. He knew because earlier a car containing Joshua cruised past him and Joshua waved the weapons out the window.

Police found Joshua in the other group, and his story, of course, differed. He said it was Javier who'd been hanging out of a car holding a knife and shouting, "I want to kill you!" Nobody was arrested, as there had been no actual physical confrontation. Police explained to everyone that there were better ways to solve their differences.

The incident was important because it took place outside Javier Laboy's house, only a few feet from where Sarah Ludemann would be stabbed six weeks later.

* * *

Jamie Severino lent an insider's expertise to those troubled times. Sarah didn't do drugs—at least not when Jamie was around. Joshua and Janet Camacho smoked weed—smoked weed a lot—but Jamie never saw Sarah do it.

"I don't do drugs, either, so me and Sarah would be sitting while they'd be smoking," Jamie recalled. Not that Sarah was a saint. She was normal enough, unless the subject was Joshua; then she became "crazy, too."

Jamie, like Lisa Lafrance before her, had her tires slashed. That was in March, and she had always felt Sarah did it. Sarah admitted it. Sarah had a problem with Jamie because Jamie was really good friends with Erin.

"She didn't like the fact that Joshua was still seeing Erin," Jamie recalled. Sarah's thinking was any friend of Erin's was an enemy of hers.

One thing Jamie noticed: If she met Sarah alone, Sarah was cool with her. But when Sarah was with her friends, it was a different story.

Just two weeks before Sarah was killed, she got into another fight. This one was with Erin. "It was a fistfight. No weapons. Joshua was there. They fought each other, and that was it," Jamie recalled. "I mean, you shouldn't fight at all, but it was a *fair* fight, and when it was over, they stopped messing with each other."

After the fight, Sarah figured it out. Erin wasn't going anywhere, so she might as well get over it. She couldn't get Erin to stop talking to Joshua. They were always going to talk. They were *parents,* after all.

The young women reconciled with one another— "Let's put everything aside" was how Sarah put it—and Sarah tried to recruit Erin to fight with her against their common enemy: "She had tried to get me to go with her to fight Rachel.

"That was a couple days before her and Rachel, but I didn't go," Erin remembered.

The last time Erin and Rachel spoke, Rachel said foul things about Erin's son.

Erin explained, "I felt I was never going to get anywhere for my son if I continued fighting over Joshua."

Chapter 3

LISA

Lisa Lafrance, born and raised in Pinellas Park, had known Rachel Wade since middle school, but they really started hanging out in ninth or tenth grade. "She was dating our friend Nick, and we had grown up with Nick," Lisa explained.

Lisa and Rachel started out as enemies. The problem, of course, involved a boy. In what would become a familiar pattern, hostilities between Rachel and Lisa built up through phone calls and text messages. They had a fight on Rachel's driveway. Lisa took complete blame for that. She'd started it. Rachel didn't want to fight. Lisa had to go onto Rachel's property to throw the first punch.

"Rachel liked to talk it, but she wasn't violent. She wasn't face-to-face confrontational," Lisa said. After the fight, they became BFFs—best friends forever.

Even back then, Rachel was only "off and on" when it came to living with her parents. She began to date Nick, and then spent a lot of time at Nick's. Lisa hung out there, too.

When they were hanging out, sometimes their activities were mundane. They played cards. But they were also bad girls. "We did a lot of drugs together," Lisa remembered. Those were the days of smoking weed, snorting coke, and taking Roxies.

Lisa was with Rachel for one of their shoplifting busts: "We used to steal clothes, sell them at Plato's Closet, and use the money to buy gas," Lisa explained.

Lisa could never figure out what it was, but Rachel's home with her parents was not a happy place. Her parents were nice, and they had her back no matter what, but they couldn't prevent her from being a relentless rebel.

Constant rebellion brought animosity, which led to further rebellion. Rachel yearned to do her own thing in a world without rules—a world where she had no one to answer to.

Plus "she was boy crazy," Lisa said. "She was always with a boy. The entire time I knew her, she was *never* without a boyfriend."

She was so dependent on boys that whichever boy she was with became Rachel's absolute priority. Parents were no longer necessary. Dealing with parents became intolerable.

"Her parents were great," Lisa said. "They just didn't know how to react when Rachel grew up, being as mature as she was for her age."

Lisa noted that Rachel had a brother, who was just a couple of years older than Rachel. The siblings never got along; and in Lisa's experience, he was never around.

"Rachel used to say they she and her brother fought all the time. She said that her brother hated her. She didn't talk about him much. She didn't like to talk about him. It was a sore subject."

Rachel needed a boyfriend to validate her feelings

and make her feel better about herself. "Even though she was gorgeous and had a great personality, she needed validation," Lisa said.

Rachel's life improved immensely when she got her own apartment. Once they no longer shared the same roof, she and her parents were on even better terms with one another.

Lisa remembered the days of hanging out at Nick's as some of the best times ever. She remembered the problems she had with Jamie Severino over Jay. That got complicated: that was what had started the big fight outside Nick's with the brass knuckles and the cops.

Lisa had maybe the best perspective of the events that would follow because she had been really good friends with both Rachel and Sarah. In school, Lisa and Sarah used to hang out in the gym together. This was before Rachel and Joshua got together. Sarah and Erin didn't get along because of Joshua, and Jamie and Lisa had their troubles over Jay.

Lisa and Sarah never really had a falling-out, but they did stop speaking. With Sarah and Rachel feuding over Joshua, Lisa could no longer be friends with both, and—since Rachel was her best friend—Sarah was dropped.

During the last days of their friendship, Sarah had tried to pump Lisa for info. What was up with Rachel and Joshua? Were they hanging out? According to Lisa, Sarah asked, "Could you please break them up for me?"

Lisa felt bad about it. She understood where Sarah was coming from. Sarah had lost her virginity to Joshua.

Lisa understood what a bond that could create. For four years, Lisa was with the guy who had taken her virginity; and when another girl came around, she was always willing to fight for him.

Lisa told Sarah to her face that, out of loyalty to Rachel,

she had to stop being her friend. Sarah took it well. "Sarah and I never had problems. We had an understanding that I was going to stand by Rachel," Lisa recalled.

Sarah was awesome, a really good kid, but not as innocent as some made her out to be. She was just fighting for Joshua: fighting for his love, for his attention. She even said to Lisa, she never felt good enough for him. Erin was beautiful; Rachel was beautiful; Sarah was beautiful, too, but she was insecure because of her weight problems that had plagued her for much of her life. She was cruelly affected by all of the juvenile taunts she had heard.

"Kids used to call her 'Shrek,'" Lisa remembered. "That was so messed up—because Sarah was gorgeous."

Lisa was aware of the escalating problems between Rachel and Sarah. Rachel would call Lisa while she was coming home from work and would talk until she was safely in her apartment. She needed somebody to talk to because she anticipated an ambush some night from Sarah.

During the last weeks of Sarah's life, Lisa was no longer speaking with Rachel, either. But it was her own fault, not Rachel's. Years had passed since the days of doing lines, weed, and pills at Nick's, and Rachel had—as far as Lisa could tell—stopped taking drugs. Rachel was vocal about her disapproval of Roxies, which was like taking heroin without the needle. Rachel had seen Nick getting goofy on pills, choosing pills over everything else. That was what had broken them up.

For Lisa, however, those drug vices she had acquired while hanging out at Nick's had become habits. She had a serious addiction. "I let Roxies take over my life for three years," Lisa admitted. She tried to recall in detail the last time she spoke to Rachel before Rachel went to jail, but it was hard. She could remember events only as reflected in something resembling a whacked-out carnival mirror.

Rachel was with a friend of hers named Jeremy Sanders at the time. Rachel's friends, in fact, would have said that Jeremy was Rachel's boyfriend. He was a muscle-bound stoner, but he made Rachel "feel so safe" when he held her in his arms—his "guns."

That there was still a soap opera going on involving Joshua Camacho would have surprised many who knew Rachel—especially Jeremy, who had been told by Rachel that Joshua was a thing from the far, far past. Rachel had assured Jeremy that she wasn't even going to *think* about Joshua anymore.

That bitch on the voice mails? Those weren't the "real" Rachel. That was an act. Rachel might have sounded pretty aggressive in her voice mails to Sarah, but in reality she was insecure. Rachel had thought about the situation with Sarah and Joshua.

"I don't think I'm going to get to be with Joshua anymore," Rachel said.

Lisa didn't recall taking that too seriously. Rachel was all about breaking up and making up.

"Still, it was my understanding that she was with Jeremy at the time," Lisa said.

At one point during that final visit, with Lisa slurring her speech and bleary-eyed, Rachel gave Lisa the ultimatum: "The pills or me." It was the first time Rachel had ever spoken to Lisa that way—and it was obvious she was doing it because she wanted to help her. Rachel had lost Nick to pills, and now she was losing Lisa to them.

Sadly, Lisa chose the pills. She was high all of the time. She was high on the night Sarah died.

Chapter 4

LAST DAY

On Tuesday, April 14, 2009, in the lunchroom at Pinellas Park High, Sarah stood out from the crowd. While other seniors ate their lunch and chatted noisily, Sarah sat alone in a corner, eyes swollen from tears.

Her friend Amber Malinchock came over to find out what was wrong. It was Joshua. Again. They'd been going out for months, Sarah was in love with him, and Joshua said she was his one and only.

But it wasn't true.

He was still seeing his ex, a bitch named Rachel.

As Sarah tried to survive school all morning, with her emotional upheaval, her task was complicated by texts she was receiving from Rachel, boasting and taunting that she was back with Joshua.

Amber listened to Sarah and told her to forget about Joshua. He was a jerk and she deserved someone who could love her back. Amber told Sarah they should do something to cheer her up, go shopping, go to a movie or something, but Sarah said no thanks, she needed to talk to Joshua.

That afternoon Charlie Ludemann picked up his daughter after school, as usual. He was very concerned about her. She'd been crying again. When he tried to comfort her, she pulled away from him. She'd been dieting. He yearned for her to see the light. She'd never been with a boy before. She didn't know about all of the great guys that were out there. No matter what he said, she did what she wanted to do, and she wanted to be with Joshua.

When Sarah arrived home, she went to Myspace and checked Rachel's latest postings.

Her rival had written: Mood: Lovin' my boo ☺.

Sarah sent Joshua a text:

Whatever Joshua, you get so mad at me for everything but you don't give a shit when she puts something up or says something. You always believe her. It's like no matter what I do she's always that much better. All we fight about is her or something that has to do with her, and it sucks. I hate fighting with you. I love you so much, but this shit hurts.

No response. Sarah waited an hour and tried again:

You say you love me but you don't have the decency to text me back.

It was just past 8:00 P.M. when Joshua finally responded: Bring the movies.

Her anger forgotten, Sarah returned to her Myspace and wrote: iloveyoubaby.

* * *

It was Rachel's night off from waitressing at Applebee's. She was in her apartment with her friend Egle Nakaite, who'd come over to visit—and Rachel was kvetching. As usual, the subject was Joshua. She wanted to trust him, but she couldn't. He said he was true to her, but there was all of this evidence that he was seeing Sarah, again. Joshua had slept over the night before, but then he took off. It was like he had someplace better to be. Rachel couldn't help it. Her vainglorious mind seized at the indignity.

Rachel's friend Stephanie Pilver remembered the distress Rachel felt when she saw the Myspace New York City photos of Sarah and Joshua, accompanied by a taunting message. It was as if Joshua had "stepped on her heart."

Egle wondered what Rachel was doing that night. Maybe they could hang out at Starbucks or something. Rachel said no. She had Joshua—she hoped. He said he was babysitting for his sister that evening, but he would be available later on.

Egle, one of the many women who hadn't fallen for that ol' Camacho magic, couldn't understand what the big deal was with Joshua. The guy stood five-five tops and walked with a swagger, like he thought he was a tough guy or something. He sneered rather than smiled. One thing was for sure, he had a hold on Rachel. What was it about Joshua? That was the big mystery. He lacked prospects and any kind of a promising future. In high school, he'd worked as a cook at Chick-fil-A and Pollo Tropical, but after graduation it was as if he had retired to smoke pot. Joshua was content to be just a "playa" and a user. He didn't have a steady job. He wasn't going to school. He stayed with family members, unless he could talk one of his girls into letting him spend the night.

* * *

At twilight, Rachel was out walking her dog. Sarah cruised by in her parents' minivan.

"Stay away from my man!" Sarah screamed.

Rachel was frightened. She didn't want to be caught alone by Sarah, who was huge, or any of the friends she might be with. Rachel put a kitchen knife in her purse. That would scare them off.

Rachel also needed backup. She called her friend Javier and asked if she could come over.

At 11:00 P.M., Joshua and Sarah were playing Wii at Janet Camacho's house. Headlights pierced the window. Joshua went to look and saw Rachel's car pass.

Seconds later, Joshua received a text from Rachel: Now I know why you're not talking to me—because you got her.

Joshua texted back: That's right. I don't like you no more. Why are you down this street? Go home.

Rachel responded: No, I'll wait for her to go home.

Sarah didn't want to leave the house and drive home, knowing that Rachel was out there, waiting for her; so Sarah texted her dad and said she was going to be home a little late.

Sarah's curfew was 11:00 P.M.; so the truth was, she was already a little late.

Charlie texted back, asking when she'd be home. Sarah answered that it would be soon.

Rachel left.

Just before midnight, Sarah kissed Joshua good-bye and left. Joshua's sister Janet and her friend Jilica Smith, who'd been sitting in cars with boys out front, asked Sarah if she'd give them a ride to McDonald's before heading home.

Already late, Sarah said sure, what's a few more minutes? So all three got into the minivan and headed to get fast food. At a stop sign, they encountered Sarah's friend Ashley Lovelady, who told them she'd just seen Rachel.

Rachel was only a short distance away, hanging out with two boys in front of Javier Laboy's house. Enraged, Sarah hit the gas so hard she left a patch of rubber on the street. Janet knew Javier—and didn't like him. Javier had had trouble with Joshua over Erin Slothower. Her father had to call the cops on that jackass once for throwing an egg at their house.

Jilica sensed that they weren't headed for McDonald's anymore. As they sped along, Sarah's cell phone rang.

It was Rachel.

"I'm going to kill you and your Mexican boyfriend!" Rachel screamed. Nobody was sure if the phone was on speakerphone, but Rachel was plenty loud and everyone in the minivan heard her. Sarah drove to Javier's house as fast as she could.

There Rachel was, leaning on her car, her white tank top and white tennis shoes lit bright by Sarah's headlights. Skinny ass trying to look tough. Sarah screeched to a stop in the middle of the street.

Chapter 5

"WE NEED AN AMBULANCE. PLEASE HELP."

Twelve forty-five A.M., on April 15, 2009, the call came into the Pinellas Park Police emergency center.

A male operator said: "Nine-one-one. What is your emergency?"

"We have someone on the floor who has been stabbed. We need an ambulance. Please help," said Javier Laboy.

In the background, the operator could hear a woman yelling, words a mile a minute, barely intelligible Spanglish, except for the punctuation of bilingual profanities.

The caller, talking to the woman, not the operator, said, "Hey, Janet." It sounded like an effort to pacify her, but his words failed to break her momentum.

Multiple raised voices could now be heard. The operator asked for, and received, the address of the incident. Judging from the background noise, the dispatcher felt it was ongoing.

The operator asked, "Where was the person stabbed?"

"She's on the floor."

"Where is the person who stabbed them?"

"She's right here, too."

"Where are they?"

"Right here in the driveway."

"What is the phone number you are calling from? Help is on the way."

Javier still had the fast-talking woman in his ear. He didn't hear the question, and it had to be repeated. This time it registered and he gave the operator his cell phone number.

"And where is the knife at now?"

"It's in her hand. You'd better hurry up and get here quick."

"They're already on their way."

Just then, the operator heard a fresh urgency to the voices on the other end of the line, which he interpreted as new violence.

The caller said, "Whoa. Whoa. Janet, Janet, Janet, back up. Janet! Janet!"

"Sir?"

There was the sound of a dial tone for a few seconds; then a second operator, a woman, came on the line, "Police."

The male dispatcher said there was an assault in progress and gave the address, and that was the last the caller heard from him.

"What's going on?" the female operator asked.

"There was a fight and someone was stabbed."

"Who stabbed her?"

Again the caller was distracted by the chaos around him. "Get inside," he could be heard saying.

"Sir, can you hear me?"

"Yes."

"Sir, what happened?"

"We were hanging out. There was a fight."

"Who was fighting?"

"The girls. Oh, her eyes are rolling. God! Oh, you got to hurry."

"They're on their way. Calm down, sir. Just tell me what happened."

"There was a fight and they tried to jump her. She pulled out her pocketknife trying to defend herself. By the time we got there, it was too late and she was already stabbed. She's on the floor."

"Was it a male or a female who was stabbed? Female? It was a female who was stabbed?"

"Yes."

"A female stabbed her? Is the female still there?"

"Yes, everyone is still here."

"How many subjects are there?"

"One, two, three, four, five, six. She's stabbed in the chest."

"All right, just stay on the phone with me, okay?"

"All right."

"Where is the knife now, sir?"

"I—I—I—I have no idea."

"Okay, if you find it, don't touch it. Help is on the way."

PPPD corporal Ty Ku was the first to arrive on the scene. Sarah was on the ground next to the van, part of her legs were underneath the vehicle. A witness, who the police officer later learned was Javier Laboy, had removed his orange T-shirt, which was used to apply pressure to Sarah's upper left chest.

Sarah had a very shallow pulse and was experiencing labored breathing. Her eyes were slightly open and her stare was straightforward. Kneeling beside the victim, Officer Ku called out a request for an "officer survival trauma kit" for a puncture wound.

Officer John Coleman, who had answered several of

the Rachel Wade runaway complaints, went to his patrol car, grabbed the kit, and returned to the victim.

The kit contained a long sterile dressing. When it arrived, the orange shirt could be removed. He would later say he thought the girl's wound was the biggest puncture wound he'd ever seen.

At one point, she stopped breathing and a bubbly fluid came from her mouth. As Ku applied pressure with one hand, he used the other to reposition Sarah's head to open up her airway.

Officer Coleman tried taking Sarah's pulse along her carotid artery. There was a pulse, but it was very weak.

Next to arrive was Officer G. D. Weaver. Ku looked up from the victim for an instant and shouted that the "subject"—that is, the suspect—was inside the residence. Officer Weaver went back to his car to get his ballistic shield from his trunk, but after seeing the subject (Rachel Wade), he realized that he would not need it. Weaver noticed that a crowd was gathering; he went to assist with crowd control.

Corporal Vernard "Rick" Wagner, 2003 PPPD Officer of the Year, was in charge of securing the crime scene with police tape. On the north end of the scene, he attached one end of the tape to a neighbor's fence, the other end to another neighbor's outside waterspout.

The ambulance arrived, and was followed quickly by Officer William Peterson, who parked his car across the road to prevent anyone from fleeing the scene by car. With two EMTs and three paramedics now on the scene, Ku and Coleman left the victim. Ku retrieved his camera from his car. He took eighteen digital photographs of the crime scene, including several of Rachel Wade.

Rachel had not gone in the house, as Javier had told her

to do. She sat on a bench in front of Javier's house and watched the surreal chaos she had caused. Javier recalled that she had a blank look on her face. Javier said it didn't look like she "was there with us."

Rachel's phone rang. It was Joshua. Sarah said she had gotten hurt. What was up?

Rachel said she was at Javier's house. She'd just had a fight with Sarah and she thought Sarah *might* be hurt. Joshua hung up, ran to Sarah's house, two blocks away, and told Sarah's parents that Sarah had been in a fight and was hurt.

Together Charlie and Joshua went to Javier's house and arrived in time for them to see Sarah still lying in the street, with the paramedics frantically working on her.

Sergeant William Lowe, who was working crowd control, recalled one young man who ran down the street to the scene, screaming. He hurled threats, saying he was the victim's brother and would see his revenge. (Of course, Sarah Ludemann was an only child.) Lowe told the unidentified man he had to stay outside the police tape, but the guy kept mouthing off, using words that could only inflame the situation: "Someone get stabbed, someone gonna get stabbed." Other police at the scene identified the troublesome bystander as Joshua Camacho.

Officer M. Turner and the search dog Dax reported to the crime scene, the same human/canine team that was once sent to the Wade household to search for a runaway Rachel. The team had just arrived as Joshua went berserk at the crime scene. Dax was positioned between Joshua and EMS activity. The dog remained in that position until Joshua retreated to the end of the street.

Charlie Ludemann couldn't move quickly, but he could move relentlessly. He pushed past police tape and toward his daughter, until Sergeant Tina Trehy intercepted him and talked him away from the van. But not before the father got a good look. Charlie said he was going back home to get his wife.

Charlie's memories came in the form of horrible snapshots and sound bites. Lights everywhere. Flashing. Areas taped off. Rachel sitting there as if nothing had happened, smoking a cigarette. Charlie yelling his daughter's name. Sarah not responding. Sarah as a little girl singing. A police officer in his face, asking him who he was.

"That's my daughter lying on the ground," he said. Sarah lying in a pool of blood.

Charlie trying to get her to respond to him, but she couldn't even lift her head. Charlie knowing she was dead, and there was nothing anyone could do.

Rachel sitting on a bench, like nothing had happened. Rachel smoking a cigarette. Charlie screaming that Rachel was a "stupid bitch." Why did she need a knife? Why couldn't she fight with her hands?

Detective Kenneth Blessing asked Janet Camacho what had happened. Janet said that she, the victim, and their friend Jilica Smith were on their way to McDonald's when Rachel threatened to stab Sarah. They met in the street.

Rachel had been the complete aggressor, Janet said. She murdered Sarah.

"What happened to the knife?" Detective Blessing asked.

"I think she snuck it to one of her boyfriends," Janet said, meaning Javier and his friend Dustin Grimes.

Detective Joe Doswell interviewed Jilica Smith, who also said that Rachel had threatened to stab Sarah, but she claimed that the victim had shown her a text to that effect.

She'd seen a red car driving by when she was outside Janet's house, with a couple of girls in it.

Later, when they got to this scene, Sarah had barely made it out of the minivan before Rachel charged her and the fight started. Jilica said she got a good look at the knife. It looked like a kitchen knife to her, and she would never forget the way Rachel smiled as she held it.

When Blessing finished with Janet, and Doswell concluded his interview with Jilica, both women began walking home. But they didn't make it far. They were intercepted, put into a patrol car, and were parked in it so that they could see the front of Javier's house.

Did either of them see the person who stabbed their friend Sarah? Sure, they said. It was Rachel Wade, sitting right there on that bench.

Officer William Peterson separated Javier Laboy and his friend Dustin Grimes; then he took their written statements. Peterson later characterized those statements as "evasive."

Javier and Dustin told identical stories. All three women got out of the van simultaneously. They charged at Rachel, yelling. Sarah, in particular, was yelling as she aggressively approached Rachel. At first, Sarah and Rachel went at it; then there was a moment when Sarah and Janet were beating Rachel at the same time, two on one. Officer Peterson thought both witnesses needed to be interviewed again and said so when he turned them over to Detective Blessing.

Sergeant Tina Trehy was in charge of keeping an eye on Rachel Wade. Police would wait for a less hectic moment to interrogate her. They wanted to get this right.

As Trehy observed, Rachel kept moving her tongue to her bottom lip and bottom teeth. She complained that she thought she had cut the inside of her mouth during the fight.

Paramedics lifted Sarah Ludemann onto a gurney and put her in the ambulance.

Officer John Coleman escorted the ambulance to the hospital, which arrived at 1:21 A.M. Doctors and nurses worked over her for one hour and eight minutes.

PART TWO

THE INVESTIGATION

Chapter 6

THE LEAD INVESTIGATOR

PPPD detective Michael Lynch might have gotten a relatively late start in his career as a cop, attending the academy when he was twenty-six, but law enforcement as a career choice had always been in the back of his mind. Some of Lynch's work history before the police academy served him well in readying him for life as a peace officer. He'd been a dive technician, working on dive equipment in a little shop. He was in the insurance industry for a while. He was a tour operator, working for his mom, taking groups of senior citizens to Europe and Alaska. Putting those experiences together, his job history prepped him well for police work. He didn't think he would have been an effective police officer right out of school. A few years of maturity helped him immensely.

And he *was* an effective officer—awarded the 2007 Officer of the Year Award to honor his work on a series of high-profile bank robberies in Central Florida, with the suspect being dubbed the "Band-Aid Bandit," and for the successful conclusion of a murder case, which went to trial that year.

He loved working in investigations. He enjoyed solving mysteries, assembling jigsaw puzzles. He wouldn't have been happy as a road officer his entire career.

Lynch joined PPPD in December 1997, was a patrol officer for two years, and after that a detective. In 2000, he joined the agency's SWAT crisis negotiating team.

Lynch was a lifelong resident of Pinellas Park. As it happened, he had been a senior at Pinellas Park High School when Jason Harless and Jason McCoy came to school with guns and murdered Assistant Principal Richard Allen.

That incident made the national news and gave the city a reputation for youth violence, but Pinellas Park didn't deserve that tag. During his years as a cop, Lynch had come to believe that the kids of the city were no more violent than anywhere else in the country. Sure, there was youth crime, but it predominantly consisted of fistfights. He was used to reporting to scenes and finding the victim with, at worst, bloody knuckles and a broken nose.

In the past couple of years, there had been a rash of bullying-type crimes: online bullying cases that had made the news; people bad-mouthing each other on Myspace or Facebook; a lot of words flying back and forth. Enemies, who might in the past have cooled off when they were apart, were now linked via cell phones and the social networks. They could insult one another at any time of day or night, and do it in virtual public. Everybody saw it, everybody heard it, and it spread like wildfire—so that embarrassment blended with anger, forming a potentially violent cocktail.

There had also been a tick upward in youth crime due to a new drug problem in the area—prescription pills. Back in the late 1990s, the city went through a heroin phase and police got used to reporting to the scenes of overdoses.

But that went by the wayside; and a few years back, there had been a rash of robberies of local pharmacies, with major thefts of pills with codeine in them. Those pills had been used to hook an unacceptable percentage of the area's juveniles.

Drug dealers discovered that Floridian kids, the ones who were out for kicks, were more apt to pop a couple blue Roxicodone pills than stick needles in their arms. Business improved.

Despite this, Detective Lynch was unaware of another local youth fight that could rise to the level of violence he saw that night in front of Javier Laboy's house. This was new. He could only hope it was an isolated incident.

Detective Lynch saw only the occasional girl-on-girl violence, which he called "she-looked-at-me-wrong" fights. They happened, but they rarely involved weapons or serious injuries.

Lynch arrived at the scene of the stabbing about an hour after it had happened. Since he was the on-call detective, he became the case's lead investigator. The first thing he did was talk to the first responders, who "gave him the lay of the land."

"Victim's name?"

"Sarah Ludemann."

The detective felt his shoulders slump just a little. He was familiar with this case. Sarah's father had contacted him in the past about his daughter being harassed by another girl.

In some ways, the early investigation was easy. For one thing, no apprehension would be necessary. All of the parties were still on hand. The accused was right over there, calmly sitting on a bench. All of the eyewitnesses were also present, which again simplified things. The witnesses had naturally divided themselves into two camps. The Rachel witnesses were standing in a driveway. Sarah's friends were down at the other end of the street.

In addition to the young adults who'd been on the scene since the stabbing, several curious and concerned neighbors were on the street. Lynch was told Sarah's parents had been there earlier. As Lynch looked around, he felt a sense of déjà vu.

He'd been on this street before, for another murder not long before. He recognized some of the family members from that other case standing nearby and observing. In fact, the boyfriend of a family member from the earlier case was among those who attended to Sarah as she lay in the street. Lynch saw him now, stained and shocked.

The detective canvassed the scene, paying particular note to the bloodstained articles of attire on the street next to the victim's minivan. About two feet away from the driver's door was a portion of a light-colored bra, cut off Sarah by the EMTs so they could better access her wound. Almost under the vehicle was a pair of bloody white sandals, which Lynch correctly assumed were Sarah's. Ten feet from the van was a blood-soaked orange T-shirt, which Lynch would later learn was Javier Laboy's.

He made sure that a line of communication was kept open with the hospital in case there was an update on Sarah's condition.

The priority at the crime scene shifted to finding the weapon. The canine team searched but was unsuccessful.

Rachel said, "Knife? What knife? They came over to jump me. I don't know where the knife is."

Lynch spoke with Dustin Grimes and Javier Laboy, who said that yes, they knew she had a knife with her, but they had no idea where it went.

Sergeant Mark R. Berger grabbed Lynch by the arm and

pulled him aside. He'd just heard from Lieutenant Kevin Riley that the victim was not good. This was probably going to end up as a homicide investigation.

Lynch thanked him. They agreed to keep that under their hats for the time being.

Sergeant Tina Trehy was still staying with Rachel Wade in front of Javier's house, and was now joined by Officer C. D. Burns.

"I was just defending myself," Rachel kept saying. "It was obviously really stupid, because it did not change anything."

Rachel described how frightened she had been that Sarah and her friends were planning to jump her. She claimed to have called 911 earlier in the night when she thought they were following her. She discussed the swerving car that had almost hit her and had preceded the arrival of the van by a couple of minutes. She thought the swerving vehicle was a Jeep.

"After the fight, Javier told me to go inside the house, but I didn't want to disturb his mother so I stayed outside," Rachel babbled.

Officer Burns frisked Rachel and confiscated from her person a phone, keys, and a pack of cigarettes.

"Have any weapons?" Burns asked.

"No," Rachel replied.

At no time did she seem upset. At no time did she ask how Sarah was. Rachel complained that she was chilly. Her light blue jacket had been ripped off during the fight. Trehy went to her car, grabbed a sterile yellow blanket—each blanket was sealed in plastic and was thrown out once used—and gave that to Rachel.

Javier's mother, who'd been asleep, was up now. She came outside and talked to a police lieutenant for a few minutes. He asked if they could search her house for the weapon, and she said fine.

Seeing that Rachel still looked cold, even with her sterile blanket, Javier's mother went back in the house and came out with a jacket for Rachel to wear.

Trehy searched the kitchen and did find a black-handled knife next to the kitchen sink, but it wasn't the weapon. There were still small pieces of food adhering to the blade.

Detective Adam Geissenberger, who had been so busy during Rachel Wade's runaway phase, did not take an active part in the investigation into the death of Sarah Ludemann. His brief written report from that night does, however, provide one interesting tidbit. Joshua Camacho had arrived at the crime scene, screaming and hurling threats that blood would be shed in retaliation. Police took this seriously enough that a "suspicious person" call was put out over the radio for Joshua's brother Jay, who was, according to one report, in his car and on his way to Javier Laboy's house. If he was on his way, Jay never arrived.

Meanwhile, Joshua went with the Ludemanns to the hospital, trailing the ambulance. Sarah was wheeled into the emergency room, where ER doctors frantically attempted to save her life. Gay went with the gurney. Charlie and Joshua stayed in the waiting room.

The mother turned to the doctor and pleaded, "Please take her to surgery."

"I can't," the doctor replied. "I have to have a pulse first."

Gay held her daughter's hand and rubbed her legs. She begged her daughter to respond, telling her that they were going to stop trying to save her if she didn't respond.

At 2:29 A.M., Sarah was officially pronounced dead.

A doctor invited the Ludemanns and Joshua Camacho to view the body.

"You ought to come," Charlie said to Joshua.

"No, I can't see her like that," Joshua said.

"You're the reason she's like that!" Charlie said.

Joshua left. They didn't see him after that.

Charlie later recalled, "I walk in there. There she is. Pale. Cold. I lost it."

Gay added, "She was our life. We lived and died for her. And she's not here."

Amy Tyson, a victim advocate, arrived at the hospital and tried to comfort Sarah's parents.

Detective Lynch was still canvassing the crime scene when he received a call from an officer at the hospital informing him that the victim had expired.

He notified the state attorney's office that this was now a confirmed homicide investigation.

After that phone call, Lynch kept the information to himself. Rachel Wade didn't know, and he wanted to keep it that way—until the time was right.

Since Rachel Wade was still not under arrest, Lynch asked her if she would be willing to return to the police department to talk to him some more about what had happened between her and Sarah. She voluntarily agreed to come. Lynch then talked her into signing a Consent to Search form, which meant police could go over Rachel's car thoroughly without first obtaining a search warrant. The search of the Saturn yielded nothing of evidentiary value.

Lynch ordered that Rachel's car be moved to the driveway, where it could be picked up at a later time by her parents. Detective Doswell and Sergeant Trehy would accompany Rachel from the crime scene to the police station. Rachel rode to the PPPD headquarters in the front seat of Trehy's car. No handcuffs. Doswell followed close behind.

Lynch asked Trehy to transport Rachel to the police department, so Rachel was put in the back of Trehy's patrol car.

"You okay?" Trehy asked.

Rachel said yes, for the most part, but she did have a headache and her stomach was upset. At the station, Rachel was placed in an interrogation room and was told to wait for Detective Lynch.

Back at the crime scene, the minivan was impounded at the request of the forensic team from the county sheriff's office. A truck with "JOE'S TOWING" painted on the side arrived and removed the victim's vehicle.

Finished at the scene, Lynch went to the hospital to observe Sarah's wounds. A hospital staffer escorted Lynch to the body and pulled back the sheet so he could see. The victim, whose clothing had earlier been collected, had "two significant stab wounds" to her upper left chest. Stab wound number one was in the victim's upper left shoulder, just below the shoulder blade.

Comparing it to the face of a clock, the wound was oriented to a position of one o'clock at the top to seven o'clock at the bottom. Stab wound number two was directly over the area of the left breast. It was oriented from twelve to six o'clock.

The wound over the breast was larger than the wound in the shoulder—two to three inches long. The shoulder wound was one to two inches long.

The detective noticed no defensive injuries—that is, injuries the victim might have suffered while trying to protect herself, which are most commonly found on the hands or arms.

After Lynch concluded his examination of the victim's body, he called Investigator John Rush, of the Pinellas County Medical Examiner's Office. Rush said he would send the county transport to the hospital to bring Sarah's remains to the medical examiner's (ME) office. An autopsy was scheduled for ten-thirty in the morning. An employee of the ME's Office, Steve Sellick, took custody of Sarah's body.

Lynch needed to speak to Charlie and Gay Ludemann, who were still in solemn discussion with victim advocate Amy Tyson.

Lynch introduced himself to the Ludemanns and "let them know where we were at in the investigation." He stressed the importance of the upcoming autopsy.

"Did you have any advance knowledge of the events leading up to Sarah's death?" Lynch asked.

The parents said they were unaware of the night's events, except for what they'd been told since the stabbing.

Charlie said, "My daughter left our house at eight-thirty to go to Taco Bell, and she never came back."

Detective Chris Piccione remained at the crime scene and went door-to-door speaking to neighbors to see if anyone saw or heard anything. No one was helpful.

John Wilkes heard loud voices but saw nothing.

Brent Godels, who was visiting his grandmother, also heard shouting, plus a loud pop that he thought might've been a gunshot.

Binh Nguyen heard loud screaming right outside his house, but he didn't know what it was all about until the ambulance arrived.

* * *

After what seemed like an eternity of waiting around while the nightmare refused to end, Janet and Jilica were through, as far as the cops were concerned. Done for the time being, anyway.

Someone would want to do a follow-up interview in the next couple of days. Detective Blessing gave the pair a ride to Janet's house.

Was it possible that less than three hours had passed since they left in Sarah's van? It was only two hours and forty minutes later, but it felt so much longer than that, like part of a lifetime.

Rachel was upstairs in police headquarters, in the criminal investigation section, in the second of three small windowless interrogation rooms.

After Detective Lynch finished with his rounds of official duties, he returned to the police department. With Detective Joe Doswell also in the room, he began questioning Rachel Wade at a few minutes past five in the morning.

There were preliminaries: before anything, Lynch had Rachel sign an Acknowledgment of Rights form, signifying that she had been advised of her Miranda rights.

At the time of the interview, Rachel was five-four, weighing 110 pounds. Her hair was sandy, and her eyes blue. Her birthday was February 27, 1990.

She had five tattoos: One said TRUE; another said NICK. There were flowers on her right hip. STAY was on her right arm, and a rosary draped her right leg. Lynch jotted it all down.

Rachel began by talking about her relationship with Joshua. They dated from June of 2008 through November 2008. It was that October that she first realized she had a problem with Sarah Ludemann, another girl who was interested in Joshua. Sarah had made many threats, even threats to kill her. She admitted that she never really believed that Sarah was going to follow up on any of her threats, and this was the first time that the two had fought.

Lynch asked about the events that led to the fight.

At about five o'clock that evening, Joshua texted her, saying he wanted to come over and spend the night. Two hours later, Rachel claimed, she received a text from Sarah.

The girl wrote: Stop texting my man.

Sarah said Rachel could forget her plans because Joshua was going to be with her that night. There was a threat. Sarah said Rachel had "something coming" if she didn't leave Joshua alone.

Rachel said that Sarah stopped at one point sending her texts, but Joshua continued to text her and call her throughout the night.

"He was encouraging me to fight Sarah," Rachel said. "If I loved him, I would fight for him."

And so Rachel went to Javier's house, and she was on the phone with Joshua when a car, maybe a Jeep, with an unknown driver, swerved and tried to run her over in the street. Then the van pulled up. Sarah, Janet, and a girl she didn't know got out.

Sarah hit her a few times and she tried to fight back. Sarah grabbed her by the hair. Janet hit her in the head. Janet had her by the hair and was dragging her around.

Rachel heard Sarah call out for Janet to get back in the van; it was time for them to go. It seemed about that time the cops arrived.

Lynch asked, "When Sarah got out of the minivan, did she come over to you?"

"Yeah, she hit me a couple of times."

"Where did she hit you?"

"On the side of my face and the back of my head."

Lynch explained that her story didn't match the facts. It didn't match what others were saying—not just the statements of Sarah's friends, but the statements of her own friends as well.

"She was there to fight you. How do you think Sarah ended up getting stabbed?"

"I don't know."

Detective Lynch explained that he knew what had happened, and she needed to know what happened, too.

"I know you had the knife," Lynch said.

Rachel admitted to bringing the knife with her. She was scared of Sarah and her friends. She thought the knife would scare them. She admitted to approaching Sarah with the knife in her hand. She said Sarah backed up a couple of steps and then started to swing at her.

"I began to swing in Sarah's direction."

"With the knife in your hand?"

"Yes."

"Did you stab Sarah?"

"I don't know. Janet came over and started hitting me at that point. I never meant to hurt anyone. I just wanted it all to end."

"You stabbed Sarah," he said. "And here's another piece of information you need to know. She is dead."

"Oh my God." Rachel was instantly hysterical. She said she never intended for anyone to get hurt. She never wanted anyone to die.

"And she *died* as a result of these stab wounds she had. All this over Joshua?"

"I just didn't want them to terrorize me anymore. They follow me everywhere. They come to my job. They come to my house."

"Well, she's not going to follow you anymore because she's dead now."

Rachel wailed: "Oh my God. I just wanted her to fight me and get it over with. I don't care anymore. A guy is not that important to me."

"Well, this guy has now completely ruined your life," Lynch said.

The detective asked Rachel if she had ever threatened to stab or kill Sarah before that night. Rachel assured Lynch that she had not. Lynch asked where the knife was. She said she'd thrown it in the direction of the house next door.

Lynch called Detective Kenneth Blessing back at the crime scene and informed him of this revelation. After getting a set of keys from the homeowner to open a gate, Blessing, Officer Burns, and Dax, the canine, as well as a couple of the crime scene technicians from the sheriff's office, looked around the grounds next door and found nothing.

There was only one other possibility: "The roof," Blessing said.

The county technicians had a ladder with them.

Blessing climbed up on the neighbor's roof. Using a flashlight, he quickly located one bloody kitchen knife, which the crime scene technicians photographed and collected.

Back at the police station, Rachel and Lynch parted ways. Rachel had a favor to ask: Would Lynch talk to her mom and dad, explain what happened, please? Lynch said he would do that.

So Detective Lynch called the home of Barry and Janet Wade to tell them that their daughter was under arrest.

"I felt just as bad talking to Rachel's parents as I had

talking to Sarah's," Lynch admitted. "I know that sounds strange. I knew one lost a child and the other one was still alive, but . . . when I gave the news to Rachel's mom, she just dropped the phone. I could hear her screaming through the house."

That afternoon he visited the Wades in person, to give them the keys to Rachel's car.

"The mom was just catatonic, sitting there in complete disarray," Lynch recalled. "To her, it was all too surreal, and there was no way for her to completely register what was happening. The dad was just as bad. He managed to speak with me, but I could see that he was completely in shock."

Barry Wade told Lynch that when Rachel would become involved with "these guys," and he didn't mention any names, they were *"Fatal Attraction"* things. Whoever she ended up with, he was the one, the sole focus of her thinking, and the breakups were always bad.

Rachel was booked and fingerprinted. Her mug shot was taken. Rachel flashed the saddest of all possible eyes.

At 8:00 A.M., the sheriff's office forensic specialist came by to confiscate the evidence on Rachel's person. Her clothes—white top, blue jeans, bra, thong—were taken away from her, to be used as evidence.

She stood naked for a moment; then she eagerly donned a white jumpsuit.

Understanding that she was about to be put in a cage, Rachel wept.

Rachel was transported from the PPPD's criminal investigation section to the Pinellas County Jail. In charge of transportation was Corporal Michael Bingnear, winner of the department's 2006 Officer of the Year Award.

Lynch told Bingnear that Rachel was ready for transport.

Bingnear handcuffed Rachel's hands behind her back. She was barefoot—exposing little painted toenails.

Bingnear escorted Rachel downstairs and into the parking lot on the building's south side. They ran into a Pinellas County Sheriff's Office (PCSO) forensic technician, and Bingnear asked if the tech had a spare pair of protective shoe covers. Rachel put her feet in those to walk the rest of the way to Bingnear's squad car.

He put her in the passenger-side backseat of his car, and neither spoke as they made the fourteen-minute journey to the jail. She silently gazed out the front windshield for the whole trip.

Corporal Bingnear stayed with Rachel until she was booked into the jail on a charge of murder, second degree. She was told to sit and wait for Detective Lynch. She did as she was told, and, with adrenaline crashing, she managed to doze off for a few minutes.

Back at the crime scene, Detective Blessing took another crack at getting something out of Dustin Grimes, who, along with his buddy Javier, had seemed less than forthcoming during the initial interview, a few hours before.

Blessing interviewed Dustin, who now described the stabbing in some detail. The eyewitness explained that Rachel Wade had approached the van the instant it pulled to a stop, even before Sarah had an opportunity to open her door.

However, Dustin still insisted he didn't see what had happened to the knife.

In the meantime, Charlie Ludemann pulled out his cell phone and called his daughter's number. He knew that it would go to message, and he wanted to hear her voice one more time, even if it was just a recording.

At the sound of the beep, he left a message of his own: "Yeah, Sarah, it's Daddy. I know you're not with us no more. I'm hoping somebody's listening to this phone. My daughter was killed last night. I just want a little closure."

Three or four times a week, Charlie called.

That was all he had left.

Erin Slothower, such a large player in the events that led up to Sarah's death, was sound asleep when the tragedy occurred. She had turned her phone off so she would be able to read her texts, she remembered. She fell asleep; and when she woke up, she had a long list of messages and voice mails.

Erin heard about the fight in the street and went to Janet's house. There she learned that Sarah was dead.

Jamie Severino, the other Camacho baby mama, was also home at the time of the stabbing, with her daughter, minding her own business. When her phone started to ring, she didn't answer at first. She'd had an argument with Jay earlier in the evening, and she thought it was him calling. But it was Erin, who was texting that Sarah had died. Jamie thought it was some stupid lie they'd conjured up to trick her into going over there.

Finally Jay spoke to Jamie on the phone, and he was crying. "Sarah's dead. You got to get over here fast," he said.

It wasn't a joke. It was like a nightmare.

Half blind with tears, Erin drove over to Janet's house; there were cop cars all over the place. Everyone was hysterical.

According to Jamie, Erin—who couldn't stop crying— received a voice mail that night, only hours after Sarah's death, from Gay Ludemann. The message said, "You don't have to worry about Sarah anymore. My daughter's dead. Now you can have Joshua all to yourself."

After that, Erin was somewhat surprised when police never asked her questions. The press did try to interview her, but the young mother was a woman of few words.

All she managed was "It's all so sad." What else could she say?

Chapter 7

POSTMORTEM

From the hospital, Sarah Ludemann's body was delivered to the District 6 medical examiner for autopsy. The ME's office was next door to the sheriff's office, and the ME was Dr. Jon Russell Thogmartin, a balding and bespectacled man. Attending the procedure for the PPPD was Detective Blessing, who had hours before found the bloody knife on a rooftop.

In addition to being a licensed doctor in Florida since 1990, Dr. Thogmartin was also licensed in Texas and Alabama. A graduate of the University of Texas Health Center at San Antonio, he trained for another five years, first as a resident in Texas in anatomic and clinical pathology, then in Dade County, Florida, for a year in forensic pathology. He was board certified in anatomic, clinical, and forensic pathology, and had been doing forensic pathology ever since completing his fellowship in 1996. He was the District 6 medical examiner since December 2000, and he had performed approximately 2,500 autopsies.

The autopsy began at 11:00 A.M. on April 15, about ten

hours after the stabbing. In cases in which the deceased died at the scene of the crime, someone from the ME's office was often sent there to help determine what had occurred. Since Sarah had died in the hospital, this was not done in her case.

Dr. Thogmartin performed both an exterior and interior examination on the body, found her to be "about five foot nine, 166 pounds, fully developed, about eighteen years old."

With the exception of her stab wounds—two wounds, one small, one very large, the large one on her left breast—she had nothing wrong with her.

In order to distinguish her wounds, he numbered them one and two, not ordering them by severity but rather by location. The topmost wound was one; the lower, more severe wound two.

In an autopsy's written report, right and left referred to the decedent's right and left. The front of a body referred to the side that faced forward as a person was standing with their palms facing forward. The palms and knees, for example, were both on the front of the body. Up and down referred again to when the body was standing; even though, obviously, the body was prone during the autopsy.

Wound number one was a slitlike elliptical skin defect caused by a sharp object, 2.1 by 0.4 centimeters. Dr. Thogmartin probed the wound to determine its depth and direction. It was only a half an inch deep, and too shallow to determine the angle. If the wound had been any deeper, it probably would have severed a couple of large blood vessels, but that had not occurred. It might have caused a little bleeding, but that was about it. If wound number one had been the only wound, treatment would have involved cleaning it out well, a couple of stitches, and maybe some antibiotics—nothing more.

Even without outside knowledge of the case, the ME

would have assumed that this was a knife wound. The lower corner of the wound was rough and squared. The upper corner was sharp—particularly when he examined it with the skin pushed together.

He could tell the weapon was most likely a single-edged blade. A double-edged dagger with sharp edges on both sides would have created a wound of a different shape. The weapon had one dull and one sharp edge.

Even at first glance, wound number two appeared to be the fatal wound. It was not a slit but rather gaping. The wound was open so far that he had to re-approximate it, push the skin together to get a better idea. The weight of the decedent's breast falling to one side stretched the entrance to the wound open, so that he had to compensate for the gravity and tension when measuring: eight centimeters by four millimeters.

Accurately measuring the wound's depth was tricky, perhaps impossible. That depth would change, depending on whether the victim was inhaling or exhaling. With lungs full, the wound would have been a full two inches deeper than with lungs empty. In his written report, the ME recorded that the second wound was about two and a half inches deep.

The wound went into the fatty tissue of her chest and her pectoral muscles, cut through her fourth rib, and—as her left lung overlaid her heart in that area—into her left lung, through her pericardial sac—the sac that held the heart—and into the right ventricle of her heart, where it terminated. The medical examiner made it official: it was the fatal injury.

When he performed his internal examination, Dr. Thogmartin looked for the quantity of blood loss. There was blood coming out of her heart and her perforated lung. The blood coming out of her heart accumulated in the sac around her heart. Three hundred milliliters of blood was found there. An additional two liters of blood was found in her chest cavity. Her lung collapsed due to the accumulating blood.

A woman of Sarah's size may have four and a half liters of blood, give or take, and she had lost more than two, so she'd lost about half of the blood that her body contained outside of her blood vessels. That would have caused severe shock.

As wound number two was being created—perhaps when the knife was going in, but more likely when the knife was being pulled out—the cutaneous portion of the wound, meaning the opening created in the skin, was stretched and enlarged. This enlargement was caused either by movement in the victim's breast or movement by the stabber or the victim.

Dr. Thogmartin filled out Sarah Ludemann's death certificate. He listed the cause of death as a stab wound to the chest. He listed the manner of death as homicide.

A blood sample was taken and sent to toxicology. Tests were run to determine if she had alcohol or other drugs of abuse in her system. Sarah Ludemann's remains were tested for amphetamines, barbiturates, cocaine, all sorts of opiates, and methadone. No test was made for marijuana. All tests came back negative.

Lisa Lafrance heard the bad news on the morning of April 15, when she arrived at work for her waitressing job at Mugs 'N Jugs Restaurant & Bar in Clearwater. The "Jugs" in the name of the restaurant referred to—as was the case with Hooters—the large breasts of the youthful waitresses.

"I was just about to start my shift, and my phone started to ring. It was Nick, Rachel's old boyfriend. He said, 'Did you hear about Rachel?' And I was like, 'What happened?

Did you guys get back together?' They were always breaking up and getting back together. He's like, 'No, she killed some girl named Sarah.'"

It took Lisa a few seconds to register what he'd said and that he was for real. She freaked out. Through her tears, she put on the news. She had to explain to Nick who Sarah was.

She knew immediately that Sarah and the others were the aggressors. She recalled the physical fight she'd had with Rachel years before, and she remembered how Rachel was all mouth. She had to *really* be provoked, punched in that case, before she would become physically violent.

"She just wasn't the type to go after someone," Lisa recalled.

Rachel would go down in history as a very angry girl, which struck Lisa as ironic. Rachel wasn't angry at all. She was the type of girl who *didn't* let things get to her. Obviously, matters involving guys were the exception to that rule. She had been spoiled by her own popularity.

Every guy fell head over heels in love with her, twisted around her little finger, and she had grown accustomed to having the upper hand when it came to boyfriends. Then came Joshua, who saw other women, frightened her, and made her feel wonderful. She *so* wasn't in charge. Joshua was every bit as much of a control freak as she was, and he was winning the game of control. She was challenged in a way she wasn't used to, and that frustrated and angered her.

"Every girl likes a challenge," Lisa said, "but Rachel took it to the extreme." Sarah was aggressive when it came to her dibs on Joshua Camacho, further aggravating Rachel.

Lisa remembered hanging out with Rachel at her apartment and was there when Sarah would call, hurling insults and asserting her right to Joshua. And Joshua was no help.

Instead of smoothing things out, according to Lisa, he was "feeding into it."

As the news of Sarah's death and Rachel's arrest sank in, Lisa felt more than just grief. She felt guilt. She had abandoned her best friend. It was the damn Roxies. If she hadn't been so strung out on drugs, she would have been with Rachel that night. She would have talked her out of bringing the knife with her. Sarah would still be alive and Rachel would be a free woman. They would be free to drive around in Lisa's car like they used to, listening to Rachel's favorite performer, Trina, on CD.

Rachel had always been loyal to Lisa. Their relationship had started with a fight, and there was something about that, forging a friendship that way, that made the bond stronger. The thought made the Mugs 'N Jugs waitress burst into tears all over again.

During the early daylight hours of April 15, 2009, Lane DeGregory reported for work at the *St. Petersburg Times,* unaware that it was going to be a very busy day.

DeGregory was a native Floridian, born in Gainesville, but she grew up in Rockville, Maryland, suburban Washington, D.C. Since she was four years old, she knew that she wanted to be a journalist.

"That was all I ever wanted to do. When I was little, my dad would read Watergate stories to me," DeGregory said. She was the editor of her high-school newspaper. She attended the University of Virginia, edited the newspaper there, and graduated with a double major of English and communications studies. She later earned a master's degree at UV. After graduation she worked a series of newspaper jobs, including one at a small paper in Charlottesville, Virginia, ten years with the *Virginian Pilot* in Norfolk, and since October 2000 with the *St. Petersburg Times,* where she started as a general-assignment feature writer.

DeGregory was best known for a feature story that ran in the *Times* on July 31, 2008, called "The Girl in the Window." The excruciating tale—of a child neglected and abused into a feral state, then saved—was a devastatingly effective piece of reporting and writing. Everyone who read it blubbered, and DeGregory was nominated for a Pulitzer Prize for it.

On that Wednesday morning, DeGregory was working out of the newsroom. She hadn't even had a chance for a cup of coffee when she and photographer Lara Cerri were sent out to Javier Laboy's house to cover the death of Sarah Ludemann. When they arrived, there was still blood in the street. A small memorial to Sarah Ludemann had been built already at the side of the street.

DeGregory knocked on the door to Javier's house, but no one answered. Rachel Wade's car had been moved into the driveway. She looked in the windows, saw nothing noteworthy, so they left. First they went to Sarah's house, and then to Joshua Camacho's house, searching for someone willing to talk about that morning's tragedy.

"We were unsuccessful," DeGregory recalled. "At the Ludemann house, there was a sign on the lawn reading 'No Media, Please.' I ended up getting Sarah's mom on the phone. Police were still there questioning them."

Rachel's parents didn't want to talk, either. "The mom had broken down and the dad just seemed confused—like he wanted to talk, but he couldn't quite grasp what had happened," DeGregory recalled.

Joshua Camacho remained elusive. He was in hiding, at a series of friends' houses, briefly at his parents' home, then somewhere else. DeGregory and her photographer were always a step or two behind. The reporter managed to get Joshua's mom on the phone, but she was not helpful.

So DeGregory spent most of the morning leaving notes on the back of her card at different houses. It wasn't until that afternoon that she got her first interview. Ashley Lovelady agreed to talk about the incident, and limited her responses to what a great kid Sarah was.

The reporter eventually discovered a stark contrast between researching Sarah Ludemann's background, and digging into Rachel Wade's past.

"With Sarah," DeGregory said, "I found friends that dated back to preschool—girls who had been friends with her most of her life. Rachel's friends were comparatively brand-new. Most of the ones I spoke with were the Applebee's girls that she only had been working with for a year or two."

One of those Applebee's girls was Ashley DeCosta, who remembered girls coming into the restaurant and "harassing Rachel. Rachel is just a sweet, sweet girl. She was so in love with that guy. And she put up with so much."

DeCosta had just spoken to Rachel, who called her from jail. "She told me she just wanted to come home and take a bubble bath."

Lane DeGregory remembered the case well. The players were so young and emotions were so high. She remembered covering the death of Sarah Ludemann for another reason as well. It was while writing her first article on the subject that she learned she'd won the 2009 Pulitzer Prize for "The Girl in the Window."

On the Wednesday afternoon after the stabbing, Sarah's friends gathered at the scene of her death. They added to the small memorial already on Javier's lawn, now placing at that spot a white cross with roses, carnations, and alstroemeria lilies.

One friend, eighteen-year-old Dani O'Leary, said,

"I knew that it was just a big mess. I knew that it was all stupid to begin with. But I didn't know it was going to go this far."

A statuette of an angel rested on a table, along with a plaque that read: *Death leaves a heartache no one can heal, love leaves a memory that no one can steal.*

Sarah's tearful friends remembered her as a girl who enjoyed life, who enjoyed painting her nails the color of the season.

Detective Lynch, in his attempt to understand the back-story, confiscated all available cell phones. Text messages were read. At first, he couldn't access Sarah's voice mails. There was a password involved.

Lynch recalled: "Since the phone was both in Sarah's and her parents' names, Charlie Ludemann tried different pass-words to see if he could help us get to the voice mails."

Sarah's dad even contacted the phone company in hopes that they would know the code, but they couldn't help. Finally, after many tries, Charlie hit upon the right com-bination, a four-digit code, and the voice mails became available.

The messages were from Rachel Wade at her "mean girl" best. When investigators heard the messages, they were surprised at the level of hostility and violence in Rachel's verbiage.

"I'm going to . . . murder you," she said. Not "kill" but "murder." Rachel's prosecution, already under preparation, had just received an essential component. The voice mail system also supplied investigators with the precise date and time of each call.

* * *

At two in the afternoon, April 16, Javier Laboy joined Detective Michael Lynch in the criminal investigations section of the PPPD for a follow-up interview.

Laboy had already given a written statement from the crime scene. There were inconsistencies in Javier's story. Lynch insisted that Javier write and sign a second statement.

Now, in a small, windowless interrogation room, Lynch wanted to focus on Laboy and get into more detail.

"My first question is—why did you leave some things out of your story when you first wrote it down, and why did you later add things to your story?" Lynch said.

"The first one was written just as everything had happened, and I was trying to get everything in there and I was all bundled up and I couldn't. It was the first one that I'd ever done," Javier replied. "I kept asking the officer, 'Should I add this? Should I add that?' That explains why I started the same paragraph over three times on my first statement."

"You've never filled out a Witness Statement form before?"

"No. This is the first time anything like this happened. . . ."

"The second statement is longer and more detailed. Was it written after you'd had a chance to sit and reflect on what happened?"

"Yes."

"In addition to inexperience and lack of time to reflect, is it possible you left some things out of your first statement to protect your friend Rachel?"

"No. Absolutely not."

Lynch went over the chronology of Javier's tale. Getting a call from Rachel was the first thing. She was upset, crying. She'd found out Joshua was cheating on her. *Again.* It was nothing new, but it upset her as much as ever.

Rachel thought she was supposed to spend the night with her man, but she learned that Joshua was at his sister's house with that *Sarah*.

According to Javier, Rachel and Joshua were boyfriend and girlfriend for a period of time in 2008. They broke up because of Joshua's cheating. But they got back together again recently, and she had just found out that Joshua was still playing her, so it was déjà vu for Rachel. Javier invited Rachel over. A few minutes after the first call, Rachel called back. She was lost, driving around, trying to find Javier's house. Javier gave her directions. Five minutes later, his friend Dustin Grimes unexpectedly showed up, stopping off on his way home from his girlfriend's house. Rachel arrived at 10:45 P.M. and parked her red Saturn on the street. Rachel, Dustin, and Javier hung out in the driveway. Javier's mom was asleep in the house. Rachel told Javier that she'd been fighting with Sarah and Joshua all night on the phone. That seemingly continued after Rachel arrived at Javier's. Javier heard her yelling into the phone during the time she hung out in front of Javier's. Rachel said Sarah wanted to fight her over Joshua.

"Did you hear the contents of any of those conversations?" Lynch asked.

"No, she walked away when she was on the phone, once all the way to the end of the street. Usually, when she had a phone call, she stood down by the street and leaned on the hood of her car. I couldn't tell what she was saying, but I could hear her yelling."

Each phone call lasted two or three minutes and they continued for upward of an hour. Javier was under the impression that "most of the phone calls were from Joshua. Just a couple of them were from Sarah."

Javier explained to Lynch that he told Rachel not to fight Sarah, that Joshua wasn't worth fighting over. Not that Javier wasn't biased. He had feelings for Rachel. He and Joshua had their troubles in the past.

Actually, Rachel had two modes while on the phone that night: yelling at Sarah and crying at Joshua. Sarah wanted to come over and fight. Joshua said everyone should chill, and they would talk about it tomorrow.

"He's cheating on you. He obviously doesn't care about you. You have too much to lose," Javier told Rachel between phone calls.

"Did Rachel tell you about any threats she might have received?" Lynch asked.

Rachel talked about threats from the past, but she didn't mention new ones. Those girls had gone to her house and threatened to beat her. Rachel knew Sarah was with Janet Camacho, who had wanted to beat her up for some time.

"I know Sarah said she wanted to fight Rachel. Did Rachel say she wanted to fight Sarah, too?" Lynch asked.

"Yes," Javier replied. "She said she was tired of crying all the time and being afraid that those girls were going to beat her. This time Rachel said, 'If they want to fight, I'll fight.' She was tired of them thinking she was scared. She was tired of them blowing up her phone every night. She just wanted to get everything over with."

"Did she say anything about Joshua encouraging her to fight?"

"She did. She said Joshua told her that if she really loved him, she would fight for him. I'm pretty sure he told the same thing to Sarah."

"Kind of pitting the two of them against each other?"

"Correct."

"At what point did you first see the knife that Rachel had?"

"I never actually saw the knife. I knew she always carried it."

"Wait, she *always* carried it?"

"Yes, she always carried a knife on her for protection."

"The same one?"

"I don't know if it's the same one or not. Her old knife was one of those flip-open pocketknives. She told me hers got stolen. I don't know what kind of knife she had after that. As far as I knew, it was on the floor in the back of her car. When everything started, I never saw her go to her car to get the knife."

"Did the knife come up in conversation that night?"

Javier said it did. After learning Janet was with Sarah, Rachel told Javier that it was a good thing she had her knife with her, in case those girls "tried anything funny." Rachel believed those girls were capable of bringing weapons to a fight; they'd been known to have brass knuckles. Javier told Rachel she didn't need the knife and to leave it where it was. "Nothing is going to happen. We are just going to leave," Javier had said.

"How did those girls know where to look for Rachel?"

"That's what we were trying to figure out. They know I'm friends with her, and that we used to date. They know that if she has a problem, she'll either go see her parents or call me."

Then there was the swerving car. That happened during one of the last phone calls to Rachel.

"Was it a white Corolla?"

"I don't remember what color it was. It was a light-colored Corolla. It came down the street, saw us, moved to the left side of the road, and sped up. I had to pull Rachel out of the road so she wouldn't get hit." He had no idea whose car it was. "I never saw it before," Javier said. There were no phone calls after that. It was just two or three minutes between the swerving-car incident and when "Sarah and Janet showed up."

Javier described the violent sequence. He drew a diagram to show how the vehicles were positioned, and where

Rachel was—first when the van arrived, and then when she fought Sarah. Javier said Rachel didn't move toward the van until Sarah was already out and the two combatants walked toward one another. They met between cars: Sarah in the headlight beam of her own vehicle, Rachel just outside that beam. There was no talking. The girls immediately fought with a quick frenzy of movements, a "frantic flailing." Sarah grabbed Rachel's hair with one hand and pummeled her head with the other. Rachel fought back. Janet got out of the car. Rachel and Sarah separated after Janet jumped in.

Javier figured the whole thing took less than ten seconds. He and Dustin had only been fifteen, twenty yards away, but Sarah and Rachel were finished by the time they got there.

Lynch read aloud for Javier excerpts from statements made by Janet and Jilica as to the positioning of Rachel and Sarah as they fought. Those girls said Rachel rushed toward Sarah, stabbed her right by the driver's door to the van, and walked away. Javier said it wasn't like that at all.

Lynch said the evidence, the blood, seemed to indicate that the girls were telling the truth and Javier wasn't. All of the blood was either in the van or right next to the driver's door.

Javier said that when Janet jumped in, Sarah returned to the front seat of her car. "Rachel walked away and headed for the back of my car." According to Javier, Sarah was able to yell at that moment: "Get back in the car. We've got to go!" Janet and Rachel began to fight, and the third girl in the van—Javier didn't know her name— screamed that Sarah just fell and was bleeding.

Javier called 911. At the same time, he took off his shirt, handed it to Dustin, and said to use it to put pressure on Sarah's wound.

Later, when the police were there and everyone was

getting chilly, Javier's mother brought out jackets for Rachel, Javier, and Dustin.

Soon after finishing with Javier, now about five-thirty on the afternoon of April 16, Joshua Camacho tentatively entered Detective Michael Lynch's interrogation room. Joshua might have had a cold. He sniffled and sounded congested.

"How long have you known Rachel Wade?" Lynch asked.

"Fourth grade. We had class together in fourth grade, and then we didn't see each other again, until two years ago," Joshua replied. He and Rachel had only dated for two months. That was about a year ago. "I moved in with her for two months," he added.

"She told me June of last year. Does that sound about right?"

"No."

"When was that?"

"It was . . ." Joshua's mind seemed to drift off. "I don't remember." He sounded a little sleepy. Lynch pressed him twice for an answer. "Maybe August," Joshua said. They went very fast from seeing each other to living together. That was right at the beginning of their relationship.

"You moved in August-ish and moved out October-ish?" Lynch asked.

"Yes," Joshua said. He lived in her Shadow Run apartment. "I moved in with her and her roommate, and there was a problem with the roommate. We broke up, and after that we were just friends."

"Would it be fair to say that you and Rachel frequently talk on the phone, texting, leaving messages?"

"Yeah. She texts. She would text me, but I wouldn't text her."

"But you would call her and talk to her every day?"

"I would not."

"How did you come to talk to her on the phone, then?"

"When I did talk to her, it was always about me having a question about something she said, about what someone might have said about me, or whatever. You know, confronting her with a question. That was the only time I would talk to her."

"You make it seem pretty simple. You went out for a while and then you broke up and you've been friends since then. According to her, it's a lot more deeply involved," Lynch said. "She says that you and she have been together, off and on, and it was a volatile off and on. We've got a lot of background here, and I would like to clear some of this up. You make it sound like you never spoke to her. You know, it's not going to get you in trouble. It just lets me know her mind-set, and it also gives me insight into the mind-set of Sarah because Sarah is not innocent in this thing, either. I understand that she ended up dead over this, but her going over there is a problem."

"Yeah," Joshua said. "After Rachel and me broke up, she had a mess of boyfriends, and that was one of the reasons I didn't want to talk to her."

Lynch had the police record showing that Joshua and Javier Laboy—Rachel's new boyfriend—had gotten into an altercation, and Lynch considered that unlikely unless Joshua and Rachel still had romantic feelings.

"You fought with Javier and then got back together with Rachel, right?"

"No, I never went back out with her again after we broke up," Joshua said. "I never went back out with her after I moved out."

"But you did talk to her occasionally on the phone, correct?"

"Yeah, that's true."

"If I say something that is untrue, please correct me and tell me what is true."

"All right. And the fight with Javier wasn't about Rachel. It was about my son. Back before Rachel, me and Erin had a kid, and then she told me it wasn't mine. During that time, Erin and Javier went out, and she was putting pictures in Myspace and calling Javier 'the daddy of my son.' So I had hate toward him because of the kid."

"Before yesterday, when was the last time you spoke with Rachel?"

"It was before I went to New York." Which was when? "It was the twentieth. Uh, I forgot what month it was. What month is this?"

"April," Lynch said, now with an edge of impatience.

"The third month. What is that? August?"

"The third month is March!"

"That's it. It was March. That's when I went. The twentieth."

"Did you go up there with any of these girls?"

"I went up there with my brother, but Sarah went up the next week."

"I understand there was a problem between Sarah and Rachel about when you were in New York, something Sarah posted on Myspace. That ring a bell?"

"Yeah. Rachel called me and said Javier was telling her I was in New York with Sarah."

"Well, you *were* in New York with Sarah. . . ."

"Not when she called," Joshua said.

"Where were you?"

"I was in New York, but Sarah hadn't gotten there yet."

"Rachel called you about you being in New York with Sarah before Sarah got there?"

"Yes. I said, 'No, Sarah wasn't up there, and I didn't know why people are telling you that.'"

"Okay, but why would she care, if you had broken up a

long time before? Why would Rachel care if Sarah's there or not?"

"I know!" Joshua said. "That's how she is. That night she was texting my phone, driving by my house—I mean, my sister's house."

"Okay, we'll get to that. I'm not done talking about New York. How did Sarah feel when she found out Rachel had called?"

"I didn't tell her anything about that," Joshua said. "What happened next was that Rachel started putting things up on Myspace." He didn't remember the exact words. "Something like, 'My baby's in New York.'"

"'My baby,' meaning you?"

"Yeah."

"Did she put your name on Myspace?"

"No. Just 'my baby.'"

Lynch was incredulous: "Somehow this enrages people? Words on a computer screen? This upsets people? Are we being serious?"

"Yes."

"You realize how absolutely ridiculous that is, right?"

"I know. I have told Sarah plenty of times."

"So Sarah sees the mention of 'my baby' on the computer. Why does Sarah care enough to look at Rachel's Myspace page?"

"That's what I'm saying."

"No, you are not. Tell me. Why did Sarah care so much about what Rachel was saying?"

"Because I don't know. Because I don't get what you are trying to say."

"If Sarah thinks that you and Rachel aren't dating, why is she looking on Rachel's Myspace page? I'm not saying that it's illegal or a problem. I just want to understand. Why in hell does Sarah care what Rachel has to say?"

"I asked Sarah that question so many times, too!"

"And what did Sarah say?"

"She said, 'Because you're mine.' That's what she always said. That's what they would do. One would put something about the other on Myspace and they would get mad, even if it's not true."

"Did Sarah tell you that she had called Rachel, that she bitched her out or anything like that?"

"No, Sarah never told me when she did anything."

"But you do know she was upset about something Rachel had posted on there?"

"Yes."

"Was it normal for Sarah to get upset about things on the Internet?"

"Yeah, and they knew that. That's why they did it." He only knew about Rachel baiting Sarah with online comments. He didn't know if Sarah retaliated.

"You said 'back and forth' before . . . ," Lynch pointed out.

"Yeah, but the texts came from Rachel," Joshua said.

Lynch asked if there were any more incidents in the three weeks leading up to the tragic night? Joshua said there were not. The detective said he knew Joshua's relationship with Rachel was tumultuous, to put it mildly. Lynch had read the police report: Rachel called the cops on him, Joshua Camacho, for kicking in the front door of her apartment. When did all that stuff occur?

"That was before I went to New York," Joshua replied.

"Rachel's been working at Applebee's. Have there not been incidents out at Applebee's involving you or Sarah, or anything like that?"

"No."

"So there were no incidents during the three weeks before. Okay. In that case, what happened yesterday, or maybe the night before yesterday, that led up to all this?"

Joshua said it was about eleven o'clock on Tuesday

night. Joshua and Sarah were playing video games at his sister Janet's house. Rachel texted his phone.

"You don't want to be with me because of Sarah," Joshua remembered one text reading.

He texted back: No, I don't want to be with you because I don't like you no more.

Now Rachel was texting that she was going to get Sarah, that she was all staked out, and Sarah was going to have to come home sooner or later. Sarah's parents were also calling, saying that she had to go home. Joshua told Sarah that for security reasons, he didn't think she should leave.

Janet had a full house. Sarah and Jilica and his brother James, and his niece and nephews, were all there. Joshua knew Rachel had driven down the block a few moments before because Janet was outside smoking and saw it. So he texted Rachel: Why are you down this street. Go home.

Joshua said that Rachel texted back: I'm waiting for Sarah to come out.

"Before your sister told you about the car on her street, you were conversing with Rachel. Isn't that correct?"

"She had texted me."

"Did you call her back?"

"No, I did not."

"I want your complete honesty here, because I am going to take your phone records and compare them against what you tell me. If I see you are calling her when you say you weren't calling her, I am going to have a problem with that."

Joshua said that was fine. He did not talk to her. He only texted her. They should check his cell phone, which was in his name. T-Mobile had the records.

Lynch became direct with Joshua. This data he was getting made a lot more sense if Joshua was sneaking over to

visit Rachel every now and again. That would be the thing
that would explain why Rachel and Sarah feuded, the
reason why tempers were running so hot. They really were
sharing a man.

Lynch said he had every reason to believe all of that was
true. He'd heard a lot about Joshua. "The bottom line is
you're a player," Lynch said. "You are stringing all three of
these girls along—Erin, Rachel, and Sarah."

"The reason I see Erin is because of my baby."

"I understand that, and you're just trying to be involved
with the baby's life, right?"

"Yeah."

There was a pause and Joshua took the opportunity to
correct something Lynch had said earlier. When he said
there were no incidents during the three weeks before the
stabbing, he didn't mean that he and Rachel hadn't had
conversations. Well, they had had the same conversation
several times.

"Rachel wanted to be with me—and I told her no,"
Joshua said. He said no because, to be blunt, because of
the *skank* factor: "Guys who knew where Rachel's apartment was would come up to me—say, I was in a store—
and they would say, 'Hey, you know Rachel Wade?' And
they would think that I was still having sexual relations
with her—but I don't." She had a mess of boyfriends, so
many that Joshua couldn't convince people he wasn't one
of them.

The way Joshua spoke made it seem as if there was a lull
in the drama, Lynch analyzed, and then, all of a sudden,
Rachel was suddenly furious with Sarah, texting threats
to her.

Joshua agreed that there was a suddenness to it. "That's
why I didn't want Sarah to go out there," he added.

"But Sarah is twice Rachel's size," Lynch said.

"Rachel is small, which meant she had people with her,

or she had *something*. Nobody in her right mind would want to go fight somebody. . . ."

"What was the exact wording of the text? What was she going to do to her?"

"She said she was going to 'beat her ass. I want my one-on-one.'"

"Are you aware of other incidents involving the two of them, chasing each other in cars all around the city, and crap like that?"

"Yeah."

"And you couldn't put a stop to that, right?"

"No."

"So she was on your sister's block. At some point did she leave? Did you go outside to see Rachel?"

"No, I didn't want to go outside. I knew that Sarah would go outside, too, if I did. My brother went outside to smoke a cigarette and said that Rachel's car had gone by again."

Joshua sent Rachel a fresh text, telling her to go home. She just said she was going to get Sarah. "If I don't get her now, I'll get her at home," Joshua recalled Rachel texting.

And all this time, Sarah's stress level was on the rise, like one of those cartoon thermometers that pop, as her parents called telling her to get home. Sarah didn't want her parents to worry so she didn't tell them about Rachel's threats. She lied and said she was in the middle of a video game and would be home soon.

Sarah finally said, "I'm going to go home."

Janet Camacho said, "I'm not going to let you go by yourself."

Since Sarah and Janet were going, Jilica went, too. His brother Jay left around that same time also, so Joshua was stuck at the house to watch Janet's kids.

"And then I got a call," Joshua said, voice quavering.

"They were going to go and get McDonald's. Know anything about that?"

"No. I thought Sarah was going home."

"If Sarah drove, how were Janet and Jilica going to get back home?"

"They were going to walk. We don't live far from Sarah's house."

"How far?" Lynch asked. When he received no response, he added, "Are you sure that's why they got in the car?" Lynch pointed out that from Janet's house, Sarah's house and Javier's house were in opposite directions. One did not pass by one on their way toward the other.

"I don't know what happened after they left, honestly."

"Well, you've talked to your sister about it, obviously."

"No, not that night. After that, I went to the hospital, and I—"

"No, I said you talked to your sister since it happened, right?"

"Yeah, I talked to her, but I didn't talk to her about that."

"They didn't think Sarah was capable of driving home alone?"

"No, my sister wanted to make sure Sarah had people with her for when she got out of the car, in case someone jumped her outside her house."

"So Janet wanted to be there as protection for Sarah?"

"Yes."

"After they left, did you call or text your sister, or Sarah, or Rachel?"

"I called Sarah at one point and I said, 'Where you at?' And she was like, 'I'm going to call you back in a minute.'" He didn't know why she said that.

"That ride from your sister's house to Sarah's house should have taken two minutes. During that time, you called her?"

"Yes. I called right after they left. I asked her what she

was doing. I wanted to make sure she wasn't going to go after Rachel or anything like that."

"When she called back, what did she say?"

Joshua started to cry. "She said, 'It hurts,'" he said with a gasp. "I asked her, 'What hurts?' And the phone just went dead. I called my sister and I heard screaming. I ran to her dad's house, and I had him drive us down to Javier's house, and she was lying on the floor."

"You mean to tell me she called you and said, 'It hurts'?"

"Yes, and when she said it, I didn't know what she was talking about."

"When you called your sister's phone, what did she say?"

"She didn't say anything. All I could hear was screaming."

"Then how did you know that they were at Javier's house?"

"My brother told me. My brother had drove by there."

"Was your brother driving a little white car, by any chance?"

"No, it was a brown car." He knew nothing of a white car. "Right after he called Janet, I called Jilica. She was like, 'We are outside that boy's house.' And I said, 'What boy?' And she was like, 'Sarah got stabbed.'"

Lynch tried again to get Joshua to talk about conversations he might have had with his sister or her friend about that night. Joshua emphasized that he had not seen his sister since that night. There had been conversations, but not about this.

The last time he saw Janet, he called her from the hospital that night and asked her to come pick him up. When she did, he told her that Sarah had died, and Janet cried.

They started to drive away, but Janet had a panic attack and was hyperventilating. Joshua took over the wheel and drove Janet back to the same hospital from which they'd come.

"After that, I went to my parents' house," Joshua concluded.

"Are you telling me that you haven't spoken to your sister or Jilica about how they ended up at Javier's house that night?"

"That's what I'm telling you."

"Well, I don't believe that for a moment," Lynch said. "I want to be sympathetic toward you because you are obviously upset about Sarah, but please do not insult my intelligence. Anyone who was in this position would want to know what the hell happened. You can't tell me you didn't talk to your sister about this."

"I am telling you the truth. I don't know how that happened."

"They were the last two people with your girlfriend when she died."

"Every time I try to talk about it, I just start crying. I can't talk about it."

There was a pause as the detective wrote notes.

When Lynch resumed the interview, he returned to an old point. "Why were Sarah and Rachel on the phone? Why were they texting each other?"

"I don't know. I know that Rachel said, 'After I stab you, I'm going to stab your Mexican boyfriend.'"

"How would you know that?"

"Because my sister told me."

"You told me that you hadn't talked to her about any of this."

"She talked to me before."

According to Joshua's time line, the Mexican boyfriend comment arrived on Sarah's phone while Sarah was in her car, still in Janet's driveway. Janet ran into the house to give Joshua the house keys and told him at that point the kind of stuff Rachel was texting.

"Why would you need the keys to the house if they were going to drive the few blocks to Sarah's house and walk back?"

"You see?" Joshua said. "That's the part I don't understand." All he knew was that Rachel said what she said, and everyone heard because of speakerphone. "And I was like, 'Just take her straight home and come back.'"

Lynch was getting angry. "Why did Sarah go to Rachel looking for a fight? Did you ever ask your sister? Why did your sister take your girlfriend, who is now dead, to that house? Did you ever ask her that? She would still be alive if you had just taken her straight home. You didn't say that to your sister? You sent your sister with Sarah to protect her, right? And, instead, they end up going to a house looking for a fight. Are you pissed at your sister? Are you going to say anything to her? Do we need to get your sister in here and ask her why, while you're here? Why didn't she take Sarah home, like she was supposed to? Why is that? Can you explain it to me?"

Joshua said he didn't feel that Janet was responsible for what had happened.

"You sent her to go."

"I didn't tell anyone to go. I told Sarah to stay there. I told my sister—"

"You said, 'Please escort her home.' Isn't that right?"

"I told Sarah not to go. She said her dad was going to be pissed."

"And you told Janet and Jilica to go with her to protect her, right?"

"No, I didn't tell them to go with her at all. I didn't ask her—"

"How do you detour from going to Sarah's house to going over there and getting into a fight? I'd be pretty pissed at my sister if I lost a girlfriend that way," Lynch said. "And you haven't even asked why they changed destinations."

"I haven't talked to anybody."

"I have more than one person confirming that you were on the phone with Rachel, talking on the phone, last night. Rachel sat in front of that residence for an hour on the phone. With you and with Sarah. And I'm telling you these cell phone records are not going to lie."

"I'm telling you, the only time I talked to Rachel that night was while I was running to Sarah's dad's house."

"I'm talking before that."

"Before that, I didn't talk to her at all."

"How many text messages did you leave?"

"There was a lot."

"So you were texting her."

"Yes. A whole lot. That was when I told her to go home, when she was on my sister's street."

Lynch again said that wasn't what he was talking about. Rachel was in front of Javier's house for an hour before the incident, on the phone, arguing, growing agitated. Joshua said there were just texts; and if it was true that he was still communicating with her when she was at Javier's house, he didn't know where she was at the time.

"How do you think your sister, your girlfriend, went— instead of going to where it was safe—went to where Sarah was in danger? How did it happen? Why couldn't they just do the safe thing? Have you asked yourself that question? Do you know what it sounds like to me? Sounds like the three of them were going to a beat down!"

"I know how Sarah is," Joshua said. "If anyone says they want to fight her, she doesn't care who it is, she doesn't back down. Before she left, she said she was going home. If she had said she was going looking for Rachel or going someplace to get in a fight, I would have never let her leave."

Lynch reiterated the bad job Janet did of protecting Sarah. He added, "I was told by Rachel that you were encouraging her to fight Sarah. That you said, if she loved you, she would fight for you. Is that true?"

"That's a lie. I would never want Sarah to fight nobody."

"What about Rachel? Did you care if she got into a fight?"

"No, I don't care about her. I only cared about her when we were living together, and it all went downhill from there. That's why I never went back out with her."

"That's not the way it's being portrayed. Everybody is saying that you are playing the field, and seeing this girl behind her back, and seeing that girl behind her back."

"No, that's not true. I know everybody is saying that, but it's not true."

"I'm not saying that. The newspapers are saying that. Sarah's own parents are saying that. Where are they getting that information?"

"I don't know. People talk. They say things about me that aren't true."

"This is a girl that you say you loved. Why are Sarah's parents telling me that you were screwing around behind their daughter's back?"

Joshua was angered at the mention of Charlie and Gay Ludemann. "That's what I don't understand. If they were saying those things, then why wouldn't they tell their daughter?"

"They did tell her," Lynch said, his voice rising with excitement.

"Then why wouldn't Sarah tell me?" Joshua asked.

"Because she loved you. Her parents tolerated you."

"No parent would tolerate their child getting played on."

"Unfortunately, they did—and it was the same thing

with Rachel's parents. They are devastated and destroyed as well. Same thing. So you are telling me that you are the kind of guy who has one girlfriend at a time?"

"That's right. I wasn't—"

"And you weren't pitting these two against one another? You didn't say to both of them that they should fight, with the winner getting you?"

"No. That's why she was at Janet's so late. I didn't want there to be a fight."

"Okay. What about Rachel? She's saying you cared for her. That she should fight Sarah—and you would be the prize."

"I never said that. I never sent it in a text."

"Okay, you said that your phone was shut off."

"Yeah, I went to the company about that and they say I got to pay an extra thirty dollars because that's how the psychics [*sic*] work."

"What do you mean?"

"Thirty dollars for when my phone turns off. Nothing would get erased—my call logs or anything. And I told them that was bull. Why would I have to pay them thirty more dollars added onto my bill every month just so my stuff could get saved."

"Everything worked fine until that night?"

"Yeah, my phone died at the hospital that night."

"Just mysteriously stopped working at that point?"

"Everything went away."

"That's a miracle, huh?" Lynch said.

"It had happened before. That's why I went to the company."

"Why would it delete?"

"It doesn't delete from them. They still have it, but it deletes from my phone."

Lynch reiterated that Joshua was in big trouble if the T-Mobile records deviated from what he was saying. One call, one text different and, as Lynch put it, "you and I are going to be back in here again, and it isn't going to be as friendly as it is now."

"I understand you."

"Because that's what Rachel is telling me. She's telling me that she was so afraid Sarah and Janet constantly chasing her around. And that she'd finally had enough and wanted to end the situation."

"That's what I don't get. If she is so afraid of my family, then why is—"

"She wasn't saying you. She was saying Sarah and Janet. She was upset with you, obviously the dating thing. She was under the impression that you guys were still together in some capacity. She said she only found out that night that you were breaking up with her."

"The last time I talked to Rachel, I swear, I was running over to Sarah's house. I asked Rachel where she was and she said she was still in front of Javier's house."

"When was the last time prior to that, that you spoke to Rachel?"

"I don't remember. That was the only time I talked to her that night. All the rest was texts."

"So during that hour she was at Javier's and she was yelling into the phone and getting upset? Who was she yelling at?"

"Was she at Javier's house before she drove down my block?" Joshua asked.

"No, this is all after," Lynch said.

Joshua knew that wasn't true. There was no way an hour lapsed between Rachel being on his block and Sarah getting stabbed. It wasn't anywhere near that long.

"That's impossible," Joshua said.

Lynch wanted to make sure he had the order of events right: Sarah called Joshua and said, "It hurts." Joshua called his sister, Janet, Jilica, and then Rachel. Was that correct?

Joshua said it was.

"What did you say to Rachel?"

"I asked where she was at. She said she was at Javier's house. And I told her I was going to kill her. She said, 'Okay, Josh.'"

Lynch verified that Joshua himself had not heard the "Mexican boyfriend" comment, but had been told about it an instant after it occurred, as it occurred before the minivan left Janet's house.

"You went to the scene. You didn't ask Janet or Jilica what happened. You didn't yell at Rachel?"

"I didn't see Rachel. I was screaming—"

"I understand that you were being ridiculous. I'm not going to get on you about that. Obviously, you lost someone you cared about."

"The only thing Janet said to me was 'I didn't know she stabbed her.'"

"And you didn't ask her what they were doing there, what happened?"

"No, I just started crying when I saw Sarah was on the floor."

"Your sister took off her flip-flops and beat Rachel up in Javier's front yard. She didn't tell you any of that?"

"No."

"Why was your sister the one who was punishing Rachel for what she'd done?"

"My sister had hatred for Rachel because after we broke up, Rachel was talking about my sister."

"So she's saying things about her. They're words. Who cares? Now somebody is dead. And when I was out there at one o'clock in the morning, in charge of cleaning up this mess, I keep hearing that your sister and you and your family were going to get even for what happened. Is that what we really need here? Do we need someone else to die? Did you know that Javier tried to save Sarah's life? Took his own T-shirt off and was down there on the ground putting pressure on Sarah's wounds. Did you know that Javier ripped his own shirt off his own back and was trying to save her?"

Joshua couldn't answer. He could only cry.

"If I hear one word about retaliation, we're all going to have problems," Lynch said. "Those three women made a huge error in judgment when they went over to that house that night. My question is, how did they know Rachel was there? Do you know how they knew? Did Rachel tell them?"

"I don't know. I didn't ask."

"Are you mad at Sarah for going over there? That would be natural."

"I told her not to go!"

"I also have a report that a little white car drove by Javier's only a couple of minutes before Sarah showed up there. I believe that was someone you know, someone they know, who told them where Rachel was. Do you know who that was?"

"I don't."

"Are you sure?"

"I promise."

"You're aware that they went to where Rachel was, right? Rachel didn't find them."

"You'll have to check the phone records, see if she said where she was."

"You know that I am the one in charge of building a case against Rachel. I was the one who arrested her. I interviewed her. I charged her with murder in the second degree. You understand that?"

"Yes."

"And I'm not happy with what your sister told me about how they found Rachel that night."

"I need to use the bathroom."

"Okay, we're almost done. Janet said Sarah had your phone that night."

"I had my phone. Sarah had her own phone."

"Any idea why your sister said that?"

"No."

"What does your dad know about all of this?"

"After I left the hospital, I went to my dad's house, talked to my mom and dad."

"Did they know anything about this before that?"

"No, just when they saw it on the television."

"They didn't know anything about the problems beforehand?"

"No."

"I need to know what brought Sarah to that house," Detective Lynch said, and concluded the interview.

Charlie and Gay Ludemann had kept Sarah's room just the way it was, as a sort of shrine to her memory. Just the same, but with one exception. All photos of Joshua Camacho were destroyed.

Gay ran events through her head, again and again, but the outcome never wavered. Normal night, Sarah out with friends. Said she'd be home soon. Gay was waiting up. Phone rang. Joshua calling with the bad news. Arriving at the scene while the paramedics were still working on Sarah, getting there too late. Sarah never got to hear her mother say, "I love you, Sarah." Gay said it over and over, but Sarah couldn't hear. Sarah was a good, loving girl. Gay's heart was broken. Gay felt her heart breaking. Just a teenager. Simple pleasures. Movies, bowling, the beach. She was making straight A's, going to college next year. . . .

And Joshua? Gay's heart went out to him. But here was

another thing: she knew he was a big part of the reason Sarah was killed.

A few days after the stabbing, Lisa Lafrance went to the county jail to visit Rachel. They had stopped speaking because of Lisa's drug habit—but this was a crisis. Lisa still considered Rachel her best friend.

"I don't know if it's true, but she told me she blacked out and she didn't remember anything about the stabbing. The last thing she remembered, Sarah and Janet and their friend jumped her. She said she didn't know what she was doing," Lisa recalled.

To a certain extent, Lisa believed her. She knew Rachel really well, maybe better than anyone, and Rachel would not just run up to Sarah and stab her. Rachel was afraid of being beaten up. That would have been the reason why she brought the knife in the first place. She had been afraid of getting jumped by Sarah and her friends for a long time. Months.

She wasn't very big, but she had a big mouth. In Lisa's experience, when crunch time came, Rachel lacked the courage to back up her words.

Sarah obviously wasn't in a position to defend herself, but Lisa would always believe that Sarah was the one who went to that location looking for a fight that night.

Rachel said that she brought the knife because she thought it would scare them off, and that made sense to Lisa. Imagine how the situation must have looked to Rachel, Lisa said. Rachel was already scared of Janet. The third girl was big. This was the nightmare scenario, the very thing that Rachel had been dreading for months, the reason that she used to call Lisa when she was on her way home from work and kept her talking until she was safely inside her apartment. Arming herself when she knew the attack was coming was exactly the sort of thing Rachel would do. It wasn't the smart thing to do, of course, but it was in keeping with the way Rachel's mind worked. She was attacked. Three on one. The stabbing was *reflex.*

At five o'clock in the evening, on April 15, nearly seventeen hours after the stabbing, Sarah's minivan was towed from in front of Javier's house to a PCSO garage for automotive evidence.

With PPPD detective Kenneth Blessing observing, a crime scene technician processed the van for latent prints, took samples from the various blood drops, and thoroughly photographed the vehicle.

When processing was complete, the vehicle—blood drops and all—was returned to Charlie Ludemann. Blessing glanced at his watch: 6:30 P.M.

Rachel Wade's parents did not skimp when it came to their daughter's legal representation. They hired forty-five-year-old award-winning defense attorney Jay Hebert, who had his own law firm, the Hebert Law Group, in Clearwater, Florida. Hebert was a Floridian born and raised, having grown up in Winter Park, just outside of Orlando. He earned his law degree at Stetson University and had been practicing law since 1991. In addition to being a top local trial attorney, Hebert was also a board member of the Pinellas County Sheriff's Police Athletic League (PAL) and Tampa Bay Junior Lightning Ice Hockey.

During one of Hebert's first interviews of Rachel Wade, Hebert tried to get to the crux of the matter. Why had this situation been allowed to stew for month after month until it finally exploded into violence, bloodshed, and death?

Well, Rachel told him, if you looked at it in one way it was Joshua's fault. He'd encouraged her.

Pinellas County judge Paul R. Levine was not the sort of man who would send people to prison, or keep them in jail, for emotional reasons. In fact, he was a reasonable man, who believed that different crimes should be handled differently. He was, for example, a proponent of keeping serious alcohol offenders (domestic abusers and drunk drivers) sober rather than incarcerated, and he supported the use of alcohol bracelets, which enabled authorities to check the defender's alcohol level continuously. One drop, and off to jail they went. Most stayed sober, thus saving that jail space for those who needed to be removed from society.

At the bond hearing for Rachel Wade, on April 16, 2009, Judge Levine found himself face-to-face with a woman who'd had her heart ripped out by violence. Again he would need to forget emotions and let the letter of the law inform his decision.

Standing before the bench, Gay Ludemann said, "Rachel Wade murdered my daughter Sarah in cold blood. And for what? A boy. A boy. How sad is that? . . . We miss and love our daughter. She is never out of our thoughts. Rachel Wade should not be allowed out of jail."

Judge Levine explained that he had to give Rachel Wade bail because this was not a capital case. If the police had charged her with first-degree murder, he would have been able to order her held without bail. However, since it was a charge of second-degree murder, bail was mandatory.

He ordered that Rachel be returned to Pinellas County Jail on $500,000 bail.

This angered Sarah's mom. "Rachel Wade knew where

my daughter lived. She was coming after her." Her whole family would feel unsafe if Wade was allowed to walk the streets again. "Are you going to let her back on the street so she can murder someone else?"

"No, ma'am," Judge Levine replied patiently. "She has to post five-hundred-thousand-dollar bond in order to get out. That's quite a heavy burden, I would think. The other thing, and I don't mean to argue with you right now, I know—"

"And I'm not arguing with you, either," Gay said. "I'm letting you know how my heart feels, the pain. My daughter is on a cold slab in a funeral home because of this girl! She took my daughter's life. She knew if she stabbed Sarah in the heart, she would die."

The question that the grieving mother was trying to ask was: Why wasn't Rachel Wade charged with first-degree murder? Why wasn't it a capital case, which would have meant no mandatory bail? Rachel brought the knife with her. How was that not premeditated?

Gay Ludemann would not get an answer to her question at the bond hearing. Afterward, the case's lead investigator took a crack at it.

According to Detective Lynch: "One of the things we looked at before presenting the case to the state, and one of the things we looked at very hard, was whether or not there was some form of self-defense here."

If Rachel brought the knife with her in order to protect herself, then the fact that she had the knife at the scene of the fight was not, in itself, evidence of premeditation.

"We knew, for example, that Sarah had driven to where Rachel was, that there were three girls in the van," Lynch said. "Rachel, on the other hand, although she had two male friends on the scene, was the only female there on her side."

Lynch felt it would have been difficult to prove to a jury's satisfaction that Rachel had premeditation using the knife to kill Sarah.

Arguing in the other direction, if this was merely a street fight that had gotten out of hand, why wasn't Rachel Wade charged with manslaughter? Would Rachel have been charged with manslaughter without the voice mails' inflammatory verbiage?

Lynch said no. He didn't believe that the voice mails were that dynamic. If they had been recorded minutes before the stabbing, maybe. As they were, recorded months before Sarah died, he didn't believe they would be a deciding factor one way or the other.

Funeral services were held for Sarah Ludemann at Memorial Park Funeral Home and Cemetery in St. Petersburg. Her family received friends on Saturday, April 18, from noon to three, and then from five to seven-thirty, at which time funeral services were held. Her family requested that, in lieu of flowers, donations be sent to the Tarpon Springs Veterinary Academy.

For Sarah's friend Amber Malinchock, it was at the funeral parlor that Sarah's death became real for her. She still couldn't get the image out of her head: Sarah lying there in her coffin, wearing her prom dress.

All of Sarah's friends attended the funeral, of course—all except one: Joshua Camacho. Charlie Ludemann had forbidden him from attending.

On April 21, in the middle of the afternoon, Jilica Smith came to Sarasota police headquarters for a follow-up interview. Jilica gave her birth date and explained that she was at the stabbing scene because she was friends with Janet and Joshua Camacho. They were like family, and she had been to their house "plenty of times." She knew Sarah because she was Joshua's friend, "because she is always there." Sarah was Joshua's girlfriend. Jilica hadn't known Sarah long—not to have conversations and chill with—not really until Janet moved to Pinellas Park, whenever that was. Sarah was always good for a ride, if they needed to get to a store or something.

She didn't know Rachel. She'd heard Sarah arguing with Rachel on the phone, and Rachel's name was repeatedly mentioned during conversations. "I only know what she looks like because of that night," Jilica said. She had heard that there were previous confrontations between Sarah and Rachel, but she had not been around for any of those.

On the night it happened, she'd been hanging out at Janet's house with Joshua, Sarah, Janet, and maybe the other brother Jay, who was in and out. They were hanging out, sitting on the couch and playing video games. Joshua was getting text messages from Rachel that said that she wanted to fight Sarah. Rachel wasn't mad at Joshua, just Sarah. Joshua showed the texts to Jilica, but at first didn't tell Sarah about them.

Sarah's dad called a couple of times and reminded her that it was a school night and she needed to get home. Sarah said she'd be home soon.

"Joshua didn't want to get drama started because he knew if he told Sarah about it, Sarah was going to get mad," Jilica explained. Rachel had been seen outside, repeatedly "riding up and down the block."

Eventually Sarah did find out what was going on, although Jilica didn't remember a specific moment when that had occurred. Sarah was calm one second, mad the next, when she somehow discovered what was going on. She was being taunted, and she could not let that stand.

After that, Jilica went outside and sat in a car with her

boyfriend. Janet was also outside in a car. Jilica wasn't sure who she was with, but she thought it might be a family friend.

The red car went by again after they were outside. Jilica was impressed with the driver's staying power. It felt like she'd been cruising the block for a long time.

At one point, the red car parked at the end of the block at the stop sign and blinked its lights. Jilica thought it odd, but she made no comment as she was otherwise occupied. The red car left, but she wasn't aware of when.

After about fifteen minutes, Janet announced that they were getting rid of the boys, and just the girls were going to go to McDonald's. Sarah was driving. Jilica said that sounded good. They got into Sarah's van.

Jilica didn't remember which McDonald's they planned to visit. She said that she didn't want to eat, anyway, so she was in her own little world, sitting in the back, behind the front passenger seat where Janet was. Sarah and Rachel were on the phone with one another, and Sarah had the phone on speaker. Jilica had her own phone out and was texting someone. Jilica had not picked up on the level of hostility—it was just talking smack—until she heard Rachel say, "I'm going to stab you and your Mexican boyfriend." That caught Jilica's attention.

"I was like, 'Hold on, what's going on?'" Jilica said.

She admitted to Detective Lynch that she had no way of recognizing Rachel's voice and had to rely on the word of Janet and Sarah that it was Rachel who made the threat. Lynch wanted to know what the anger between Rachel and Sarah was about. Jilica said Sarah was just trying to figure out Rachel's problem.

Sarah was asking, "Why you talking crap? Why are you saying these things about me?" Sarah said, "Where you at? Where you at?" And that was when Jilica knew they weren't going to McDonald's anymore.

Jilica began to fret aloud from the backseat: She didn't know this girl. She didn't know who she might be with. This just didn't feel right. Word on the street was that Rachel was crazy. She wouldn't want anything to do with Rachel, and she hoped Janet and Sarah didn't want to have anything to do with her, either.

At some point during the ride, maybe before the phone call, they ran into a girl named Ashley at a stop sign. Jilica didn't know whose friend Ashley was, but Sarah and Janet knew her.

Ashley said, "Hey, Rachel is at Javier's house."

That got Detective Lynch's attention. Here was the missing piece of the story!

Jilica didn't know Ashley's last name. And she was not sure what color Ashley's car was. Maybe white. She didn't know the make. Ashley was by herself, though. She was a white girl, a teenager, looked like she might be Italian, a little bit on the darker side, but not Spanish. Jilica remembered that.

She was pretty sure that at some point during the ride, they'd cruised by Sarah's house because she remembered seeing Sarah's dad's car, which was easy to notice because it was a taxicab. Jilica wasn't sure why Sarah drove past her own house, unless it was to see if Rachel was there. That was the reason that made the most sense.

Jilica apologized to the investigator. She realized that she was there, and all, but she still felt like she didn't know anything. "I'm still pretty confused about what happened myself," she said.

Sarah had not stopped at her house. No one got out of the van until they pulled up behind the red car. They got there quickly. No one had a chance to think things through. No one in the van had a weapon of any kind. As they pulled up, Jilica saw Rachel crossing the lawn, heading toward the street, toward them. Lynch showed her a diagram that had been made from Janet's version of the facts. Jilica said that Janet had the position of the cars correct, and the spot where Javier and his friend were standing, but the diagram was wrong when it came to Rachel. Janet said Rachel was leaning on the front of her car when the van pulled up. Jilica disagreed. She clearly remembered Rachel crossing the lawn. Janet and Jilica agreed that when Sarah first got out of the van, when her feet first touched the ground, Rachel was already between the vehicles and approaching fast. It was when she crossed in front of the van that Jilica got her first look at Rachel's face.

"I saw the knife," Jilica said.

It was in Rachel's left hand and held in a threatening manner. She didn't see the stabbing; and the next thing she remembered, she was holding Janet around the waist, holding Janet back, protecting her because that girl still had the knife in her hand.

The confrontation between Sarah and Rachel was quick—two or three seconds, no more than that. As soon as she saw Janet coming, Rachel backed off. During the ruckus, Jilica dropped her phone and somehow it managed to end up underneath Rachel's car. She had her shoes off and she went under Rachel's car, trying to get her phone. It was too much at one time to process properly. She retrieved her phone. When she got back up, she saw Sarah standing there, just inside the van's open driver's door, holding her chest.

Janet and Rachel were fighting on the lawn. Janet had a shoe in her hand and was trying to knock the knife out of Rachel's hand with it. Jilica managed to get her own sandals back on. Janet had the same pair, but she lost her shoes that night. Two pairs of sandals were recovered at the scene: one black, Janet's; one white, Sarah's. It seemed crazy now, but at the time Jilica thought Sarah was okay, and that her real worry was Janet's safety.

Rachel was still waving her arms wildly, still had the knife, and Jilica remembered saying, "Janet, no," and pulling her friend away from Rachel, toward the van. She glanced back at the van and didn't see Sarah anymore. Janet went around to the other side of the van and screamed that she saw blood. Jilica got down on the ground with Sarah.

Janet headed back for Rachel, who had run up between houses. After that, Rachel didn't have the knife anymore. Sarah's phone was ringing. It was Joshua. Jilica told him Sarah was down and bleeding. Then she called 911.

As she gave the lady the info, she noticed that Javier was on the phone; she realized they had called 911 simultaneously. The operator gave Jilica instructions for first aid. She needed something to apply pressure with; Javier gave her his orange shirt. Other people were showing up. At some point, a man showed up and took over tending to Sarah.

Jilica stood up and began screaming at Rachel, "You just stabbed someone! You are going to jail!"

Jilica again tried to pull Janet away from Rachel, now fearful that the cops were going to arrive any second and might not be quick to figure out the good guys from the bad guys.

"It's not about us now," Jilica recalled saying, thinking the focus should really be on safety. "Think of your kids," Jilica said to Janet.

Rachel kept saying, "I'm done, I'm done!" She didn't want to fight anymore. Rachel tried to go in the house; but for some reason, she didn't. Instead, she took a seat on a lawn chair. She was smiling. No remorse!

Lynch asked, "At any time, did you ever hear Joshua encourage Sarah to go fight Rachel?"

"No," Jilica replied.

Had she ever heard Joshua encourage Rachel to fight Sarah? Jilica silently shook her head.

Jilica again apologized. Everything caught her by surprise that night. Back at Janet's house when Joshua showed her the texts from Rachel, she wasn't impressed because—as it had been explained to her—Rachel was crazy and she did this sort of crap all of the time. Rachel and Sarah were perpetually threatening to kick each other's asses, but they never did. Jilica had no idea why this night was different.

Lynch tried to probe Jilica's theories as to why this all happened and found Jilica unwilling to speculate.

"It was just a bunch of high-school foolishness taken to the street," she said.

Jilica left, and Janet Camacho came in and sat down in Jilica's seat.

Lynch continued his follow-up questioning.

Janet said she was aware that Joshua had once dated Rachel, but it wasn't for long. "A few weeks, I'm not sure," she said.

When was that?

"Maybe last year," she said.

Janet never met Rachel, just saw her from afar a few times, but she just heard a lot about her. Everything she knew was based on stuff Joshua had told her. She'd heard rumors about Rachel, heard she did it with her brother Jay Camacho, too—but that was not verified information. Jay denied it, but who knows?

When did Joshua start dating Sarah? Janet didn't know. She just knew that they were always together, every day. According to Joshua, he and Sarah dated for a year and then broke up, but Janet couldn't verify that. In the chronology of Joshua's love life, Janet said, Erin Slothower came first, but she and Joshua had broken up already by the time she learned she was pregnant. Joshua had been there for her because of the baby, but they were never a couple after that. Janet admitted that there had been friction between Erin and Sarah, mostly jealousy over Joshua. Janet knew of no fights between Erin and Sarah. Other than Erin, Sarah, and Rachel, Janet didn't know of any other women in Joshua's world.

Janet had no use for Rachel. She was a bad influence, introducing Joshua to a destructive lifestyle, which included alcohol and pills. This was not recent.

Once, while on the phone as she was going to the store, Janet told Rachel about her feelings.

"How did she react?" Detective Lynch asked.

"She had a mouth on her!" Janet replied. "She was disrespecting me, and after that, I didn't have nothing else to say to her."

The only other contact Janet had with Rachel came during autumn 2008, after Joshua moved out of Rachel's apartment. All Joshua wanted to do was return the house key to Rachel. Seemed like simple enough, right? Rachel was such a loose cannon that Janet went along with Joshua to have his back. Janet and Rachel had another sharp verbal exchange on that occasion.

During the days leading up to the stabbing, had Joshua ever talked to his sister about new problems with Rachel? Janet said no. How about Sarah? Did she mention new problems with Rachel?

Janet shook her head. Sarah liked to come over to Janet's house and play with her kids or whatever, but they didn't have a relationship where Sarah would confide in Janet.

Janet described the scene in which Rachel drove past the house a few times and then parked at the end of the block. Janet was in a car with a friend, and didn't know at first that Rachel was in the car parked at the stop sign. It was too dark to tell the color or make of the car. Joshua came out of the house and told Janet that Rachel was waiting for Sarah to go home because she wanted to fight her—and that was when Janet put two and two together and realized Rachel must be in the car at the end of the block. Janet flashed the lights on her friend's car, and Rachel flashed right back. Rachel was watching. Sometime after eleven at night, Rachel left.

Janet and Jilica's company left. Janet said she felt hungry and went in the house to recruit Sarah to take her to McDonald's. Jilica agreed to go along for the ride. The closest McDonald's was closed down for the night, so they planned to go to the twenty-four-hour franchise, which was farther away. Janet said she thought it might be on Park Boulevard, but she wasn't sure because she'd never been to that one before.

Sarah wasn't angry, but she was concerned because she knew Rachel was out there looking for trouble. Janet explained that she and Sarah and Javier all lived very close to one another, but Rachel's place was relatively far away. It was therefore slightly unnerving for Rachel to be cruising around their neighborhood.

So it was wrong to think that Sarah was out looking for Rachel. Sarah and Janet were *home;* Rachel had come to their neighborhood and was looking for trouble.

Sarah might not have been angry when she first got into the car, but her anger quickly grew. Instead of heading straight for McDonald's, Sarah went to her own home, first—a minor detour—but Rachel was nowhere to be seen.

Janet told Detective Lynch about the "stab Sarah and her Mexican boyfriend" comment. She didn't remember if she was on speakerphone. It was possible Rachel's unbelievable mouth could be heard throughout the minivan without amplification.

Sarah replied, "Where you at? You say you're at my house and want to fight me. I'm at my house. Where you at?"

During the phone call, Janet said she and Jilica kept their mouths shut because they didn't want Rachel to know they were in the car.

The mood in the van relaxed a little. The little bitch was all bark. That was when they encountered Sarah's best friend, Ashley—Janet didn't know her last name, someone Sarah went to school with at Pinellas Park High—who said Rachel was right down the block. Janet wasn't sure what kind of car Ashley was driving. After that, Sarah went directly to Javier's house.

Michael Lynch gave Janet a piece of paper and asked her to draw a diagram, a map of what the scene outside Javier's looked like. Where were the cars? Where were the people? Where did the fight take place?

The cars ended up almost "face-to-face," Janet said, but there was room enough between their snouts for people to walk back and forth. Illustration was not Janet's forte, but she tried.

Janet said that Rachel was leaning on the hood of her car when Sarah pulled up. This disagreed with Jilica, who recalled Rachel crossing the lawn as Sarah approached. Janet remembered that Javier and his friend were standing in the driveway. Once the van stopped, Rachel came quick. Sarah didn't even have a chance to close her car door when Rachel was on her, attacking her with a knife, which Janet thought was in Rachel's right hand.

Sarah said, "What you going to do with that knife?"

At first, Jilica and Janet stayed in the car, but Janet got one glimpse of the knife and got out to assist Sarah, who had no weapons. Sarah was trying to defend herself and hit Rachel also. The fight was so fast—two, three seconds.

By the time Janet got to Rachel, she'd already turned around and was heading back toward Javier's house. Janet removed one of her slippers and used it to try and knock the knife out of Rachel's hand. But she couldn't do it. There were a few seconds there when Janet thought Sarah was okay. Janet decided they should get out of there. She looked in the minivan's passenger-side front window and saw blood on the front seat. She heard Jilica scream that Sarah was "on the floor, bleeding."

Janet ran around the front of the van, saw Sarah was down, and attacked Rachel a second time.

Janet remembered screaming, "You stabbed her!"

Rachel said, "I'm done," and acted like she didn't care.

After the second fight, Rachel kept walking back toward the houses. Janet told her she was watching her; she knew she was trying to get rid of the knife.

"You stabbed my friend. You're not getting away with it," Janet remembered screaming.

Lynch asked if Janet knew if Joshua was seeing Rachel behind Sarah's back.

"I don't have no clue," Janet said.

Joshua knew that Janet disapproved of Rachel, so he probably would not have shared that kind of info with her.

"Was Joshua encouraging Sarah to fight Rachel, or vice versa?"

"No. Joshua always tried to keep Sarah from fighting anybody. He wanted Sarah to go home because it was past time for her to go home."

At no time did Janet have phone contact with Rachel. Lynch warned her that he would be subpoenaing her phone records. Janet repeated that she didn't even know Rachel's number.

"How old are you?"

"Twenty-seven."

"Did it ever occur to you as you headed over to Javier's that this was a bad idea?"

"I had talked to her plenty of times about all this drama."

"Were you in the van saying, 'Come on, let's go over there and kick her ass'?"

"No! Even if I told her to stop, she wouldn't have listened."

Janet then bragged that Rachel didn't come around her house. "She didn't want to deal with me," she said. "Rachel was waiting for Sarah to go to her house, because she knew she would be alone—and I wasn't going to let that happen."

Janet felt that just the fact that she was in the minivan in front of Javier's house would have been enough to make Rachel back off. But it didn't work.

Detective Lynch also conducted a follow-up interview with Dustin Grimes, but his recording mechanism malfunctioned so he later had to summarize the interview from memory.

According to Lynch, Grimes verified the swerving-car incident, saying it was definitely a smaller car and light in color. He said that Rachel walked out into the street when the van arrived and met Sarah "just to the driver's side of the minivan."

He didn't know who "Ashley" was.

It didn't take Lynch long to figure out that Ashley was Ashley Lovelady, the victim's best friend. Ashley Lovelady became the last of the witnesses to be interviewed by police. It was an occurrence further delayed when Ashley was hesitant to speak of that night, unsure of how much trouble she might be in.

When Ashley did arrive at the police station, she was with her dad, who explained to Detective Lynch that because Ashley was underage, he wanted to sit in. The father was also worried that his daughter might be in legal trouble. Even though Lynch explained that Ashley was not in any trouble, she was very closed-lipped during that initial interview.

Ashley told Lynch that she was Sarah's best friend since forever—from preschool! Next to Sarah herself, she probably knew the most about the problems Sarah was having with Joshua. He had at least two other girlfriends, one of them being Rachel Wade.

Rachel left threatening voice mails, horrible stuff. Ashley had tried to talk Sarah out of Joshua, but no way. She loved him. Ashley last spoke to Sarah about a half hour before her death. She admitted to driving her car in the vicinity of Janet Camacho's house that night, but she claimed that this was the extent of her involvement.

Ashley got the impression that Detective Lynch knew the truth about her role that night. She could tell by the way he pressed the point. She said she was out driving in a gold-colored Camry, which belonged to her boyfriend's mother. Yes, she did run into Sarah and Janet on the road. Sarah was mad.

"Did Sarah mention anything about Rachel?" Lynch asked.

"Yes. She said, 'I can't take it anymore, I'm going to find her.'"

"Did you see Rachel Wade at any time that night?"

"No," Ashley said.

Lynch ended the interview by telling Ashley that she could call him at any time and that his door was always open to her because—and he told her point-blank—her story was not consistent with what he had heard from Janet Camacho and Jilica Smith.

The very next day, Ashley did call Michael Lynch back. She admitted that it was she who had spotted Rachel Wade outside Javier Laboy's house, and subsequently had told

Sarah Ludemann where her archenemy was located. She denied being the driver of the swerving car. She apologized for not being completely truthful the day before. When she was talking to Sarah for the final time that night, she gave her the old mantra: "He wasn't worth it. He wasn't worth fighting about." Sarah Ludemann was "obsessed" with Joshua. He was her master, and she always obeyed.

There had been one telling moment during the summer when it was hot. Joshua told Sarah that he didn't like her wearing shorts. He didn't like the idea of other boys being able to see her legs. From then on, despite the heat, Sarah wore long pants.

Detective Lynch remembered that, according to Janet Wade, Rachel's mother, Joshua pulled this manipulative stunt on Rachel as well. If she *really* loved him, if she loved him *enough,* she'd wear long pants so he'd be the *only one* to see her legs.

Joshua told Sarah he didn't want her to go out at night unless she was with him. So from then on, when her girlfriends asked her to come out, she always said no. She stayed home even on nights when Camacho was out with another girl!

Joshua's Svengali-like influence was disturbing on another level: It had caused a dramatic change in not just Sarah's appearance, but in her aura. It was like Sarah's very *spirit* was altered. She dressed differently, acted differently. Her voice was different.

"Her old friends were weirded out," Ashley said.

Sarah's parents were weirded out, too. Sarah's dad found his daughter's new attitude tragic. What was it? Gangsta and slave? Great! Joshua gave the orders and Sarah obeyed. Sarah's mom remembered how Sarah was developing into a strong-willed woman, but now that was gone. In its place was a tiny person, a puppet, allowing a boy to pull her strings. Sarah's mom and dad saw the bruises on her arms. Sarah said they came from Joshua while "play-fighting on the couch."

During the first two weeks of Rachel's lengthy stint in the Pinellas County Jail, her telephone calls were recorded, just in case she said something to incriminate herself. It was not a secret recording. An automated voice informed the parties on the line every few minutes that every phone call might be monitored or recorded.

In order to talk to Rachel, a prepaid account had to be established, two dollars from which was subtracted with each call, which could be up to twenty minutes long. Only two phones signed up to be on Rachel's call list: her parents, and her muscular boyfriend, Jeremy Sanders. She talked to others when one of those two phones was set for a three-way conversation.

When Rachel's dad tried to set up the account, which was done right on the phone, punching information into an automated system, he became frustrated when he entered his credit card number incorrectly on the first try. When Rachel came on the line, she was scared, sick, and crying that she didn't want to be in jail, only hours after her arrest, and the first thing her dad did was complain to her about what he "had to go through" to call her.

Rachel had long phone conversations with her mom during which very little was actually said. Janet Wade often just sighed with disappointment. At first, there was business to be taken care of. The Wades picked up Rachel's dog, Tinkerbell, and took the valuables out of her apartment. But after a time, the conversations with her parents were reduced to minimalist audio poems of despair.

"Are you okay?"

"No, I'm not okay!"

Rachel had developed a rash in jail and this dominated

her conversations with her mother. Rachel finally "went to medical" and got some antihistamines and cream.

Rachel learned in increments that she was notorious. At first, she told those she called "not to tell anybody." Too late, she was informed; her mug shot was all over TV, front page of the papers. Reporters were everywhere. People who hadn't known her since grammar school were weighing in on her situation. Rachel wondered how she was going to get a job when she got out.

During the first calls to Jeremy, Rachel blabbed endlessly about the circumstances of Sarah's death. It wasn't her fault. They jumped her. Three of them. She blacked out. She didn't remember stabbing her, just striking out, and so on. She was injured. Janet Camacho wiped the floor with her. She had bruises, a busted lip, which Joshua had instigated.

"I went to fight her and I ended up stabbing her," she said.

"How many times?" Jeremy asked.

"Two," Rachel said.

Jeremy was often very stoned during his conversations with Rachel. His words slurred and Rachel regularly had to ask him to repeat. Jeremy had driven past the scene while Sarah was still down.

"I know she was stabbed, but I didn't know your little ass did it," he said.

"That shit's gonna be on my conscience for the rest of my life," Rachel replied.

"Why?" Jeremy asked. "Maybe that shit was *supposed* to happen."

She told him that when she was booked, they wouldn't let her wear underwear. "They made me bend over," she said.

Jeremy asked her if she was "all fucked up and shit—you know, drunk and whatever?"

Rachel was not.

"Sarah who?" Jeremy asked.

"I don't know her name. She's a senior," Rachel said. "I'm not a fuckin' murderer. That's not me. Are you dating someone? I was swinging because they were swinging at me, and I couldn't drop the knife, because I guarantee one of them would have picked it up and stabbed me."

Jeremy said he wasn't dating anyone. He had talked to a couple of girls, and that was it. He had a question for her, too: "Why did she fight you if you weren't fuckin' with Joshua?"

Rachel said it didn't matter. As long as Sarah *thought* Rachel still had feelings for him, Sarah wanted to fight.

Discussions regarding the stabbing ended after a day or so. Having talked to a lawyer, her dad told her to shut up about what had happened. He told her that she shouldn't talk to her friends. She should talk to family only. That was the best way to make sure she wouldn't say anything the prosecution could use against her.

Over the days, there was a slow realization by Rachel of the fix she was in. At first, she sobbed that she might be in jail for a couple of days; then, when bond was set so high, a lawyer told her she'd be inside at least six months to a year.

Janet Wade rejected the news. "I don't know how they can tell you that," she said to her daughter. "I think we'll just have to wait and see."

Dad blamed the environment, saying, "There were always problems" in that section of Pinellas Park where Javier lived.

A few days after the stabbing, Rachel had her period in prison and complained to her mother that not only didn't she feel good, but they wouldn't give her tampons. Pads only. Gross.

* * *

Using Jeremy's phone, Rachel was allowed to talk to Javier. Compared to Jeremy, he sounded like a professor of diction.

"Hello, beautiful," Javier said.

He told Rachel that he had seen the entire thing. He was going to testify at her trial that she was defending herself, and everything was going to be okay. She shouldn't worry. He was going to get her out of there. In the meantime, he was telling everyone not to believe the bullshit on TV. Rachel said she hadn't seen the TV coverage. Every time they started to talk about her on TV, a female corrections officer turned it off.

Rachel said she was concerned about Javier's safety. Rachel and Javier knew that Joshua had a gun, because they'd both seen it. Joshua had called her minutes after the stabbing, screaming that he was going to shoot her. Both Joshua and his brother Jay had threatened Javier for taking Rachel's side.

"Watch your back," she warned Javier.

He told her he could take care of himself.

She also talked to her "homegirls" via three-way, and they sounded very young. Perhaps overwhelmed by the gravity of the circumstance, they spoke in baby talk, but still with the easy profanity of friendship: "Hi, baby. Fuckin' love ya! Miss you *soooo* fuckin' much!"

"Everything's going on without me," Rachel cried. She said that they should play the lottery, win it, and bail her out. Her folks lacked the funds.

Over the next few days, Rachel's conversations with Jeremy became increasingly flirtatious. He was going to wait for her. He wanted her for a lifetime, so waiting for a year was no big deal.

"Will you marry me?" Rachel asked.

"Most likely," Jeremy said.

"Most likely?" she said, feigning outrage.

"Duh," Jeremy replied.

"I'm so lucky. I can stop lookin' for a fuckin' guy, 'cause I got one," she said.

The conversations turned into "phone sex." He called her "baby girl," "sweetheart," and "pumpkin." They pledged their exclusive and undying love.

The prurient talk would commence with discussions of food. She couldn't eat the jail slop, rice with some brown goop on it.

"I want some fuckin' Church's Chicken, so my fingers get all greasy," Rachel would say. "I want a fuckin' taco. You know how sick of Applebee's I was. I saw a commercial for Applebee's and I would love me some Applebee's right now. When I get out of here, you are going to buy me a different kind of fast food for every meal. I'm going to start with KFC, then McDonald's, then Taco Bell and Pizza Hut. I'm not kidding you. We're gonna eat and then we're gonna fuck. We're gonna eat and then we're gonna fuck."

"I'm gonna have to bust you out of there," Jeremy said, and Rachel giggled.

"When I get out, I'm gonna get one of them big bowls of whipped cream, and then I'm gonna give you something to dip in it," she replied.

She told Jeremy that her roommate had stood on her bed so she could look out the window and talk to a guy. The roommate said her name was "Peaches," and the guy asked if he could eat her peach. The roommate said she had a man on the outside, but she needed to make arrangements for the meantime. Rachel said she'd wait for her man.

All the girls in jail had phone sex. All she heard was "I wanna fuck."

"What's the first thing you're gonna do when you see me?" Rachel asked.

"I'm gonna grab you and squeeze you and kiss your neck," Jeremy replied. "Then I'm gonna pick you up and *ummmm*. What you gonna do?"

"I'm gonna go crazy! I like sex. You know how much I like sex. When I get out, I am going to go crazy."

"They don't feed the girls sausages in there. They're afraid you use 'em as dildos."

"There's a sixty-five-year-old woman here. She's flashing a guy out the window. Ewww."

"You flash anybody out that window?"

"Fuck no. Why would I flash somebody? Ewww, now she's talking about some guy who came all over his window. I wanna throw up. The only person I want to see come is you, baby." Then she faced facts. "But there's nothing physically I can do for you now. Do you think you can behave? Even if I'm in here for six months to a year, you can do it?"

"I hope so," he said. "Right now, I'm lying in bed trying not to pass out."

"You know I can't imagine being with anybody else but you."

"Not even Lil Wayne?"

"He doesn't have your personality, but he is Weezy."

"You got a point," Jeremy agreed.

He told her that when he thought about her, he could feel a tingling sensation in his stomach, and he developed superhearing, like Superman's, so he could hear through walls.

"That's just withdrawal from not seeing me," she said with a laugh. "When I get out of here, I'm going to take a shower, and then I'm not going to leave your bed. Never. You and me are going to do some freaky shit."

"You're a beast," he said. "You're my little head monster."

"Is that what you're going to call me? Your little head

monster?" Rachel asked with a throaty laugh. She sighed and said, "You and me and Tinkerbell, lying on top of both of us like she does." She said all she could think about was sex. "Me and you takin' care of business!"

"I'm going to give it to you good, pumpkin," he said.

She let out a quick earthy laugh. "Oh, baby, it feels so good when you say that. You can do whatever you want to me, baby, as soon as I get home."

The hot chats didn't last. Jeremy became impatient with Rachel's pledges of fidelity. He knew her. She *needed* it. Needed it *bad*.

He began to say things like, "You say that now. You only been there a week. Wait till six, seven months. You be doin' sick shit in there."

"Nooo," she said.

"You and your roommate be doin' it."

"No, Jeremy."

"No, it's cool. Weren't you gay once?"

"Yes, but there are no girls in here that I . . . Well, there's one girl that I would consider—but no. No, thank you. It's you and me, all the way, when I get out."

"But it ain't cheatin', baby."

"I don't want that. I want you. I don't want a girl. I don't."

"You guys are going to be spending a lot of time together."

"I don't care. I don't care. I'll do it myself. I got hands."

"So she's going to sit there and watch you?"

"No, she sleeps underneath me."

Jeremy heard from a homeboy that someone in jail asked Rachel if she had a boyfriend, and she said, "I don't know. Kind of. Not really, no."

What was that about?

Rachel assured him that her days of promiscuity were behind her.

"I fucked up once. I'm not going to fuck up again. Believe me, Jeremy, this has been a *huge* reality check for me. Now I know who cares about me and who doesn't care about me, and I know who I'm going to be with."

But she spoke too fast.

"What?" Jeremy asked.

"That's the old me, Jeremy!"

"What, a week ago?"

Besides the deteriorating trust issue, Jeremy's life was in flux. He had to move out of one apartment, for unstated reasons, but he managed to move into another apartment, which was on a lake. There was an island in the lake and a little rowboat, so he could go on the island and chill.

But paradise was short-lived.

During her second week in jail, Rachel called Jeremy and found him a paranoid wreck. When the conversation started, he was smoking a joint outside his front door. He saw four cop cars go by and freaked out. Without dropping the joint, he ran and jumped a fence.

"I was straight, man, like the wind," he told Rachel. He was on the phone, panting in an alley.

Rachel said, "Jeremy, what are you doing? What are you *doing*? Jeremy, drop what is in your hand."

Jeremy said he couldn't talk because he saw flashlights.

That call was followed by a period of Jeremy ignoring her calls. When he finally did answer, he told her that he had been kicked out of his lakeside apartment and he'd been robbed.

Rachel became angry, and that was it for that romance.

By the time Rachel went to trial, Jeremy was no longer in the picture, and Javier was. Javier was the one she wanted to marry and have a family with.

Chapter 8

JUDGE BULONE

Presiding over Rachel Wade's pretrial hearings, as well as her trial, was circuit judge Joseph A. Bulone, who had manned the bench since spring 2005. Before that, Judge Bulone was lead trial attorney prosecuting felony cases. He joined the staff of State Attorney (SA) Bernie McCabe in 1985, and built up an impressive set of stats: 150 jury trials, more than twenty of them first-degree murder cases. Before that, he was an attorney in private practice working for two years in Tallahassee in the areas of personal injury, insurance defense, family law, and criminal practice. He served as a vice chair of the Bar Grievance Committee and had been an adjunct professor at the St. Petersburg College Police Academy. Prior to earning his Juris Doctor degree with honors from the Florida State University College of Law, he graduated cum laude from Stetson University with a bachelor's degree in political science.

Bulone was a veteran of capital murder cases. Earlier in 2010, he'd wielded the gavel at the trial of Richard T. Robards, a Clearwater, Florida, personal trainer who was accused of fatally stabbing two of his wealthy clients, Frank Deluca, sixty, and Deluca's wife, Linda, fifty-nine. Robards had been a competitive bodybuilder and in 1995 won heavyweight and overall titles in the Tampa Bay Classic contest. He'd also worked as a male revue dancer. But he'd fallen on hard times and was living in a Motel 6 when he murdered the Delucas because they kept a lot of cash, jewelry, and collectible coins in their house. Robards was caught after a friend reported to police that he'd tried to recruit him to help carry away the Delucas' five-hundred-pound safe. After Robards was convicted and the jury recommended the death penalty, Judge Bulone stated that death was appropriate, given the brutality of the murders. Both victims had been stabbed repeatedly, with both their throats and lungs punctured. One of them would have been alive to see the other attacked, and at least one was coughing up blood during the attack.

Going further back, in 2008, Judge Bulone was assigned the trial of Genghis Kocaker, a forty-four-year-old man with a history of violent crime who was on felony probation when he murdered Eric J. Stanton in Clearwater, Florida, in 2004. The murder was especially heinous, as Kocaker stabbed Stanton, a cabdriver, in his taxi; then he set the cab on fire, causing his conscious victim to be burned to death. The blazing vehicle rocked as Stanton tried in vain to kick his way out. Kocaker's attorney argued that there was no evidence that his client stuck around to watch the horror. He also put forth that Kocaker had a multiple personality disorder caused by sexual abuse he suffered as a child, possible mental deterioration due to HIV, and a history of substance abuse. A jury convicted Kocaker and voted eleven to one for him to receive the death penalty, a recommendation that Judge Bulone solemnly adjudicated.

On a Monday morning during the spring of 2010, Bulone had a truly bizarre experience in his courtroom. Forty-year-old Matthew Mauceri was due in the courtroom to begin his trial on scheming-to-defraud charges. Trouble was, he was flying into Florida from out of state and his flight was delayed. He could have called the court and explained the situation, and there would have been a delay, but folks who are accused of scheming to defraud often employ complex methods of problem solving. Matthew gave the matter some thought and decided not to call the court. Instead, he called his twin brother, Marcus, and asked him to sit in for him. No one would know the difference. It was Matthew Mauceri's own lawyer who suspected his client was pulling the switcheroo and instantly informed Judge Bulone that, contrary to appearances, he didn't believe his client was present. The judge ordered the "defendant" fingerprinted, and the scam was quickly exposed. Now, instead of one twin being accused of fraud, there were two. Judge Bulone ordered them jailed—in separate cells.

Soon thereafter, Judge Bulone listened to Jay Hebert's argument that Rachel Wade should not be prosecuted because she acted in self-defense under Florida's "Stand Your Ground" law. The judge rejected the argument, saying, "She's waiting there with a knife for something to happen. It's almost like Clint Eastwood saying, 'Go ahead, make my day.'"

Chapter 9

Two Girls in Jail

In May 2010, nineteen-year-old Jamie Severino, friend of Erin Slothower and mother of Jay Camacho's child, proved conclusively that her tastes in men had not matured with motherhood. (Jay hadn't matured, either. Only a few days earlier, Jay was arrested by deputies of the Pinellas County Sheriff's Office for possession of cocaine.)

These days Severino had a new boyfriend, twenty-year-old Jeff Overton (pseudonym), who lived the life of a rebel (and theoretically victimless) outlaw. This was cool, until Jamie, Jeff, and two other men got popped for operating a prescription narcotics operation.

The *St. Petersburg Times* reported that the arrests came after a man and his friend were beaten and robbed at gunpoint during a drug deal gone bad. According to the PCSO, one of the victims called Severino on a Wednesday morning, seeking Roxies. She instructed the caller to come to a St. Petersburg address. When the men arrived, the sheriff's report said, they were punched, kicked, and robbed at gunpoint of a BlackBerry and cash. The victims were allowed to leave; at which time, they called Gulfport police. The cops, in turn, reported the incident to the sheriff. Jamie's boyfriend was charged with two counts of robbery with a firearm, and dealing in stolen property. He was jailed in lieu of $320,000 bond (and eventually tried, convicted, and sentenced to six years in Apalachee Correctional Institution, East).

Jamie Severino was charged with being a principal to robbery with a deadly weapon, robbery with a firearm, and armed burglary, dealing in stolen property, and driving with a license suspended or revoked. Her bail was set at $320,250.

"I was at the wrong place, at the wrong time," she recalled. "They blew it out of proportion. My boyfriend at the time was selling drugs, and these junkies came, two dudes. One of them had been calling and calling my phone, harassing me. My boyfriend didn't like anybody calling my phone—and when they came, I didn't think anything of it. They started arguing and got into a fight. We didn't think the cops were going to be called. Junkies don't call the cops. They came to buy drugs, got into an argument, a fight, and that was it. Nothing really bad happened. When the cops got there, the junkies started lying, saying my ex-boyfriend had a gun, hit him with a gun. I don't like guns, and my ex-boyfriend never had a gun around me at all. There was no gun."

The charges might have been based on fabrication, but the effect on Jamie's life was real enough. "It really messed up a lot of things for me."

After her arrest, Jamie took up residence in the Pinellas County Jail. One day, when entering the visitation room, Jamie was horrified to see someone she knew—Rachel Wade—also receiving visitors.

"It was really, really awkward, because she used to harass me when I went to Applebee's, and stuff like that," Jamie said. "And it was just me and her in the room. So there I am in the room and I'm talking to my daughter on the visitation screen, and I could see that Rachel kept looking over and being really nosy. I don't know who she was seeing, but I could hear her saying things like, 'It's really funny who's sitting next to me right now.'"

After Jamie finished speaking to her daughter, she turned to Rachel and said, "Do you have a problem?"

"No," Rachel said.

"Why were you saying those things you were saying? What's funny about sitting next to me?"

"I don't need your shit."

"I'm not starting any shit with you."

That established, Rachel talked about her future. The way she saw it, she had one. Money talks, she said, and her family had shelled out fifty grand for a really good attorney. She was going to walk.

"I'm going home," she said.

"Why did you even do that?" Jamie asked. "Why did you stab her? Sarah *wasn't* that tough."

Rachel replied, "I tried to tell her about Joshua, but she wouldn't fuckin' listen."

According to Jamie, who was not Rachel's friend, Rachel exhibited no sadness, no regret—just the firm belief that she was going to get away with it.

Girls would come to Jamie and ask about Rachel. They knew there was a connection. After all, Jamie had a tattoo of CAMACHO. So, during her stay in jail, Jamie learned some things about Rachel through the grapevine.

Rachel had been telling bizarre lies. She claimed, for example, to be the mother of Javier Laboy's child.

"One girl said to me, 'That's so sad. Rachel is going away for murder, and she has a baby at home.' I was like, 'What?'"

Jamie set the record straight. Rachel was *not* a mommy. When Jamie and Rachel ran into one another the next time, also in the visitation room, this became a topic of discussion.

"She got really mad that I'd told everyone the truth. As we were being led back to our pod, she started screaming, 'I swear to God, if I could get away right now, I'd strangle you!'"

Same old Rachel, hurling threats. Threatening violence. Threatening to kill.

But at the same time, it wasn't the same old Rachel at all. Her words used to roll off her enemies' backs. Those days were through. Rachel's threats bore more weight now.

She had proven that she could, and would, back them up with action.

Jamie didn't have much nice to say about Rachel, but she did not think that the death of Sarah Ludemann was premeditated murder.

"Rachel lacked impulse control at the key moment," Jamie said, "but she hadn't thought it through beforehand."

The idea exploded into action before the thinking part of her brain could catch up.

"I think she brought the knife just to let everyone know 'Don't fuck with me,'" Jamie said.

Why Rachel did it wasn't the only mystery surrounding the death of Sarah Ludemann, according to Jamie Severino. There was also the question of *how*.

One thing was for sure—whether it was fear or anger or something else—Rachel was physically *charged* at the time. She was jacked when she killed Sarah.

It required some arm strength to stick a knife into somebody that far and, look at her, Jamie Severino said, "Rachel was not that strong of a person."

That same spring of 2010, more than a year after their daughter's arrest, Barry and Janet Wade finally agreed to talk to reporter Lane DeGregory, who went to the Wade home. During the quiet interview, Janet clutched Rachel's small dog to her bosom as if it were a security blanket.

Janet Wade said that she had been filled with such optimism, right up until the night of the incident. Rachel had been giving them problems for years, rebellious to the nth degree; but by 2009, they thought she had started to calm down.

After years of not-so-much socializing, Rachel was visiting regularly with them, stopping by periodically for dinner. The Wades had reason to believe their chilly relationship with their daughter was starting to warm up a little bit. They didn't worry about her being in her own place. Rachel had a nice apartment and a good job. Janet Wade felt like she could finally breathe a sigh of relief. And then this . . .

The problem with Rachel all along was boys. She was boy crazy, and then some. She couldn't live at home anymore because it was cutting into boyfriend time. Janet condensed her daughter's bitter biography, from innocence to experience: "When Rachel was little, all of the girls wanted to be like her. From middle school on, all of the boys wanted to be with her."

With a nose for news, DeGregory looked around the house, scrutinized the demeanor of the parents, sought anything that might give her a clue as to why Rachel Wade was the way she was. But there was nothing. The ambience was a completely suburban, middle-class lifestyle—*normal*.

The only missing piece to the puzzle was Rachel's older brother. DeGregory never saw him, never spoke to him. She called him, left voice messages for him, but she received no response.

DeGregory asked Rachel's parents about their son, and they replied that they were not close.

"They said they were estranged from their son, that he was quiet, and that he didn't want to have anything to do with this," DeGregory recalled.

PART THREE

THE TRIAL

Chapter 10

Day One

The Pinellas County Criminal Justice Center was an impressive four-pillar courthouse in Clearwater, Florida. On July 20, 2010, in that building, voir dire began. That was the process by which a panel of Rachel Wade's "peers" would be chosen from a large jury pool.

The jail was just south of the courthouse, on County Road 611. The sheriff's office was just south of that, so proximity led to convenience. Transporting Rachel Wade to and from the courtroom would not be difficult.

Judge Bulone's courtroom was large with seven rows of seats for spectators. Capacity was more than one hundred people, and it would be full throughout the trial.

Groups of young men and women, friends of the victim and the defendant, sat on opposite sides of the aisle. Rachel's friends included Courtney Richards, Lindsey Atticks, and Lisa Lafrance.

The first elimination came after potential jurors filled out a written questionnaire. Those that passed the first test were brought into the courtroom in small groups.

If the court took a break during questioning, Judge Bulone would ask, "Did anyone see anything about this case during the break in the hallway? No one heard anything. No hands. Did anyone see anything about the media coverage? No hands."

Every once in a while, a hand would raise and the judge would ask that juror to approach his bench. If he felt what the potential juror had experienced or overheard would prejudice that person, the potential juror was dismissed.

Each person was questioned by both the state and the defense. The defense asked questions such as, "Do you have any family members in law enforcement?" And "Do you have a set idea of what happened in this case, how it came down?"

One exchange went like this:

"Juror twenty-three, do you have anyone in your family in law enforcement?"

"Yes, I do, but he's retired now."

"Is there anything in your past that would interfere with you being a fair and impartial juror?"

"No."

Defense attorney Jay Hebert asked each potential juror the same question: "Have you ever been in a fight?"

If they had not been, he didn't want them on his jury. He needed jurors with empathy, who understood the intensity of the emotions here.

By the early morning of the following day, July 21, the six-person jury—five men, one woman—plus two alternates, were seated. Seven of them sat in the front row of the jury box, one behind. They would take turns as to who sat behind the others.

It was almost half past ten in the morning when Judge Joseph Bulone took the bench. He looked out over the full courtroom, noted the crowd of family members and young people, and warned that he didn't want to hear any emotional outbursts.

He warned, "If anyone can't control themselves, they will forfeit their right to be in this courtroom. Does everyone understand?"

Silence.

The jury was brought in.

First order of business was a stipulation. Both sides had agreed that the victim in this case was indeed Sarah Ludemann.

The judge called for opening statements: "Ms. Hanewicz?"

"Thank you, Your Honor," Assistant State Attorney (ASA) Lisset Hanewicz said.

ASA Hanewicz was a slightly stocky woman with an aggressive, almost pugilistic, stance. She wore a white suit. Her dark brown and frosted hair was cut in three lengths: into bangs in the front, shoulder length at the sides, and midback in the rear.

She turned to the jury and shouted, "*I am going to fucking murder you!*'"

Several jurors physically recoiled.

Hanewicz explained that was what Rachel Wade had said to Sarah Ludemann seven and a half months before she took a knife and stabbed her through the heart.

She had another quote. On the night of the murder, the prosecutor said, "Rachel Wade was telling her friend, 'I'm going to fucking kill that bitch.'"

That same night, Rachel Wade had a verbal argument on the phone with the victim, Sarah Ludemann, and said, "I'm going to stab you and your Mexican boyfriend."

The point was that the defendant promised to do it,

and she did it. That was the reason they were all gathered together in that courtroom.

"Because Sarah Ludemann is *dead*."

Hanewicz gave the jury the background: On April 14, 2009, Sarah was with Joshua Camacho, her boyfriend, and they were at his sister Janet's house. Also there was a young woman named Jilica Smith, who knew Janet because she was related to the father of Janet's children.

There would come a time during that evening when Joshua and Sarah were in the house, while Jilica was outside in a car with a gentleman, and Janet was also outside.

Just then, Jilica noticed a red car "zip by." She noticed that the driver was a woman with blond hair. Janet also saw the car, which pulled over and parked at the side of the street at the end of the block.

"Janet thought that was strange and wondered why that car was there," Hanewicz said.

The jury would learn that at some point during that evening, the girls got into Sarah's vehicle, her mom's minivan. Sarah was driving, Janet Camacho was in the front passenger seat, and Jilica Smith was in the back.

They were going to McDonald's. At least, that was the plan. However, they received a phone call during the ride—a phone call that changed everything. The phone call was to Sarah Ludemann from the defendant, Rachel Wade.

The passengers in Sarah's vehicle heard that phone call. They heard the arguing back and forth. They heard the voice on the other end of that call making threats. They heard that voice make the "Mexican boyfriend" threat.

That phone call came only short minutes before the physical confrontation between Sarah and Rachel. The jury would learn through eyewitness testimony that Sarah was visibly upset by that call.

"Perfectly understandable," Hanewicz said.

After all, Sarah had just received a *death threat*. The

jury would learn that this threat was just the most recent in a feud between Sarah and Rachel, which had been going on for months. It was a feud over Joshua Camacho, a young man whom Rachel used to date.

Not long after the phone call, Sarah and her friends would encounter the vehicle of another friend, a girl named Ashley Lovelady. Both vehicles stopped; Sarah and Ashley had a conversation.

Ashley told Sarah that she had just seen Rachel Wade at Javier Laboy's house; Javier was another neighborhood boy whom Rachel used to date. At that point, Sarah drove directly to Javier's house to confront Rachel. (For the first several times that Hanewicz mentioned him, she mispronounced Javier's name as Ha-VEER. As she went along though, a third syllable developed and her pronunciation came closer to Ha-vee-air.)

The jury would hear the testimony of Javier's friend Dustin, who was also there. Hanewicz explained that Dustin could not be in court in person because he was serving in the military and was in Korea. His testimony had been prerecorded and they'd be seeing it on a TV set.

Dustin would testify that he was with Javier when Rachel showed up, that she was extremely emotional, extremely angry. The word he used was "enraged." Rachel spent a lot of time on the phone, and after she got directions from Javier, she left.

The directions were either to Sarah's house or Joshua's house. Dustin didn't remember. For a while, Rachel was gone, and then she came back. Dustin also saw a vehicle go by Javier's house, which turned out to be driven by Ashley Lovelady. That was how Sarah found out where Rachel was.

Hanewicz didn't want the jury to think that all of this accidentally running into one another was a series of unlikely coincidences. All of these people lived in close proximity in the same neighborhood.

"Ashley swerved her car toward Rachel a little as she passed," Hanewicz explained. "And soon thereafter told Sarah that she'd seen Rachel at Javier's house."

The jury would hear that when Javier and Dustin realized that Rachel had a knife, they said, "You don't need a knife." Hanewicz held her arms out at her sides as she said this, a gesture meaning that what the boys were saying could not have been more obvious: You do not bring a knife to a fight. Only bad things could happen when you brought a knife to a fight. *Everyone knows that.*

The boys told Rachel to put the knife away, and they thought she had. When trouble started, Dustin and Javier didn't know that Rachel still had the knife on her.

As soon as Sarah found out that Rachel was at Javier's house, she forgot all about going to McDonald's. She headed directly to Javier's, pedal to the metal.

The jury would learn that Jilica Smith, who was sitting in the back of the minivan as it zoomed through the streets of Pinellas Park, had no idea what was going on.

Jilica didn't even know Sarah very well, having only met her once or twice at Janet's house. Jilica had just happened to be at Janet's house at the same time as Sarah, and just happened to come along when Sarah volunteered to make a McDonald's run.

Hanewicz explained that Sarah's minivan, moving as fast as it was, arrived at Javier's house very quickly. As Sarah drove down the street, her headlights were in Rachel's eyes. Sarah stopped her car right in the middle of the street.

Rachel's car was facing in the opposite direction; it was parked at the side of the street. Rachel was standing near the hood of her vehicle, on the driver's side, right in front of the left headlight.

According to the prosecutor's scenario, the defendant grabbed the knife the instant the minivan screeched to a halt. With the knife in her hand, she walked across the front of her car and then across the front of the minivan.

She was heading straight for Sarah.

"Everyone agrees that it all happened in less than five seconds," Hanewicz said.

As Rachel was walking between the vehicles, Sarah got out of the minivan. She left the driver's door open, and took no more than a couple of steps toward the front of the minivan, when the confrontation occurred.

"It happened right there. Right there on the driver's side of Sarah's vehicle!" Hanewicz exclaimed. "Near the front of the minivan."

Hanewicz's scenario had Rachel moving fifteen feet in the time it took Sarah to open the car door and take a couple of steps. Who was the aggressor? There could be no doubt.

Rachel wanted to get to Sarah as fast as she could, and she didn't just have a fistfight in mind—evident, to the prosecutor, from that kitchen knife Rachel held tightly in her right hand.

"And it is immediate," Hanewicz said, switching to the present tense and crisply clapping her arched palms together. "It is not as if words are exchanged. It is *boomboomboom,* just like that."

It happened so quickly that all of the eyewitnesses, some of whom were only a few feet away, did not know immediately that Sarah had been stabbed.

There had been a blur of action in the street. Hair was flying, arms were flailing. Then it was over. It just stopped, and Rachel turned around and she just walked away.

But Sarah *had* been stabbed in the heart. Gravely injured, she managed to call out, "We got to go."

"Sarah Ludemann tried to get back in her minivan—but

she didn't make it. She eventually ended up down on the ground," Hanewicz said, rigidly gesturing toward the courtroom floor with outstretched arms.

And Rachel thought she was just going to walk away. But Janet Camacho had something to say about that. Janet looked down and saw the knife in Rachel's hand.

"'What are you doing?'" Hanewicz quoted Janet as saying. "'What are you going to do with that?'" Janet had asked, referring to the knife.

Janet Camacho was fearless. Knife or no knife, she confronted Rachel; and a second fight began. Jilica moved forward, in a small attempt to get Janet away from the girl with the knife, but they were so caught up in their own ruckus that none of the girls noticed that Sarah was on the ground.

"Interestingly, Rachel never tried to use the knife on Janet," Hanewicz noted.

People do unexpected things sometimes when in the throes of hand-to-hand combat. Janet Camacho, for example, took off her flip-flops and smacked Rachel with them. While smacking Rachel in the head with the flip-flops, Janet used her other hand to try and get the knife away from her.

The fight didn't stay in one place, as Rachel retreated and Janet pursued. They moved out of the street and onto Javier's front lawn. Jilica noticed for the first time that Sarah was lying in the street on the driver's side of the minivan, just below the still-open driver's door.

Jilica began screaming.

Hanewicz promised the jury that it would get to hear the 911 tape. At some point in the fight, still on the lawn, Rachel managed to get away from Janet Camacho. She ran toward the back of the house and, in the prosecutor's words, she "ditched something."

When Rachel returned to the front of the house, no

knife. There was a lot of commotion. Emergency vehicles screamed onto the block. Paramedics were approaching on foot, carrying equipment.

"There was someone on the ground, stabbed, lying in the middle of the street," Hanewicz said. "And while all of that commotion was going on, *she,*" the prosecutor said, gesturing toward the defendant, just so there could be no mistake as to whom she was referring, "*she just sat there, in the back, showing no emotion whatsoever.*"

Like nothing had ever happened.

Hanewicz told the jury that she was confident that after they heard all of the evidence in this case, they would find Rachel Wade guilty of second-degree murder, and that she *did not* act in self-defense.

The prosecutor thanked the jury for their attention, and then she sat down. She had spoken for fourteen minutes.

Judge Bulone asked if the defense was ready to deliver its opening. Jay Hebert said that the defense wished to reserve its opening statement until the beginning of their case-in-chief.

"Very well. In that case, the state may call their first witness," the judge said.

Assistant State Attorney Wesley Dicus, a slender, bespectacled man, stood up and said, "Your Honor, the state calls Ashley Lovelady."

Prospective witnesses were kept in a witness room until it was their turn to testify. Keeping them out of the courtroom prevented testimony from being affected by the testimony that preceded it.

The message—"Ashley Lovelady to the stand"—was relayed out into the hall, and from there into the witness room. After a short delay, a young woman entered the courtroom, rolling her shoulders with a tough-girl gait. That walk spoke eloquently. She did not play.

Ashley had a massive calamity of hair over her shoulders and down her back. She wore a dark blue sweater over a gray dress over dark leggings. As she took the oath and sat in the witness chair, Rachel Wade was watching her closely, pausing now and again to scratch notes in her yellow legal pad.

As ASA Dicus stood to begin his questioning, Ashley Lovelady suddenly did not seem so tough anymore. She was filled with anxiety, perhaps near tears, trying to control her breathing and closing her eyes tightly in an attempt to remain composed.

There was a natural urge to think that since Ashley's hair was big, her voice would be also. But this was not the case. When Dicus asked how she was doing, Ashley replied something, perhaps "fine," in the tiniest of all possible voices.

Judge Bulone immediately piped in that Ashley was going to have to speak up. Ashley shuddered as if she'd been admonished by the voice of God.

Dicus gently suggested she move her chair forward a little bit so that she was closer to the microphone. Ashley liked that idea and complied immediately.

The prosecutor asked her if she had ever testified in court in front of a jury before, and Ashley admitted that she had not.

Was she nervous?

"Yes," she said, showing a small smile.

No, she wasn't employed. She was a student, although she did not actually attend a school. She took a couple of courses online.

In between questions, she was still closing her eyes tightly as if holding back tears. She said she was trying to finish up some credits for school, trying to get her diploma. She lived with her parents in Pinellas Park.

"Did you know a girl named Ashley Ludemann?" Dicus inquired.

Ashley Lovelady looked at the prosecutor as if he had two heads.

Dicus repeated his question, word for word, and had to be informed of his problem by a voice that sounded like a prompter during a play feeding an actor his forgotten lines.

Before he could correct himself, the witness said, "You mean Sarah?"

He did. Yes, Ashley knew Sarah. Very well. They had been best friends, in fact. They'd known each other since *preschool.* Since *forever.*

Ashley told the court that Sarah had gone to two high schools. She started out at Tarpon High, and then transferred to Pinellas Park. She had been attending Pinellas Park High School during the spring of 2009. Sarah lived with her parents and had no job. She didn't have her own car. When she needed to get around, she borrowed her mother's vehicle, a minivan.

Dicus asked Ashley if she knew Joshua Camacho. She did, but she was uncertain as to how long she had known him. After some haggling, they settled on the phrase "for a substantial period."

Ashley knew Joshua because he was Sarah's boyfriend, Sarah's *only* boyfriend.

"Did Joshua consider Sarah his exclusive girlfriend?" Dicus asked.

"No, he did not," Ashley said firmly.

Ashley testified that she knew the defendant as well because Rachel Wade was Joshua's ex-girlfriend. The witness was aware that during his relationship with Sarah, Joshua had continued to see Rachel.

What did the witness mean by the verb "see"?

That meant he continued to have intimate relations with Rachel, Ashley patiently explained.

The prosecutor asked how Joshua's continued intimacy with Rachel "affected everyone."

Ashley said it caused a lot of drama and arguing.

"Between who?"

"All of them."

Dicus wanted to know how long the drama had been going on. Ashley, well rehearsed, instantly replied that it had been eight months in duration. For eight straight months, the drama and arguing brewed and grew.

Did she know a boy named Jay Camacho?

He was Joshua's older brother, and the witness's ex-boyfriend.

Dicus asked what Ashley's relationship with Jay was during April 2009.

Ashley again closed her eyes tightly, battling her emotions. She built up her courage, took a deep breath, and blurted out, "We were friends with benefits." Again her eyes were closed tightly.

Spectators got the impression that though the phrase was common enough, she herself had never used it before; and now that she had, she couldn't believe she'd done so in front of a courtroom full of people, many of whom she knew.

Dicus cocked his head as if he were unfamiliar with the phrase. "Friends with benefits? What's that mean?"

Ashley explained that it meant friends who have sexual relations—and she began to cry.

Dicus forged on, and Ashley quickly regained her composure.

Yes, she knew Janet Camacho. That was Jay's sister. Janet was older than both Jay and Joshua. She had her own place and her own car.

And yes, she knew Javier Laboy. He had dated Rachel

According to Jamie Severino (pictured), Rachel Wade once threatened to "slit her throat." Sadly, Rachel's bloody threats had a desensitizing effect. She was a barker, not a biter. When she started in with Sarah, nobody blinked. It was Rachel being Rachel. *(Photo courtesy Pinellas County Sheriff's Office)*

Jamie Severino didn't think Rachel Wade premeditated Sarah Ludemann's murder: "I think she brought the knife just to let everyone know, 'Don't f*** with me.'" (Photo courtesy Florida Department of Corrections)

Sarah Ludemann's shirt, slit over the left breast by Rachel Wade's kitchen knife. (Photo courtesy Pinellas Park Police Department)

A forlorn Rachel Wade stands in front of Javier's house only minutes after the stabbing, not a drop of blood on her. *(Photo courtesy Pinellas Park Police Department)*

Blissfully unaware of any future irony, Rachel Wade posed for this joke photo. She is sitting on a bar in torn stockings, wearing a bonnet, holding a handgun, and the caption reads, *Wanted!*

The victim was a big girl, five-nine, and had struggled with a weight problem. Once she had a man, though, she went on a crash diet and lost thirty pounds. *(Photo courtesy Lisa Marie Lafrance)*

A late bloomer, Sarah Ludemann was a senior in high school when she had her first boyfriend. Her willingness to fight for him proved fatal. *(Yearbook photo)*

Sarah Ludemann died in the street, a gaping stab wound in her left breast. The first cop on the scene called it "the biggest puncture wound" he'd ever seen. *(Yearbook photo)*

Rachel's friend Egle Nakaite said, "People sometimes thought Rachel was prissy, but she wasn't, once you got to know her." *(Photo courtesy Pinellas County Sheriff's Office)*

Javier Laboy's house. The street in front of the house is well marked with rubber patches, laid down by cars entering or exiting the scene hurriedly.
(Photo courtesy Pinellas Park Police Department)

Rachel Wade was thoroughly interrogated, only hours after the stabbing. At first, she said she had no idea how Sarah was stabbed.
(Photo courtesy Pinellas Park Police Department)

When she was informed that Sarah was dead, Rachel Wade burst into tears and admitted that she was the one who'd wielded the knife. *(Photo courtesy Pinellas Park Police Department)*

Journalist Lane DeGregory was covering Sarah Ludemann's death for the *St. Petersburg Times* when she learned she'd won a Pulitzer Prize for feature writing. *(Photo by Tucker DeGregory)*

Rachel Wade (right) dropped out of high school and left home so she could spend more time hanging out and hooking up. *(Photo courtesy Lisa Marie Lafrance)*

Lisa Lafrance, who has described her body type as "more to love," shows off her beach body in a photo she took of herself for her Facebook page.

(Photo courtesy Lisa Marie Lafrance)

The Camacho boys were playas—and fertile. Jay (pictured) had a baby with Jamie Severino. His younger brother Joshua impregnated Erin Slothower, and was sexually involved with both the victim and her killer. *(Photo courtesy Pinellas County Sheriff's Office)*

According to Jamie Severino, the Camacho brothers disciplined their women. Jay (pictured) hit Jamie, and Jamie had seen Joshua hit Erin. *(Photo courtesy Florida Department of Corrections)*

The knife that killed Sarah Ludemann was recovered on a neighbor's roof (pictured). *(Photo courtesy Pinellas Park Police Department)*

Friend Lisa Lafrance said she and Rachel Wade were bad girls. "We did a lot of drugs together. We used to steal clothes, sell them at Plato's Closet, and use the money to buy gas." *(Photo courtesy Lisa Marie Lafrance)*

Rachel Wade's jailhouse phone calls and letters suggested that her obsession with sex didn't calm down just because she was behind bars.
(Photo Courtesy Florida Department of Corrections)

Blood in the interior of Sarah Ludemann's van. *(Photo courtesy Pinellas Park Police Department)*

The front of Javier's house, with the white lawn chair where Rachel took a seat after the stabbing and asked for a cigarette. *(Photo courtesy Pinellas Park Police Department)*

The minivan, just as Sarah Ludemann left it. The driver's door remains open and there is blood and debris in the street from the paramedics' urgent efforts to save her life. *(Photo courtesy Pinellas Park Police Department)*

Items in the street, such as Sarah Ludemann's white sandals and Javier Laboy's blood-soaked orange T-shirt, were marked and numbered as evidence. *(Photo courtesy Pinellas Park Police Department)*

This angle shows that only the front half of Sarah's van was visible from Javier's front door; the rear was screened by the neighbor's tree line. *(Photo courtesy Pinellas Park Police Department)*

The lead investigator was Detective Michael Lynch, a former Pinellas Park Police Department Officer of the Year. *(Photo courtesy Pinellas Park Police Department)*

also, although Ashley wasn't sure if they were still dating at the time of the incident.

Dicus called the witness's attention to the early hours of April 15, 2009. She was in her car, bringing Jay a spare cell phone because his was broken. She first tried to deliver the phone to him at his parents' house on 102nd Avenue. At Jay's parents' house, she learned that Jay wasn't there. She got back in her car, called him, and learned he was at his sister's. (Some jurors may have wondered on what phone Ashley called Jay, as his was supposed to be broken, but the question went unasked.)

So Ashley drove toward Janet's house along a route that took her past Javier's house. Dicus probed this point until it was clear to the jury that Ashley believed she drove more or less a direct route to Janet's house and did not go out of her way to pass Javier's home.

It was impossible to tell if this was true, however, as Ashley knew none of the street names and used her hands to explain in which directions she turned.

Dicus asked Ashley if she knew Javier's address. She did not.

Did she know what time it was? A little after midnight.

What did she see when she drove by? She saw Rachel, Javier, and "another guy" standing in the driveway. Seeing Rachel stood out in her mind because of "everything that had been going on" between Rachel and Sarah.

The prosecutor asked the witness if she saw Rachel Wade in the courtroom; and if so, could she point her out? Ashley pointed at the defendant, and she identified her as the "girl in the black shirt."

When she drove past Javier's house and saw the defendant in the driveway, did she say anything? She did not.

Did she swerve? No.

How fast was she going? About the speed limit.

What was the speed limit on that street? No clue.

Dicus said he thought it was probably twenty-five miles per hour. How fast did she think she was going?

"About that," Ashley said.

Dicus asked her if she, like a lot of teenagers, spent a lot of time on the phone. She said she did.

Was she talking on the phone when she drove past Javier's house? She said she didn't remember, but it was possible.

As long as they were dealing with possibilities, Dicus asked if it was possible that Ashley turned a little wide onto Javier's street in such a manner that it might have *appeared* that she swerved toward Rachel as she passed.

Yeah, it was possible.

After that, Ashley drove to Janet's house. Jay came outside and she gave him the phone. She and Jay talked for about a minute. Just as she was about to leave, Janet, Jilica, and Sarah came out of Janet's house. Then she left. She saw them get into Sarah's mom's minivan.

Dicus questioned Ashley about Jilica. The witness said she knew who Jilica was now, but she did not at that time.

Sarah and Ashley pulled away from Janet's house at approximately the same time. Ashley was first, but it was nearly simultaneous.

At the four-way stop sign at the end of the block, Sarah pulled up alongside Ashley's car. Sarah rolled down her window. Ashley thought she looked "upset, angry, and frustrated." She looked "shaky."

Had she ever described Sarah's demeanor in a different way?

She had, in her deposition for the defense. At that time, she'd said Sarah was "in a rage." She explained that she changed that part of her story to make it more correct; saying Sarah was in a rage made it seem like she was ready to "go out and kill somebody," but that was not the case at all. That was an exaggeration. Ashley explained that Sarah looked more frustrated, like she was just "done with the drama."

Sarah complained that Rachel had been texting her, driving past Janet's house and leaving threatening messages like, "You have to go home sometime tonight," and that she was outside Sarah's house waiting for her to come home.

Had anyone in the car asked Ashley if she knew where Rachel was?

Yes, Janet had. Ashley said she'd just seen her at Javier's house.

Ashley admitted that she hadn't always been up front about the fact that she was the one who told the girls where they could find Rachel. When she initially spoke with the police, she did not mention telling Sarah where Rachel was. Later, however, she called the detective back, and admitted that she had told Sarah where Rachel was that night.

Why had she held back at first?

"Because I didn't want people to think differently of me," Ashley testified, sobbing, "that it was all my fault and I'm the reason she's not here today." She bowed her head and put her hand over her face.

"Did anyone tell you to call the detective back and tell the truth?"

"I did it on my own."

She hadn't thought there was really going to be a fight. After all, this had been going on for eight months, and no one had yet struck a blow—and the only weapon that had been used was Silly String.

Dicus established that Ashley could not only recognize the defendant but, because she had spoken to Rachel Wade on a number of occasions, she could also recognize her voice. Ashley said that she had heard Rachel on Sarah's voice mail phone messages where Rachel had threatened Sarah.

The prosecutor handed the witness a disc marked state's exhibit number two. This was a disc that the witness had earlier listened to, initialed, and dated.

Had she recognized the voice on the disc? Yes, it was Rachel's.

Ashley testified that she had heard Rachel making threats to Sarah in the past, threats previous to and different from those contained on state's exhibit number two.

After a short shuffling of papers at the prosecution desk, Dicus said he had no further questions at this time.

Judge Bulone looked to the defense table.

Jay Hebert stood to cross-examine.

Under defense attorney Hebert's questioning, Ashley reiterated that she was Sarah's best friend and that Joshua Camacho was the love of Sarah's life. Sarah and Joshua met while he was working at the Chick-fil-A at the Park Place Mall in Pinellas Park.

When Sarah met Joshua, they didn't start dating right away, but sometime after that. When Sarah and Joshua began dating, Joshua was still dating a young woman named Erin Slothower. Yes, he was cheating on Erin with Sarah.

"At some point in time, you know Sarah had a baby by Josh, correct?"

"You mean Erin," the witness said patiently.

Grown-ups couldn't keep anybody's name straight.

"Erin," Hebert corrected.

"Yes," Ashley replied.

More than anything else, Jay Hebert wanted to make the jury see the defendant as normal, a regular teenager who was dramatic, loud, abrasive, obscene, and impulsive, just like every teenager in the world.

So he asked about the relationship between Erin and Sarah; there was drama there, too, right?

Ashley said there was.

Another lengthy sidebar interrupted the flow of Hebert's cross-examination, and Rachel—who was not wearing makeup—began to look heavy-lidded at the defense table, ready to put her head on her folded arms and take a nap. But she battled to stay alert.

If Hebert had wanted to ask the witness if it was true that Sarah and Erin had had a fistfight not long before the incident, in order to establish that the victim had a history of violence, he didn't get that opportunity.

So, instead, the defense attorney reminded the witness that they were discussing the relationship between Joshua, Rachel, Erin, and Sarah. Wasn't it true that Joshua did not like to give titles to the women he had relationships with, that he didn't like the term "girlfriend"? If he called one of them his "girlfriend," that would mean he was cheating on her with the others. He thought of them as "friends with benefits," a term Ashley herself had used on the witness stand during direct examination. Wasn't it true that he liked to think of himself as a guy who could sleep with any number of women, and yet not be committed to any of them?

Ashley said all of that was true.

In fact, according to her testimony, she was in a relationship much like that with Joshua's brother. Did she know that Joshua wanted those girls to *fight* for him?

Wesley Dicus was on his feet with an objection before Hebert had an opportunity to complete the question. His grounds were relevance, hearsay, and that it was improper character evidence. He called for another sidebar, and again Hebert's momentum was squelched.

Hebert was suspicious of Ashley's testimony that she had passed Javier's house by accident that night, because it was on the easiest route between the houses of Jay's mother and sister. He asked her to confirm the addresses of those two houses. Ashley said she couldn't do that. She didn't know the addresses. She didn't even know the names of the streets. She only knew how to get there.

"You took the most direct route to Janet's house?"

"No, I took the most easiest route in the direction my car was pointing. Instead of turning around, I just went in the direction I was."

Hebert pointed out that Ashley had to go quite a ways out of her way to pass Javier's house, that she had to go north and then south and then north again.

Ashley said she was just "working her way through the neighborhood."

"Snaking your way through the neighborhood?"

"Yes."

"Taking the most direct route?"

"Yes."

"Not talking with Sarah that night?"

"No."

She hadn't spoken to Sarah or texted Sarah. She did not know that Sarah was looking for Rachel.

Hebert did get Ashley to admit that although she may not have specifically known about problems between Rachel and Sarah that night, she knew that there was a "pattern of drama" between the two.

She knew, for example, about the Myspace and Facebook exchanges between Sarah and Rachel. She knew about Sarah posting pictures of herself and Joshua at the beach. She knew that there had been comments about Sarah posted online.

Ashley agreed that the Sarah/Rachel drama was a two-way street.

Hebert asked Ashley if it was true that she once said about Sarah: "There was no stopping her that night."

The witness agreed that she had said that.

When she was first interviewed, wasn't it true she had not admitted telling Sarah how to find Rachel, the very point that had earlier made the witness cry because it made her feel responsible for her best friend's death?

The question brought a quick objection, stating that it was redundant and that the question had already been asked and answered during direct examination.

Judge Bulone overruled the objection, and Ashley agreed that she had indeed lied to the detective about her role in the night's activities. There were no tears this time when she said it. Instead, her chin tilted upward and she gave the defense attorney her best look of defiance.

Attempting to chip away at her strength whenever he could, Hebert pretended he didn't hear her answer. He made her repeat it—which she did in a manner sure to be heard in the back row of the courtroom, perhaps in the hallway.

Wasn't it true that five months later she called Detective Lynch and told him a different story?

"I called Detective Lynch the *next day,*" Ashley said firmly. Hebert's attempts to fluster her weren't working. She had her shoulders square to him and was ready for anything he could dish out.

Hebert tried some rapid-fire questioning, getting Ashley to reiterate the events at Janet's house, dropping off the phone, seeing the girls come out of the house just as she was about to leave.

But Ashley answered in rapid-fire fashion as well, and Hebert's attempt to make her contradict herself backfired. He asked her if she got out of the car when she got to Janet's house. She said no, she stayed in the car; Jay came outside to get his phone. She put space between her words as she might when talking to a mentally slow person.

She didn't talk to the girls when she was at the house.

She did not talk to the girls until they were at the end of the block, at the four-way stop sign.

Yes, it was Janet Camacho who asked where Rachel was.

Hebert was scoring some points here. Ashley was expecting the jury to believe that just as it was a coincidence that she had driven past Javier's house in the first place, it was coincidence that Janet had asked her if she knew where Rachel was, and—*what do you know?*—she'd just seen her just a few moments before.

Ashley explained that when the two cars stopped, they were both pointed in the same direction. Sarah rolled down her window and Ashley leaned across and rolled down her passenger-side window so they could talk. Was this brief conversation at the stop sign the only time she spoke to those girls that night? Ashley said it was.

Hebert showed the witness defense exhibit number three, an aerial photo of the pertinent Pinellas Park neighborhood, and he asked if she recognized it. After a long pause, Ashley said she did not.

The defense attorney pointed out Javier's house on the photo and asked if this helped her to orient herself to what the photo showed. She said it did. He tried to show her which direction she was going when she passed Javier's house, but she corrected him and said she'd been headed in the opposite direction.

Hebert asked to introduce the photo into evidence, but before he could do that, Dicus requested that he first be allowed to ask the witness a few questions in voir dire. Judge Bulone said okay.

Dicus held up the same photo for Ashley and asked her if she could tell which way was north. She said she could not. Despite that, she tentatively acknowledged that the photo accurately depicted Javier's neighborhood.

Because there was no compass on the photo, wasn't it true that she couldn't tell which direction she was headed when she passed Javier's house? Ashley very softly said that was true.

Of course, she had already testified as to which way she'd been driving when she passed the house, and matters of east-west, north-south, had nothing to do with it. She knew which side of her car Javier's house had been on when she passed.

Hebert placed the photo on an easel facing the jury, and Ashley was allowed to get down from the witness stand to get a close-up look.

Rachel's lawyer stood off to one side, a few feet, with his arms crossed over his chest. He tried to get the witness to figure out where on the photo Jay's house was, based on him pointing out where Javier's house was. She reiterated that she just knew how to get from one place to the other, not the names of streets or anything.

She also couldn't find Janet's house on the photo. She was, however, able to show Hebert which direction she was headed when she passed Javier's house, and at which corner she had made the wide turn that might have been mistaken for swerving.

Hebert asked whose car she was driving, and she said it was a gold Camry, which belonged to her boyfriend's mom. Her boyfriend wasn't Jay at that time, but rather a guy named Jeremy.

Under rapid-fire questioning, Ashley maintained that when she saw Rachel, Javier, and the other guy standing in the driveway, she neither swerved nor sped.

"If somebody said that happened, they lied, correct?"

"I didn't see it happen," Ashley said. It was not a wholly satisfying response.

"Are you saying that you drove past that location fast?"

"I'm saying I drove by at a normal speed."

"Okay," Hebert said, removing the photo and the easel. Ashley was allowed to return to the witness stand.

Hebert made her acknowledge once again that Sarah was looking for Rachel that night. Ashley said this was true, repeating that it was because Rachel was sending her threatening texts.

"Would you agree with me that when Sarah is mad, she's mad."

"Yeah, she's mad. She's upset. Yeah."

"And, in fact, there was no stopping her that night."

"No, she . . . no."

Hebert used this response to return to the discrepancy between Ashley's defense deposition and today's testimony, wherein she had withdrawn the phrase "in a rage" from her description of the victim's demeanor.

Ashley now said that she had originally used the term to describe Sarah's angry and frustrated demeanor. She did not want to imply that "her head was about to pop off, or anything."

When she said Sarah was in a rage, that was also the time when she said there was "no stopping her"?

Yes, she agreed.

With that established, defense attorney Jay Hebert sat.

Wesley Dicus had a few questions on redirect. He wanted to make sure that the jury understood it was *normal* for someone to look at an aerial photo of a neighborhood and have difficulty determining directions.

The prosecutor asked Ashley if she had ever seen the neighborhood from an aerial perspective. Had she ever flown over Javier's house in a helicopter, or anything like that?

The witness said she had not, and repeated that she couldn't tell for sure from that photo which streets she had driven on or in what direction.

She then described the route she had taken for ASA

Dicus in her own terms, again sometimes not even saying "left" or "right," but using her hands to gesture.

In his cross-examination, Jay Hebert repeatedly used the phrase "no stopping her." Three or four times. He used it as a way to describe Miss Ludemann's demeanor.

Did she remember that?

She said she did.

He asked if that phrase, when she used it, had anything to do with fighting.

Ashley said no, it just meant that she was going to do what she wanted to do, and no one was going to talk her out of it.

On his recross, Jay Hebert sounded sick of the semantics and had a "let's get real" tone to his questioning.

Wasn't it true that Ashley knew that Sarah wanted to find Rachel and "end the drama?" And what could that phrase mean if it didn't mean she was going to fight her?

"Not to fight, to confront," Ashley said. "Not to have it end the way it ended, no. I didn't think they were going to fight. They had never fought before."

"You knew she was going there to fight."

"No! I didn't!"

And with that, Ashley Lovelady was allowed to step down from the witness stand and exit the courtroom, using the same shoulder-rolling strut with which she had entered.

Sitting in the spectator section of the courtroom, glaring at Ashley as she testified, was Jamie Severino. The two young women had long been enemies because both laid claim to Jay Camacho.

Jamie said it had nothing to do with them being enemies,

of course, but she knew for a fact that many of the things Ashley had testified to were complete bullshit.

"She said that night she went to Janet's house to give Jay a phone," Jamie later said. "That was completely false. I had just bought him a phone. This was around tax time, so I had just bought him a brand-new phone, brand-new clothes, everything. She didn't come by to give him a phone. I was over there that day and she came by to see what he was doing, to be *crazy*! She was stalking—kind of like what Rachel was doing. She didn't talk to Jay. She didn't come in the house. She didn't even get out of her car. She drove by, and that was it. She parked outside for a second."

Jamie didn't even believe that Ashley was telling the truth about driving by Javier's house and then relaying Rachel's location to Sarah. Her theory was that Rachel told Sarah herself where she was.

This theory, however, failed to explain the car that sped down Javier's block and, according to some witnesses, swerved in an attempt to intimidate Rachel.

The jury was hearing a story that made events seem so accidental, random, as if coincidence and fate had brought Sarah and Rachel together in front of Javier's house.

Jamie didn't believe it was that way at all. She thought it was all planned. Sarah and Rachel agreed to meet at that time, at that spot. Coincidence had nothing to do with it.

Jamie claimed the very premise—that Ashley was Sarah's friend, and that was why she snitched out Rachel's location—was faulty.

Ashley and Sarah were *not* buddies, Jamie insisted. In fact, Ashley had done some serious shit to Sarah, not just to Sarah but to the Ludemann family. They were *never* going to be friends.

Jamie had a theory: "Ashley was just *pretending* to be Sarah's friend so she could get close to Jay."

You would've thought that things would smooth out,

become significantly less dramatic, after Sarah's death, but that hadn't been the case. Ashley had continued to bother Jamie, and a senior relative of Ashley's even got into the act, saw Jamie at the store in November 2009, and chased her in her car. They both were pulled over. They both had to go to court. Charges against Jamie were dropped, but Ashley's relative was nailed for reckless driving.

"The state calls Jilica Smith."

Jilica was a black woman who wore part of her hair in a ponytail, and had a cascade of hair falling down the right side of her face. She wore tight white pants, a pink shirt, large hoop earrings, and had her voluminous black purse slung over her left shoulder.

Lisset Hanewicz did the questioning.

Jilica said she was twenty-one years old, and had been twenty at the time of the incident. She knew Janet Camacho because Janet was the mother of her cousin's children. With a deep and musical voice, Jilica came off as far more mature than the previous witness. She explained that she knew Joshua because he was Janet's brother, and she'd known Sarah through Joshua.

She did not know Rachel Wade. Not then, not now. On the night of April 14, 2009, Jilica had been at Janet's house on 59th Street in Pinellas Park. She was living with Janet at the time. She didn't live with Janet anymore. There were four people there that night: she and Janet, Joshua and Sarah. At some point, Jilica was outside with a friend, sitting in a car for about thirty minutes. Janet was outside, too, at some point. "She was in a green van, I think." Janet was in a car parked "in her yard," and the witness was sitting in a car "parked across the street."

ASA Hanewicz asked if a vehicle caught her attention as she was sitting.

Yes, it did, Jilica replied. She saw a red car pass by. It caught her attention because it was speeding. She didn't recognize the driver, but she saw blond hair.

"I couldn't really make out if it was a boy or a girl," Jilica testified. The car came to a halt at a stop sign at the end of the block, and maybe "she" drove past a second time.

"I don't know. It was just driving by," Jilica said.

When the vehicle was approaching, she was facing it. After it passed, Jilica had to turn around to see it. The vehicle Janet was in was facing in the opposite direction, so she could more comfortably watch what the car did after it passed.

At some point during the evening, Jilica was standing outside the house "texting or something," when Janet and Sarah came out of the house and announced they were going to McDonald's. That sounded good, so Jilica decided to ride along with them. The three young women got into Sarah's green minivan.

Hanewicz asked the witness to whom did the car belong. Jilica said she didn't know—just that Sarah was always driving it.

From the witness stand, Jilica snuck a quick peek at Rachel, sitting at the defense table. This slightly unnerved Jilica, who crossed her arms across her chest, suddenly chilly, and stared downward for a moment.

"At some point, when you were in the vehicle, did you overhear a conversation?" Hanewicz queried.

Jilica said she did. She heard a girl's voice on Sarah's phone, a voice she didn't recognize, and she clearly heard it say, "I'm going to stab you and your Mexican boyfriend." She couldn't hear everything that was said on the other end of the phone connection. In fact, that one sentence was the only thing that caught her attention.

Hanewicz wondered what made that one sentence stand

out. Jilica said it was because of what it said. That would catch *anyone's* attention.

Was Sarah screaming?

Jilica said, "She was kind of arguing back. They were just two people going at it." Although the voice wasn't familiar, it was identifiably female.

What was Sarah's reaction to the outrageous threat?

Sarah didn't seem to take it seriously. She just said "really," or something like that.

Once Sarah started to drive, where did she go?

Jilica couldn't be sure. She wasn't that familiar with Pinellas Park, but they passed a couple of streets and she thought they went by Sarah's house. She saw a cab parked out front and knew Sarah's dad was a cabdriver.

At one point, they did stop; and Sarah talked to another person in a car, a girl, but Jilica didn't know her. She didn't overhear much of that conversation. She remembered hearing the name "Javier," but that was about it. She didn't know what was going on. She knew Sarah was mad at someone—but she thought they were still going to McDonald's. It all concerned people she didn't know, so it didn't register. Not at first. Slowly it sank in. Sarah's agenda had shifted. After the conversation with the girl in the other car, Sarah's driving changed. They "whipped around a couple of corners" and ended up in front of "some guy's house."

Hanewicz produced a large board, upon which were glued nine photographs, which she referred to as state's composite exhibit 3a through 3i. She asked the witness if she recognized those photos.

Jilica said she did; they were from "that night." She pointed out the minivan in which she was sitting, ran through again where she was sitting, and where Janet and Sarah were sitting. Jilica testified that when they arrived at the location, there were two boys and a girl there. The girl was standing in the yard, on the grass, on the driver's side of the red car between the front tire and the front door. The boys were standing in the yard, closer to the house.

As soon as Sarah's minivan came to a stop, she opened her door. The blond-haired girl was walking toward her, "sort of fast," with her right hand held up beside her face, something held tightly in that hand. Jilica didn't recognize the blond girl or the two boys standing in the yard. She had never been at that location or seen any of those people before.

"What did you see in the girl's hand?"

"I saw a knife."

Jilica saw the girl with the knife walk right up to Sarah. They "locked heads" in confrontation. For a moment, all Jilica could see was a bunch of hair flying around.

Hanewicz made the witness spell it out so that it was clear: The blond girl had been the one to close the distance between the two combatants. The blonde walked all the way from the side of the road to the driver's side of the minivan, while Sarah had barely taken two steps out of her car. Jilica was still in the backseat when she saw the blonde walk right in front of the minivan.

The witness knew now that the blond girl must have stabbed Sarah, but she didn't see that. She just saw a flurry of motion, and then the blonde walked away.

It all happened very fast, "not even ten seconds." And it was at that point, after the fight, that Janet and Jilica got out of the minivan.

Jilica had concentrated her efforts on trying to calm Janet Camacho down because Janet had seen what had happened and was very mad. Jilica looked at the blonde and she was just standing there with a smirk on her face. She hadn't seen the blonde's face immediately following the confrontation with Sarah because she was walking away, and all she could see was her back. But when the blonde turned around, and they were face-to-face, Jilica saw she was smirking.

Was Janet upset? Jilica did not remember Janet crying.

Did Janet want to fight Rachel? Jilica had no idea what was going through Janet's head.

"Okay, fair enough. What did you see Janet do?" ASA Hanewicz asked.

Janet hadn't been able to do anything. That was because Jilica had her arm. Janet Camacho was trying to get to the blonde.

"But I didn't know if the girl still had the knife, so that was why I was holding her," Jilica testified.

"Where were the boys at this time?"

Jilica said the boys had not been quick to react, that they were "pretty much just standing there."

How did Jilica learn that Sarah was hurt?

"I turned around and I saw that Sarah wasn't standing up anymore."

Jilica could tell that Sarah needed medical attention. She grabbed for her purse, but she was nervous and dropped the phone. It hit the street and the back popped off. By the time she managed to get the plastic piece back onto the back of her phone, she looked at the blond girl, whose name she now realized was Rachel. She could see that she no longer had the knife. She let go of Janet and walked around the rear of the minivan, which she referred to as "the truck."

"I saw Sarah lying on the ground, and I scooped her between my legs and I was holding her chest a little bit."

"When you saw, did you scream anything at Rachel?" Hanewicz inquired.

"Yes. I said, 'You stabbed her! I saw you stab her, and you're going to jail!' That's exactly what I said to her."

"Do you see the person who stabbed Sarah in the court-room today?"

"Yes, ma'am."

"Could you please point to her and identify her by an item of her clothing."

"She's right there, wearing a black jacket," Jilica said, pointing at Rachel.

Hanewicz showed Jilica a CD that had been listened to and signed by the witness, who testified that it was a recording of the call she placed to 911 moments after the incident.

According to the police, Jilica's 911 call was made at precisely 12:45 A.M. Now the CD was played for the jury.

"Nine-one-one. What is your emergency?" the dis-patcher asked.

"Oh my God! Oh my God!" Jilica replied.

The dispatcher tried to get her to give an address, but Jilica only knew the name of the street she was on, not the cross street or the house number.

The dispatcher asked what city she was in. Jilica said Pinellas Park.

"Pinellas Park. Okay. What happened?"

"Fucking Rachel fucking stabbed her."

"Okay. What is the address? Ask what the address is."

"What the address is? Sarah is not even . . . What ad-dress is this?"

Voices are heard in background relaying information.

Jilica started to relate the address but interrupted her-self to say, "Don't let her get to her! Janet, come here!" Jilica finally managed to get out the address.

"Where on her body was the patient stabbed?"

"I swear to God this is . . ."

"Where on the body is the patient stabbed?"

"She's stabbed in the chest. It's Sarah."

"Where is the person who did this?"

"She's right here."

"This is a female patient?"

"Yes."

"All right, my name is Margaret. I'm going to put you right through to the police. There is already an ambulance on the way. Okay?"

"Okay. Don't hang up."

"I'm not hanging up."

On the recording, there was the sound of a phone ringing as the dispatcher tried to patch the call through to the police.

Jilica, obviously impatient, said, "Come on, come on, come on!"

Margaret finally came back on the line, the original dispatcher.

"We got a girl on the ground and she's passed out. I don't know if she's alive," Jilica said.

"All right, we have some help on its way. You say she's passed out?"

"I don't know. She's like coming and going. She's trying to breathe."

Margaret again reassured Jilica that help was on its way. "I'm going to tell you what to do for her, okay? Is the knife out of her?"

"She's stabbed in the fucking chest. The knife is out."

"Is there serious bleeding right now?"

"Yes, there's bleeding. Sarah! Sarah, stay with us."

"All right, you say she's stabbed in the chest. Is there more than one wound? Was she stabbed more than once, or is there just the one wound?"

"Just the . . . I don't know. I didn't see when she got . . . I mean, I saw her get stabbed, but I don't know how many times she stabbed her. I didn't think she was going to do it. I just saw the knife. She's foaming out the mouth. She's breathing."

"And where is the person who did this, right now?"

"Help is coming, Sarah. She's, oooh, she's standing right here. All right, I think the police are coming. . . ."

"Listen to me, you need to try and stay calm."

Jilica could be heard calling out instructions, apparently to police who had arrived. "She's right there! No, not the girl in the orange shirt. Janet!"

Then there was silence. The call had been terminated.

In the courtroom, there was a pause as everyone recovered a bit from the horrible recording they'd just heard. Both Jilica, on the witness stand, and Rachel, at the defense table, had wiped away tears as the tape played.

ASA Hanewicz broke the silence by asking, "Jilica, could you please walk us through what we just heard?"

Defense attorney Hebert objected to that, saying the tape could speak for itself without color commentary.

Judge Bulone sustained the objection and asked Hanewicz to ask a more specific question.

Hanewicz asked the witness what she was doing when she first called 911.

Jilica reiterated that she was sitting on the ground with Sarah's head between her legs, trying to comfort her. She put a little pressure on her chest wound, but she wasn't sure if she was doing it correctly. She was talking to Sarah—no response.

By this time, a couple of neighbors had come out of their houses to gawk. She was limited in what she could see because she was sitting next to the car. It was hectic and she'd been screaming Janet's name, because she didn't know if they were still fighting. She didn't want her friend to get hurt.

When the cops arrived, Jilica pointed out Rachel as the one who'd done the stabbing, and made sure they didn't confuse Janet—who was wearing an orange shirt—with Rachel.

"No further questions, Your Honor," Lisset Hanewicz said.

Jay Hebert, looking angry, paced in front of the witness, setting up the easel with the photos of the crime scene pasted on it. Hebert began by asking about the time, on the night of the incident, when Jilica was outside Janet's house in a car talking to a friend.

"Who was the friend you were in the car with?"

"Justin."

"Last name?"

"I don't know."

Hebert wondered to whom Janet was talking outside the house.

Jilica said she didn't know that guy's name at all.

Hebert was interested in intoxicants. No, Jilica didn't observe anyone smoking marijuana that night. No, she didn't personally smoke any marijuana that night.

"Not that I know of," she said.

"Not that you know of?"

"I don't think I did."

She hadn't seen any vodka that night, either. She was outside most of the time, sitting in her friend's car. She wasn't sure when Janet came out and went in, but she was pretty sure Sarah didn't come out until the McDonald's run. Joshua *never* came outside.

Hebert drew Jilica's attention to the red car that passed by that night. "Isn't it true that you thought there were two people in that car?"

Jilica replied that she couldn't really see. All she saw was hair. She knew someone had to be driving; but as for whether or not there was a passenger, she couldn't be sure. She *might* have said it looked like there were two people in the car.

Jay Hebert pointed out that in her deposition, page 25, line 24, she definitely said that at first it looked like there were two people in the red car.

Jilica acknowledged that those were "probably" her words. She had said them a long time ago. The thing that drew her attention to the car wasn't just its speed, but the length of time it stopped at the corner. It had definitely *not* been "just a regular stop-sign stop."

Hebert then focused on the encounter with Ashley Lovelady. Jilica didn't know Ashley, had never seen her before, and had no idea that she was Sarah's friend. She thought Ashley might have been driving a white car.

Up until the news from Ashley, everything was calm in Sarah's minivan. In contrast to Ashley's testimony, she remembered the cars facing in opposite directions when they stopped and had a conversation.

As Jilica recalled events, the two drivers, Sarah and Ashley, could easily roll down their windows and speak to one another. Jilica wasn't "really tuned in to the conversation," but she did overhear the phrase "Javier's house." She didn't know, or didn't remember, the context.

"You would agree that it was then that all hell broke loose, and that the drive from then on, until the time the van stopped, was a completely different drive."

"Yes, I would agree with you."

"Sarah was mad?"

"Yes."

"Sarah wanted to fight," Hebert stated.

"I don't know what was going through Sarah's head. I know she was angry."

Hebert once again referred to Jilica's deposition, during which she'd been asked if Sarah was angry and wanted to fight, and Jilica had answered yes. Did she recall answering that way?

"I do recall answering that way—but that was kind of two questions in one," Jilica complained. "As for whether Sarah wanted to fight her or not, I don't know what was going on in Sarah's head. You asked me if she was upset and ready to fight, and I said yes because she was upset." And, yes, from then on everything changed. It was not a pleasant drive.

"There was no stopping Sarah at that point. Isn't that correct?"

"She was angry. I don't think we would have been able to stop her."

"Sarah wasn't going to stop?"

"No."

"And at that point, you knew you weren't going to Mc-Donald's anymore."

"Yes."

Getting out of the van was not an option then. Sarah was clipping around corners.

Hebert changed the subject to the "Mexican boyfriend" statement. Had Sarah's phone been on speakerphone?

Now aware that Hebert was using her earlier statement to make it seem as if she were changing her story, Jilica admitted she probably *said* it was on speakerphone at one time because she had heard it so clearly—but now looking back on it, she couldn't be sure. She didn't remember Sarah turning the phone to speakerphone.

"Miss Smith, you spoke with an officer that night."

"I spoke to a couple of officers."

"You spoke to an Officer Simpkins and you gave him a statement. Is that correct?"

"I don't remember the officer's name, but yes, sir, I gave a statement."

"Do you remember if during that statement, you mentioned this 'I'm going to stab you' phone call?"

"I'm not sure what was mentioned and what wasn't mentioned," Jilica replied.

Hebert tried again, but Jilica repeated that she didn't know.

"Okay, would you admit that Janet was mad that night, pretty fired up about the situation?"

"She was mad." Jilica didn't have a good feeling about things as Sarah screeched to a halt in front of Javier's house. In fact, she was pretty sure something bad was going to happen.

In order to ask the witness which direction the minivan was headed when it stopped in front of Javier's house, Hebert showed Jilica a large blowup of the aerial photo taken by the Pinellas Park police of the neighborhood.

Jilica looked at it and saw nothing she recognized. "I don't really know Pinellas Park," she said. "Is this Javier's house?"

Hebert said it was, and Hanewicz objected, pointing out that Hebert was now the one testifying. After some discussion, it was stipulated which house was Javier's, so Hebert could finally get to his question regarding which direction the van was headed.

The photo was admitted into evidence as defense exhibit number six. Still, there were problems. Jilica said she wasn't sure from which direction Sarah pulled into the neighborhood, but she recalled that she stopped "on the right side of the street."

Hebert tried again. Jilica was allowed to step down from the witness stand and look at the photos as they were set up on the easel. This time Jilica thought about it for a while and she looked at the photo carefully.

"No, I don't remember which way," she said.

Hebert gave up on the aerial photo, and showed the

witness the ground-level police photos taken of the crime scene, which depicted the vehicles in question. Jilica recognized the scene and testified that Sarah was driving fast, and came to an abrupt stop, and that Sarah and Rachel's cars were pointed in opposite directions. Even then she wasn't enthusiastic about it.

"I was in the backseat. This looks right to me," she said.

Hebert tried to get Jilica to say when Janet got out of the car. Jilica wasn't sure. Hebert asked if the car was running when they got out. Jilica didn't know. She knew Sarah stopped but couldn't recall if she took out the keys.

"Was it dark that night?"

Hebert showed her two police photos, one taken with a flash and one without. Jilica acknowledged that the one without was darker. Jilica realized at one point that she was standing so that the jury couldn't see the photos and apologized as she moved to one side. Jilica acknowledged that, according to the photos, Sarah stopped her van "somewhat in the middle" of the street, rather than on the right side, as she'd earlier testified.

Hebert asked Jilica to repeat where the tragic confrontation had taken place. She pointed to a spot near the left front of the minivan. Again she added that she'd been in the backseat, so she couldn't be certain.

That opened a door that Hebert charged through. Jilica was in the backseat and had a poor view of the action; yet she had testified that she'd seen Rachel walk across the front of the van with a knife in her right hand. Hebert asked Jilica to show the jury, using a pen, how Rachel was holding the knife. Jilica assumed a position that had the tip of the pen pointing downward.

"It was kind of down," she said, a phrase that Hebert liked so much that he had her repeat it.

"Do you know if Janet saw the knife?"

Jilica didn't think so. "I don't think she would have tried to go at her if she did," Jilica said.

Hebert asked how the girls held their hands as the confrontation began.

Jilica put her dukes up and assumed a classic boxing stance.

"Like they were defending themselves?" Hebert asked.

"Like they were fighting," Jilica replied. She saw them fight, hair being grabbed, hands flailing.

"And you saw that from Sarah? . . ."

"I saw that from both parties."

How tall was Sarah? Jilica said that Sarah was taller than she was, and she was five-six, so that would make Sarah five-eight, five-nine.

How much did Sarah weigh? Jilica didn't know, and wouldn't hazard a guess.

Was Sarah bigger or smaller than Rachel? Bigger.

Jilica was allowed to return to the witness stand.

Hebert asked the order of events and Jilica was insistent that she and Janet didn't get out of the car until after Sarah was stabbed. Hebert had to do something about that. His whole case depended on the notion that the girls had ganged up on Rachel, and that she had reasonably needed a weapon to defend herself. Hebert tried to get Jilica to say that Janet attacked Rachel. Jilica responded that Janet couldn't attack Rachel because she was holding her back.

Hebert repeatedly tried to put words in the witness's mouth, but she was stubborn.

"At some point in time, Janet did attack Rachel," Hebert said, once again coming very close to doing the testifying himself.

"Yes," Jilica said tentatively.

"You didn't see that?"

"I was with Sarah. I don't know."

"You didn't see Janet grab Rachel by the hair and drag her across the lawn?"

"Oh yes, yes, I saw that," Jilica said. "They were fighting. You said attacked."

"Janet was beating Rachel up."

"They were fighting."

"You saw Janet grab Rachel by the hair and drag her across the dirt!"

"I was the one dragging. I grabbed Janet and was dragging her away from Rachel. Janet was mad. She'd just stabbed her friend!"

"Did you see Janet take one of her shoes off and beat Rachel with it?"

"She had a shoe, her sandal, in her hand. I didn't see her hit her with it."

"You would agree with me that, at that time, that was a pretty chaotic situation. Explosive?"

"Yes."

Jilica explained that after the situation at Javier's house was over, she and Janet realized they had no way to get back home, and they had started to walk. Jilica had no idea where she was, but Janet knew the way. They were walking, and a police car pulled up. They got in, and the cops gave them a ride home. While in the car, they answered some more questions.

The prosecution wanted the jury to believe that police had separated the witnesses immediately so that there had been no opportunity for them to put their heads together and come up with a common story they were going to tell.

Hebert now asked if Jilica remembered being sequestered at any time that evening. She didn't understand the question.

"You were not put in a room and told to stay there, or put in a squad car and told to stay there?"

"No, sir," Jilica replied.

"You were able to walk around and later walked home with Janet. Is that correct?"

"Yes."

"That's all I have, Judge."

"Redirect?" Judge Bulone asked.

"Yes, sir," Hanewicz said, and began her questioning of Jilica Smith.

"Jilica, when defense counsel was asking you if you knew that Sarah and Rachel were going to fight, was there any talk of fighting, in the car, on the way to Javier's house?"

"She was mad. I don't know what was going through her head." (Jilica went to the well with that line once too often.)

"Did you talk to Sarah about fighting?"

"No, ma'am."

"Was there conversation in the car about fighting?"

"Not from me and Sarah."

"Were there weapons in the vehicle?"

"There were no weapons anywhere in that car," Jilica said confidently.

"Did you even know why you were going to Javier's house?"

"No. I kind of put two and two together because Sarah was mad, but I didn't."

Hanewicz asked if Sarah was driving with the headlights on or off. With a slight smile, Jilica said that she *hoped* they were on.

Were the headlights on when the van pulled up in front of Javier's house? Jilica thought about that. She'd seen Rachel and the two boys pretty clearly, so it was possible that the headlights were still on.

"When you talked to a police officer right after this

happened, was it a one-on-one conversation between you and the police officer?"

"No, ma'am, it was just everyone standing around."

She spoke with a number of police officers, in fact.

Hanewicz was done.

Judge Bulone told Jilica that she could leave, but that she was on standby. This meant that if she was called back, she had to come in.

Court recessed for lunch.

After the lunch break, the state called a very pregnant Janet Camacho to the witness stand. Janet had wavy black hair combed back off her forehead that fell to the middle of her back. She wore a pretty, off-the-shoulder aquamarine dress.

Janet told ASA Wesley Dicus that she was twenty-nine years old. She had known Sarah Ludemann through her brother Joshua. She considered herself close to Sarah and had allowed Sarah to babysit her kids.

She said Sarah and Joshua were "inseparable." They had dated on and off, true; but "romantic" separations didn't physically separate them. "Even when they weren't together, they were together," Janet said.

Janet testified that she knew Rachel also. She'd met her through her brother Jay.

Wesley Dicus asked if Rachel and Sarah got along.

"No," Janet replied emphatically.

"Do you know Ashley Lovelady?"

"Yes, that's Sarah's best friend."

On the day before the stabbing, Janet got home at four or five in the afternoon. She didn't remember exactly. It might have been later. She had four children, and they were home that night. Also over at the house were Sarah,

Joshua, Jay, and Jilica. Janet knew Jilica because she was family.

The witness explained that at one point that evening she was in a car with her friend Jeremy and they were talking. Sarah and Joshua were playing video games with Janet's kids. They were also sending out texts to persons unknown while talking to each other.

Two things were occurring simultaneously. Rachel was cruising Janet's street, looking for trouble, and Sarah's parents wanted her home because it was a school night.

Dicus asked Sarah how she knew Rachel was on the street, and Janet said she'd seen her. "I saw a car parked near a stop sign. I asked Jeremy to turn on his headlights."

"Was the car just stopped at the stop sign, or was it actually parked there?" the prosecutor inquired.

"It was stopped."

"The headlights were not on?"

"Right. Jeremy flashed his lights and I saw Rachel." The headlights allowed her a clear view into the vehicle. Janet identified the person in the parked car as the defendant.

Dicus asked if she did anything. Janet said yes, she had Jeremy flash his headlights. Rachel flashed back. Janet got out and started walking toward Rachel's car. Rachel left.

Later that night, Janet and Jilica decided to go to McDonald's—which wasn't unusual. They asked Sarah to drive them. Dicus asked why, and the witness replied, "She was the McDonald's queen. We always go to McDonald's. I knew she wouldn't mind taking us." Janet didn't recall the exact time—but it was late.

Once Sarah started driving, she stopped texting, but there was a phone call. Janet didn't know who called whom, but Sarah had Rachel on the speakerphone in the car. Janet recognized Rachel's angry voice, cussing, yelling. Sarah was yelling back.

One thing in the conversation stood out: Rachel said she was going to stab Sarah and her "Mexican boyfriend." That pissed Sarah off. Janet sensed they weren't going to McDonald's anymore. Instead, the hunt was on; they were looking for Rachel.

Rachel claimed to be at Sarah's house, so that was the first place they checked. It didn't take them long to get there. No sign of Rachel. Then they ran into Ashley Lovelady— the one and only person on the road that night who knew where Rachel was.

This, of course, contradicted the testimony of both Ashley Lovelady and Jilica Smith, who said the meet-up between Sarah and Ashley occurred only seconds after they left Janet's house. Janet recalled the order of events differently: they were headed toward Janet's house when they ran into Ashley, and the two vehicles were pointed in opposite directions when they stopped for a brief conversation.

Ashley said Rachel was at Javier's house. Janet didn't know where Javier lived, but Sarah did—and, zoom, off they went.

Speeding?

"A little bit," Janet said, but not so much that she felt unsafe. Not reckless. Maybe five miles per hour faster than the speed limit. It was just a few blocks, and they were there.

Janet was allowed to waddle down from the stand so she could testify regarding crime scene photographs, which were placed on an easel so the jury could see.

"When you first arrived at Javier's house, what did you see as you pulled up?"

She saw Rachel standing to the driver's side of the car, near the front, close to the grass. Sarah stopped the car in the middle of the street, in front and to the side of Rachel's car. The photos were accurate.

When Sarah stopped, Janet did not get out of the car.

She looked through the windshield and saw Rachel, walking fast, crossing in front of her own car, holding a knife in her hand. Rachel headed for the driver's side of the van. Sarah was only a step from the driver's door when the tussle started.

Janet didn't remember which hand Rachel had the knife in or how she was holding it, but she *did see* the knife. It was a kitchen knife, black handle, silver blade. She and Jilica were still inside the van.

And the tussle?

"Sarah was trying to defend herself. She grabbed Rachel by the hair." The witness waved her own hands on either side of her head to demonstrate flailing. Janet admitted that because she was on the passenger side, and the fight was on the driver's side, "there was not much I could see."

The fight lasted about five seconds. It ended when Rachel "just walked away." Then Janet got out of the van. Rachel headed toward Javier's house.

When they first pulled up, Janet noticed there were also two guys at the scene, standing on the grass. She didn't recognize them. She later learned that one of them was Javier, of whom she'd heard, but she *still* didn't know who the other guy was.

When Janet got out of the van, she had no idea that Sarah had been stabbed. Her focus was on Rachel. Janet recalled saying: "We're not Mexican. Why don't you start with me?" Rachel just said she was done, and faced Janet. She still had the knife in her hand. Janet took off her flip-flops and held them in her hand. At first, Janet hit Rachel only to get the knife out of her hand, but Rachel held tight. Rachel kept saying she was done, so Janet turned and got back in the van. Then she heard Jilica say Sarah got stabbed.

Janet was allowed to return to her seat on the witness stand.

"And what did you do when you heard that?"

"I got out of the car and went to see if it was true."

"What did you see?"

Janet started and stopped speaking a couple of times as her emotions took control. Finally she managed to say, "Sarah was on the road, foaming. . . ." She couldn't say the rest, and gestured with her hand to her mouth.

ASA Dicus took a sympathetic tone. He noted that Janet had described Sarah as "family," so seeing her in distress like that might have been heart-wrenching.

Janet nodded that this was true.

"What did you do when you saw Sarah in the road foaming like that?"

"I approached Rachel again and said, 'Are you serious? You stabbed her!' I was yelling," Janet said, glancing at the defense table with fresh fury.

Rachel focused her attention on the prosecutor. She took quick glances at the witness stand, didn't like what she saw, and quickly looked away.

"What was the defendant's reaction?"

"She said she didn't care," Janet said, now glaring at Rachel. "She started laughing and she walked toward Javier's house."

Janet was wild with fury that night. She ran up behind Rachel, grabbed her by the hair, and pulled till she fell. Rachel was still holding the knife. Janet hit her, screaming, "You stabbed her! I can't believe you did it!" She yelled that again and again.

"Did the defendant do anything to defend herself?"

Janet said Rachel managed to kick her one time, kicked upward while she was lying on the ground. In retaliation Janet dragged her by the hair across Javier's front yard, punching and scratching her.

"What did Rachel do with the knife?"

"She didn't do nothing with it."

"Nothing? She didn't stab at you?"

"No, sir," Janet said.

Jilica finally pulled Janet off Rachel. Who could tell how long it lasted? Longer than five seconds!

Now free of Janet's grasp, Rachel continued toward Javier's house with the knife still in her hand. Janet said her attention was divided at this point because of concern over Sarah's injury. The next time she looked at Rachel, the blonde was "in front of Javier's house, throwing something at his house."

Janet couldn't see what Rachel threw. After that, Rachel sat in front of Javier's house, no knife. Police arrived, and Janet ID'd Rachel.

Wesley Dicus finished with a line of questioning designed to combat a claim of self-defense, reestablishing that Rachel was the only one on that street carrying a deadly weapon—or any weapon at all, for that matter—if you didn't count flip-flops.

"No further questions, Your Honor," Dicus said, and sat down.

"Mr. Hebert?" Judge Bulone said.

"Thank you, Your Honor," Jay Hebert said, rising. "Good afternoon, Ms. Camacho."

"Good afternoon."

Hebert asked if it was Janet's testimony that at the time of the incident, her brother was dating Sarah. Janet said that it was not. Her testimony was that she didn't know. Were they friends with benefits? Janet didn't know that, either.

Hebert drew Janet's attention to a deposition she gave in December 2009, on the first floor of this same courthouse. Janet said she remembered giving the deposition, but she didn't look sure. Hebert reminded her that, at that time, a court reporter was present, and she had sworn to tell the truth. She was asked at that time if Joshua was dating Sarah, and she said no.

Did she recall saying that? Yes, she said—but she still didn't sound convinced.

Hebert wanted to know what everyone was smoking and drinking that night. Janet said she wasn't smoking or drinking. She didn't see Joshua smoke or drink, either.

Hebert asked again if Janet's kids were home "the whole time," and Janet said they were. She was aware of the drama between Sarah and Rachel, that there was a "lot of commotion" going back and forth, a lot of cell phone activity, social networking. She was less aware, however, of drama between Joshua, Sarah, and Erin. She'd heard of it, but she hadn't seen any of it.

"You testified at some point in time that you went outside and saw Rachel Wade's car parked in the street with its lights off. Is that correct?"

"With the lights dimmed," Janet corrected. "It was not totally off. There's a button where you turn it and the little lights come on, turn it again and the big headlights come on. It was not the big lights. It was the small lights."

Hebert asked if Janet recognized that vehicle as belonging to Rachel Wade, and Janet said she did not. She only recognized Rachel after Jeremy turned on his high beams so she could see into the car. Hebert asked how long the car was there. Janet didn't know. It was there when she first came out of her house. When her company came, she went outside and got in his car.

Hebert pointed out to the witness that it was her testimony that the car at the end of the block had flashed its lights at her. Janet corrected him. Rachel flashed her lights *back* "after I did it," Janet testified.

Jilica was on the other side of the street in a car pointing in the opposite direction. Janet got out of the car and began to walk toward Rachel. Sarah was still inside the house, with Janet's brother and her kids.

"There was a lot of *texting* going on during this, wasn't there?"

"Yes."

Sarah had a curfew, eleven o'clock. Sarah had made an earlier comment about her parents wanting her home.

Hebert asked a good question: If Sarah had to be home by eleven o'clock because that was her curfew, why, in fact, didn't she go home? Why did she agree to give the other girls a ride to McDonald's?

Janet said it was because "I had asked her."

"Were you aware that Rachel and Sarah had talked in the past about fighting?"

Janet thought about that for a moment and said, no, she didn't know that. She didn't know in advance that there was going to be a fight.

Hebert tried again: "During the days and weeks and months leading up to the incident, Rachel and Sarah had discussed fighting each other. Wasn't that correct?"

This time Janet said yes, but her face was uncertain. She was shaking her head from side to side.

"And up until that time, you had never paid much attention to that kind of talk because there hadn't been any action taken. Isn't that right?"

"It was always name-calling and threats. That's about it," Janet agreed.

Hebert tried to paint a picture of the inside of that minivan as it headed to get fast food.

Was Jilica sitting behind Sarah or her? Janet didn't remember.

Janet added, to the defense attorney's delight, that the minivan never did head toward McDonald's. They had barely pulled out of Janet's driveway when Rachel called, and Sarah put her on the speaker.

"So the phone call during which Rachel supposedly said, 'I'm going to stab you and your Mexican boyfriend' occurred before you ever saw Ashley Lovelady. Is that correct?" Hebert inquired.

"Yes," Janet said.

"So you are in the van when a phone call comes in, allegedly from Rachel Wade's phone, and you allegedly hear Rachel Wade's voice."

Janet said that was true.

Other than that one oft-quoted statement, did Janet remember *anything else* that was said during that conversation?

Janet recalled hearing "I'm going to kick your ass," stuff like that—but only that one comment stuck out in her mind. After the threat from Rachel, Sarah decided to go look for Rachel at her house, and they drove past Sarah's house. Rachel wasn't there.

Hebert wanted to make sure the jury understood. Sarah was looking for Rachel. Janet agreed that was true.

Even as Sarah searched, the phone call with Rachel continued. Rachel said she was at Sarah's house, and Sarah now knew that wasn't true.

"'Where you at? Where you at?'" Janet quoted Sarah as saying.

"And yet no one in that van called the cops?" Hebert asked. Janet didn't bother to answer.

Hebert said, "Sarah wanted to end it that night, didn't she? She wanted to end the drama, and she was looking for Rachel."

Janet started in again about going to Sarah's house and seeing Rachel wasn't there, so Hebert nudged her narrative forward in time: "Okay, okay, you've been to Sarah's house and now you're back on your street and you run into Ashley Lovelady, right?"

Right. Ashley offered without prompting that she'd seen Rachel at Javier's house.

Hebert, unhappy, wanted to make sure he had it straight: At no time did Janet ask Ashley where Rachel was, right? And if someone said she had, they were not telling the truth, right? They were *lying,* right?

Janet begrudgingly said yes, but she looked like she wanted to smack Hebert with her flip-flops when she said it.

"How fast was the van moving when it pulled onto Javier's street?"

Janet said Sarah was driving the same as when she left Janet's house.

Hebert wondered how familiar Janet was with the neighborhood, and the witness replied not very. Hebert asked if it was true that Janet only lived a block from Javier's house. Janet said she didn't know where Javier lived. Hebert decided a glance at the aerial photo might help. It didn't. Janet wasn't in the mood to be helpful. As Hebert put the large photo away, Janet took the opportunity to shoot Rachel another hateful stare.

Janet testified that Sarah still had Rachel on speakerphone during the ride to Javier's.

Hebert asked, "Is it your testimony that Sarah and Rachel were on the phone right up until the moment the van arrived at Javier's?"

Janet thought about that and backed off her earlier statement. At some point the phone conversation had broken off, but she wasn't sure when.

"Didn't Sarah say she wanted to kick Rachel's ass?"

Janet agreed that among the cussing and yelling back and forth, Sarah had threatened to kick Rachel's ass.

The defense attorney now spoke slowly and dramatically, an important point was being made: *"And you were going to have Sarah's back, weren't you?"*

The question made Janet's temper flare. She closed her eyes, lowered her head, and took a deep breath before responding: "Um, depending on which way you're trying to say it. I was there because I knew nothing was going to happen. I didn't think nothing was going to happen. I mean, she didn't come to my house or in front of my house because I was there. So I figured if I was there with Sarah the whole time, nothing was going to happen."

"That's because Rachel was scared of you," Hebert said. "You had threatened Rachel before, hadn't you, ma'am?"

Janet didn't recall. What she did recall was she had a problem with Rachel because she didn't want her with her brother. She was a bad influence. Up until this point, Janet had been making solid eye contact with the attorney as she answered questions. However, she gave this response with eyes lowered, almost as if she were reading the response from an invisible card. "That was it. I didn't know her like that. I just didn't want her with my brother."

"You told her to 'stay the 'eff' away from my brother,' didn't you, ma'am?"

"I don't recall that, either."

Hebert returned to the scene at Javier's house. Janet agreed that the minivan pulled up quickly, but not that Sarah got out quickly. Sarah slowly turned off her car and opened her door. Rachel was already around the corner. From the moment they pulled up, Janet could clearly see Rachel.

"You made eye contact with her?"

Janet wasn't ready to go that far. She saw Rachel, and she was sure Rachel saw her. Janet definitely saw the knife in Rachel's hand. Sarah had barely gotten her feet on the ground when Rachel was on her and the tussle began.

Hebert found a copy of the diagram she'd drawn for Detective Lynch. Janet had placed an X marking the spot where the tussle had occurred. He showed the diagram to the witness and asked if she remembered it. She said no.

He pointed out that she had signed it. She said okay. As it turned out, the X was not on the driver's side of the van at all, but near the passenger-side front of the van.

"Are you telling me that I said the fight took place in front of Sarah's van?" Janet asked.

"This is your drawing. I'm just asking you if you remember drawing this."

"No," Janet said, answering with a small smile. "That's not what happened. The fight never occurred in front of Sarah's van."

"So what you are saying is that when you drew this, and you were under oath, you were not being truthful."

"No, I'm saying that that drawing is messed up."

Judge Bulone interrupted and asked the witness if she recalled making the drawing at her deposition. She nodded pleasantly. "Oh yeah, I drew—but the fight never happened in front of Sarah's van."

Hebert tried to get Janet to commit to who started the fight, to who threw the first punch, but Janet said it was impossible to tell. Was it because she had an obstructed view? No, because everything had happened so suddenly. It was a flurry of motion all at once.

How tall was Sarah?

Janet looked off into the distance, trying to remember. "She's tall" was the best she could come up with. Hebert asked if she was about five-nine, and Janet said sure.

"So the fight was over in five seconds, and Rachel started to walk back toward Javier's house. You then attacked Rachel. Am I correct?"

Janet didn't like the word "attacked."

"I confronted her, yes."

"You confronted her and then you hit her. Isn't that right?"

"Yes."

Hebert wanted to account for Jilica. Where was she during all of this?

Janet said Jilica was with Sarah "the whole time." Hebert wanted to know how Jilica got from the backseat of the van to Sarah, but Janet didn't know. She'd been focused on Rachel and hadn't been watching. Jilica had been nowhere near Janet or Rachel, the witness concluded.

"So, at that point, Jilica wasn't grabbing you? Trying to hold you back?"

"No, not at that point."

"If somebody said that, they wouldn't be telling the truth."

"She did hold me back. Afterward."

"Oh, that's right. You had two fights with Rachel Wade that night, didn't you?"

"I wouldn't call the first one a fight."

"Oh. All right. An encounter. A-a-a—she had a knife."

"Yeah."

"So you go back, grab Rachel by the hair, and drag her across the grass. You *beat* her, didn't you, ma'am?"

Janet didn't like the word "beat." She was hitting her, sure. Hitting her with her hands. But that was after she noticed Sarah was stabbed. Janet admitted she was more violent after learning that her friend had been stabbed.

Hebert asked her, flat out, if she didn't go there to "beat Rachel down."

"No, sir," Janet said firmly. She didn't. Sarah didn't. No one did. "It takes a lot for Sarah to fight," Janet added.

There was an opening: "You've seen Sarah fight before?"

Dicus objected to the question on grounds of relevance, but Judge Bulone ruled that, now that the witness had opened the door, Hebert was allowed to walk through it.

Janet said that she had *not* seen Sarah fight before, which was "just the point" she was trying to make. She had seen Sarah in situations where other girls might have fought, but Sarah didn't—therefore the witness knew it took a lot for Sarah to fight.

In fact, that was why Janet didn't think there was going to be a fight that night. *Because Sarah didn't fight.*

"You'd seen Sarah get in a fight before, haven't you, ma'am? But not with Rachel. You saw Sarah get in a fight with Erin, didn't you?" Hebert said.

Dicus objected on the grounds of relevance, and Judge Bulone sustained. Hebert felt frustrated. He'd been trying to show that his client was in fear for her life because Sarah was out to get her. How could Sarah's history of violence not be relevant? But the ruling had been made, and the question went unanswered.

"Are you aware that your brother wanted these two girls to fight one another?"

Dicus objected both on the grounds of relevance and that the question was based upon hearsay.

Judge Bulone thought for a moment and said, "I'll sustain the objection."

"Without revealing the contents of your conversation with your brother, are you aware if your brother wanted girls to fight over him?"

"Objection, Your Honor. It is the same question," Dicus said impatiently.

"Sustained," the judge said.

Hebert was through.

* * *

On redirect ASA Dicus made it clear that even though Janet had told Hebert during her deposition that Sarah and Joshua weren't dating, she had also, during that same interview, described the pair as "inseparable."

Dicus returned to the drawing Hebert had used to imply Janet was changing the location of the tussle. The prosecutor showed the drawing to Janet and asked her, once again, if she had drawn it.

Janet figured maybe she had. Dicus asked if she was an artist.

She laughed. "No, not at all."

Dicus asked if the illustration was "drawn to scale."

Janet didn't understand. Dicus explained and she gave an emphatic no.

"They just told me to draw the way the cars were," she said.

Dicus said the drawing wasn't very good, that a kindergarten student with some talent could have done better, and Janet agreed.

"My son probably could have done better," she said, smiling.

"I see scribble and some initials. Is that what you see?"

"Yes."

Dicus asked her what the X was supposed to signify.

Janet said, "That's the thing. I don't understand what . . ."

Dicus asked, wasn't it true that during that same deposition, during which she'd made the drawing, Hebert also had asked Janet to describe verbally the altercation between Sarah and Rachel?

Janet gave an enthusiastic yes. He *had* asked many questions on the subject, questions that involved distances and where things were situated in relationship to one another.

Dicus read some of Janet's statement during the deposition, during which she had said that the fight took place almost as soon as Sarah got out of the minivan. In fact, Janet had said that Rachel was on Sarah so quickly, Sarah had not even had an opportunity to close the car door.

The prosecutor asked Janet if she recalled making those statements, and Janet said she did. Dicus asked if, indeed, those statements were consistent with the testimony she'd given today, and Janet said they were.

Wasn't it true that Janet had already described the way the fight came down when he asked her to make the scribbled illustration?

Janet said it was true.

Janet absolutely believed there would be no fight that night. Janet knew Rachel was afraid of her. As long as she was there, Janet believed there wouldn't be a fight.

Of Rachel's threats, Janet said, "I thought it was just words."

After all, earlier, when Janet got out of Jeremy's car and started to walk toward Rachel's vehicle, Rachel fled.

"Because you were sitting in the front seat of the van, plainly visible, did you believe that Sarah Ludemann was going to be safe?"

"Yes, sir."

Dicus pointed out that Hebert had earlier asked Janet about statements Janet had made to Rachel regarding the defendant staying away from Joshua, but—and this was the point—Hebert had not asked *when* Janet had made those statements.

Janet said it was true that she thought Rachel was a "bad influence" on her brother, but she did not recall having a phone conversation with Rachel during which she expressed that opinion.

Defense attorney Jay Hebert had a few questions for Janet on recross.

"Isn't it true that you knew Rachel wouldn't come to your house because she was scared of you, and you knew you could control that situation?"

"No, she . . . I mean, yeah, she didn't want to deal with me."

"She . . . didn't . . . want . . . to . . . deal . . . with . . . you," Hebert repeated slowly. "That's all I have, Judge."

Janet Camacho was excused.

Judge Bulone explained to the jury that the next witness, Dustin Grimes, was in the U.S. Army and was stationed in South Korea, so his testimony had been pre-recorded onto a DVD, and would be shown to the jury on a television monitor. The tape was made in the same courtroom, and all of the same parties—judge, lawyers, and defendant—had been present.

During his testimony, Dustin had identified and testified regarding several prosecution exhibits, so the jury needed to be shown those exhibits in a fashion synchronized with the recording. If the witness pointed out something on a map, for example, the jury would not only need to be shown the map, but also where on the map the witness had pointed. Everyone was in agreement that this was the best way to handle the situation. Since it had been anticipated that Dustin would be out of the country at the time of the trial, appropriate preparations were made.

Dustin Grimes was an athletic-looking white man. He wore a light-colored button-up collar shirt, and had a military haircut. On the TV screen, he took the stand, spelled his last name, and gave his date of birth, which was during the autumn of 1987. He was married and a resident of Pinellas Park. He was in the army and had been since September 9, 2009. He was scheduled to be based in Korea and would begin the trip there the following weekend, which was the beginning of April 2010. He would be in Korea between one and three years.

Lisset Hanewicz asked what was Dustin Grimes's relationship with Javier Laboy. They were friends since seventh grade. That night Dustin was on his way home and saw Javier outside. He stopped, and parked his car on the front lawn, just to the side of the driveway. They hadn't seen each other in a while and he wanted to see how things were going. They were just hanging out, talking in Javier's front yard.

At some point, Dustin learned that a girl named Rachel was on her way over so she and Javier could get something to eat, and to help her get over the argument she was having. He didn't know the specifics of the argument, just that this was a friend of Javier's who needed calming down. He didn't know Rachel, just *of her.*

He wasn't sure of the exact time. It was "late at night." Guessing, he'd say around eleven o'clock. Rachel arrived alone in a red Saturn, parked at the curb out front. She and Javier talked a little bit and she was on and off the phone. The boys leaned on Dustin's car as Rachel yelled about who-knew-what into the phone. She was upset.

She was pacing back and forth as she yelled, across the yard and around her car. Dustin didn't know how long that went on. At some point, Rachel showed them a kitchen knife she'd brought from home. The boys told her to "put it away," that there was "no need" for her to have it.

Dustin was under the impression that she had put the knife away. He wasn't sure how she ended up with it again. At some point, a car sped down the street past Javier's house. The car barreled around the corner and swerved toward Rachel, as if it were "trying to run her over."

Five minutes later, Javier gave Rachel directions, either to Joshua or Sarah's house. Then she did leave, but she was back in five minutes.

She told Javier what she'd done while she was gone. All Dustin remembered overhearing was that she sat in her car near whichever house she went to.

Upon her return to Javier's house, Rachel's demeanor remained the same. She was still upset, still arguing on the phone.

Javier's attempts to calm this girl down were a complete failure. Rachel, in fact, was increasingly agitated. Rachel griped aloud about Sarah, saying, "I'm going to kill that fucking bitch." She said it to Javier. Dustin overheard it, but he didn't take her seriously. He thought it was just a "figure of speech," he said.

About ten minutes later, a van pulled up in front of the house. The driver put the van in park and three girls emerged simultaneously from the vehicle. Rachel was already making her way toward the driver's side of the van and was crossing the front of the vehicle.

On the TV screen, Dustin was shown a photo of the scene that was taken on the night of the incident. He marked upon it where everyone was standing. Using an arrow, he showed where Rachel was standing when the van arrived, and where she walked as soon as the vehicle stopped. Rachel crossed in front of her own and Sarah's vehicles to the site of the fight, which took place near the left front of the van.

Synchronization went smoothly. As the video played, the jury was shown these exhibits.

Dustin said the girls "locked up" and the fight was over very quickly, lasting only three or four seconds. He couldn't tell who threw the first blow. Sarah got in three or four punches, and Rachel was punching with a downward motion, or so he thought at the time.

When it was over, Sarah got back in the van and Rachel walked away. As Sarah sat down in the driver's seat, one of the girls she was with went after Rachel, swearing at her.

Dustin couldn't tell exactly what she was saying. He didn't remember if it was the girl who had been riding in the front passenger seat or the girl who rode in the back. A second fight broke out.

The girl from the van took off her sandal and hit Rachel with it. Dustin said that he and Javier were "just standing there, not wanting to get involved." The girl who wasn't fighting screamed that Sarah had been stabbed, so the boys were hesitant to approach because Rachel, they then noticed, had the knife they had seen earlier in her hand.

Knife or no knife, the girl was "beating up" Rachel. The fight began before the girl screamed that Sarah had been stabbed, and continued after it. The girl dragged Rachel across the yard by her hair. The fight broke up after about a minute, and Rachel walked toward the back of Javier's house. Dustin didn't know what she did back there.

It was only then that Javier and Dustin first went over to Sarah to see how she was. Javier removed his shirt and used it to apply pressure to the wound.

Sarah was unresponsive on the ground, not far from the still-open driver's door to the van.

"Did you know Sarah?" ASA Hanewicz asked the witness.

"I didn't know her. I knew of her," Dustin replied.

"No further questions," the prosecutor said.

Jay Hebert wanted to get the order of events straight. Dustin Grimes arrived at Javier Laboy's before Rachel? And he was talking to Javier by the driveway when Rachel Wade first arrived?

Correct.

"You were a single guy?"

"I was already dating my wife."

Dustin knew all about the drama: girls atwitter over a boy. Javier disliked the guy, so Dustin had heard the stories. The witness didn't know, however, with whom Rachel was on the phone. But yes, it had to do with Joshua Camacho and his harem.

Rachel made a comment about "killing Sarah"—and that was before the car came down the street and swerved at her. Javier was in a position to hear the threat—in fact, Dustin believed Javier *did* hear Rachel's statement.

Dustin thought Rachel was "talking smack." He agreed that he had heard other people make similar statements without ensuing violence, and he agreed that these types of statements were "common with people" of his generation. And the witness concurred that such statements were routinely made through a variety of media, phone, social networking, and so forth.

Hebert asked about the swerving car. Dustin knew little about it. He hadn't noticed the color or make of the car—or the gender of the driver. He noticed the car immediately, though. It turned onto Javier's block in a speedy and erratic fashion. Even before the swerving car, Rachel was anxious, in anticipation of violence. He didn't think that much about it as it occurred: "I just thought it was someone being stupid," he testified. There was *no doubt* that the car swerved toward Rachel, or that it came within one or two feet of striking her.

Dustin heard Javier give the defendant directions to a house before she left and was gone for five minutes; then she returned. He wasn't sure, but he thought that perhaps she was going either to Sarah's or Joshua's house. When Rachel returned after being gone for roughly five minutes, she parked in exactly the same spot. Ten minutes after she returned, the van arrived. Hebert did the math: about seventeen minutes passed between swerving car and van arrival.

Even though Dustin Grimes was a prosecution witness, and had changed the order of events—putting the swerving car before Rachel's brief trip to someone's house—there were segments of his testimony that thrilled Jay Hebert, and the defense attorney made a show of having Dustin repeat them.

One: When the van arrived, it arrived aggressively. During one interview, Dustin said the van "really came flying in there." Two: All three girls got out of the van at the same time—in fact, they came "flying out of the car"—which touched upon the very crux of Hebert's argument. Rachel had been jumped by a gang and had a right to arm herself in self-defense. Also, Dustin agreed that Sarah had had an opportunity to move toward the front of the van before she and Rachel came together.

Hebert asked Dustin if he knew on that night which girl was Janet Camacho. The witness said he did now, but not then. That night had been the first time he'd ever laid eyes on either Janet or Jilica.

Would the van have hit the Saturn if it hadn't come to a sudden stop? Dustin wasn't ready to commit to that completely, but he did say that "it could have" struck Rachel's car. When the van arrived, Rachel was not standing next to her car but rather was leaning on it. Leaning on the hood? No, it "was more on the driver's side."

Hebert wanted the jury to consider this contrast in passive and aggressive: three girls stampeding out of a van; one girl leaning back against a car.

"I want to make sure a couple of things are crystal clear about your testimony today. You never saw Rachel attack Sarah as she was sitting behind the wheel of the minivan, did you?"

"No."

Dustin didn't know if the van's engine was still running. The fight happened near the front driver's side of the van, "halfway between" the van and the Saturn. Sarah grabbed

Rachel by the hair; although he couldn't say for sure that she pulled Rachel's hair, or that she pulled Rachel's head down by her hair. Sarah landed three or four punches to Rachel's head.

Hebert took Dustin, step-by-step, to the second altercation, the one between Janet and Rachel. He asked the witness if he saw Janet Camacho "beating Rachel down," beating Rachel "profusely." Dustin said he did. And yes, the beating lasted upward to a minute.

"It was apparent, in your opinion, when that van pulled up, that there was going to be a catfight, that there was going to be a beat down that night, wasn't it?"

"I didn't actually think there was going to be a fight. I thought they were just going to start yelling at each other, and then just leave."

"And then all hell broke loose?"

"Yes."

Hebert understood that the witness did not know Jilica Smith, but he knew which girl she was. At the time, did Dustin think Jilica was going to be part of the fight? Dustin admitted that he had no clue.

"Jilica could have been part of the gang that was going to be involved with the fight, right?" the defense attorney asked.

"Right," the witness said.

Dustin said he didn't remember Jilica physically holding Janet back and trying to keep her out of the fight, but he did remember Jilica hollering at Janet. It was something about not getting hurt for the sake of her child.

Hebert wanted to emphasize the one-sidedness of the fight between Rachel and Janet. Janet was "cleaning Rachel's clock." Wasn't it true that Janet attacked Rachel before Jilica called out that Sarah had been stabbed? That was true. The Janet-Rachel fight, in fact, "immediately" followed the Rachel-Sarah fight. It was while Janet was beating down Rachel that Jilica cried out that Sarah had been stabbed.

"No further questions," Hebert said.

On redirect Lisset Hanewicz returned to the swerving car. Had either Dustin or Javier pulled Rachel out of the way to keep her from getting hit?

Dustin said they had not, and they were not even in a position to do so, as they were still over by his car, not with Rachel down by the street. But Rachel did have to move to avoid being hit by the swerving car.

Hanewicz had been paying close attention to Hebert's word games. When he said that Rachel and Sarah first came together near the front driver's side of the van, this wasn't halfway between the van and the Saturn at all, was it? It was closer to the van than it was to the Saturn. Rachel traveled farther than Sarah to get to the point of the altercation.

Hanewicz concluded by having the witness identify Rachel in the courtroom, which he did.

The DVD ended, the TV was turned off, and the courtroom lights were brightened to normal.

That concluded the testimony for the day. Judge Joseph Bulone admonished the jury: No TV news. If they looked at a newspaper, skip the local section. No discussing the case, no research online, no news sites online. He told the jurors to be back by ten the next morning and dismissed them for the day.

With the jury gone, Hebert briefed the court as to what his game plan was: His case was going to involve a text message from Joshua to Sarah, two days before the incident, in which he advised her to put the gun in her backpack. Joshua denied ever sending any such text message. Hebert said that he didn't know if the prosecution was going to call Joshua as a witness. If they chose not to, he would call him as a hostile witness.

Hebert said he planned to discuss the gun during his opening statement because it went to his client's state of mind during the buildup to the incident. Hebert gave a quick rundown on the many ways in which Joshua's story regarding the gun had changed with time. He'd denied having the gun; he had claimed that he didn't recognize the text he sent to Sarah regarding the gun; he'd said Rachel had no way of knowing about the gun. He was all over the place.

When she testified, Rachel was going to say that not only did she know about the gun, but she had been threatened by the gun as well. Her friends could vouch for her because she told them about it at the time. Joshua pointed the gun at her and said, "You'll never leave me. You'll never leave me." The implications were clear. He'd blow her brains out if she tried. And all of that led to Rachel's heightened state of mind.

Judge Bulone looked at Hebert with a skeptical raised eyebrow. The thing that amazed him, he said, was that this was such a pivotal thing; yet Hebert had failed to mention it during earlier court hearings. The judge wanted to get this straight. Hebert was not suggesting that the defendant knew about a gun because it was mentioned in a text message from Joshua to Sarah. Hebert conceded that. The text message was important in that it corroborated that the gun existed, a gun that Rachel already knew about and would testify that she'd been threatened with. Rachel would testify that the gun was part of her mind-set when she chose to arm herself on the night of the incident.

The judge became irritated. If the defense was saying that Rachel stabbed Sarah because she thought she might have a gun, Hebert certainly could have asked Rachel that question at the immunity hearing. However, he had not.

Hebert said that wasn't quite what Rachel was going to say. She didn't know who was going to show up that night to attack her. For all she knew, Joshua was coming to get her. Joshua might have given his gun to his older sister, Janet. Rachel didn't so much think Sarah had a gun, as she feared that a gun would be brought into the picture at some point during the night, and that was why she felt justified in arming herself.

Judge Bulone characterized that argument as "pretty speculative," but he saw no reason she couldn't testify to that, if that was what her mind-set was. He ruled that if Hebert wanted to corroborate Rachel's story that Joshua had a gun and had threatened her with it, he should have Joshua testify to that, but he didn't see how the text message from Joshua to Sarah was relevant, since Rachel couldn't have known about it and therefore it couldn't have affected her mind-set.

Hebert said, yeah, but in his legal opinion, Joshua had lied during every step of the process.

The judge replied that Joshua was not on trial—and thus the first day concluded.

Chapter 11

DAY TWO

At ten o'clock the following morning, July 22, as all parties waited for Judge Bulone to enter the courtroom, Rachel Wade was already busy, writing in her yellow legal pad. She looked a little better than she had during day one, as this was the day she was scheduled to testify on her own behalf. She had been allowed to wear some eye makeup.

At three minutes past ten, the bailiff called out the "All rise!" and Judge Joseph Bulone strode purposefully into the courtroom with a Styrofoam cup of Dunkin' Donuts coffee in his hand. He took the bench and asked if there was any business that needed to be tended to before he brought the jury in.

Defense attorney Jay Hebert said he had made copies of Joshua Camacho's October 27, 2009, deposition, the one that dealt with the gun issue. During that deposition, Joshua said that he had no gun, was familiar with no gun, and had no access to a gun in his household. Did he have a gun at the time of the incident? No. However, during a deposition dated January 21, 2010, Joshua was asked if he had a gun, and he responded, "I had one."

While trying to sort this out, speaking aloud, Judge Bulone repeatedly referred to Rachel as Sarah, and twice had to be corrected.

Hebert said that it would have been nice if, at the various times Joshua was deposed, the defense had had access to the phone photos of Joshua with the gun, so that Joshua would have been unable to deny having one. The defense, however, had not gotten a copy of the photo of Joshua with the gun until two weeks before the trial.

Judge Bulone noted that the key factor, as far as he was concerned, was that Joshua had at least admitted that he had a gun at the time of the incident during the second deposition. That, in itself, was still not relevant. The only potentially relevant factor was: did Rachel know about the gun and have reason to believe it would come into play on the night of the incident? The judge said that they had a lot of things to get through before Joshua took the stand and they would deal with the subject more when the time came. He called for the jurors to be brought in.

The prosecution called PPPD patrol officer Benjamin Simpkins. After a brief pause, Officer Simpkins entered in uniform, a burly man with close-cropped hair and a round face. He took the oath and was seated.

Under Wesley Dicus's questioning, Simpkins identified himself as a six-year veteran of the force, who worked the midnight shift. He had worked continuously for those six-plus years, and had some experience in corrections prior to that. He'd graduated from the police academy, of course. In addition to that, he'd received radar laser training and courses in vehicular homicide. He was also an instructor for the department in first aid and CPR. He was a field-training officer, who worked with new recruits to get them road ready.

Simpkins testified that he was trained in being a first responder at the scene of a crime and had previously been the first responder at scenes of crimes that involved great bodily injury.

How many times?

Simpkins chuckled and replied, "Numerous."

During the early-morning hours of April 15, 2009, Simpkins was called to the scene of a stabbing. The precise time he received the call was "zero zero fifty-three hours," that is, at 12:53 A.M. He was on the scene within minutes, only a few minutes after the stabbing occurred—not the first responder, but among the first responders. The scene was "chaotic": green van in the street, bleeding young lady down, paramedics. Other police officers were already there, busy trying to quell a disturbance between unruly bystanders.

"As one of the first responders, what were your duties?"

The first priority was to save life and limb. Secondly, to make sure that no one at the scene was armed and that there was no immediate further threat to the victim or any of the bystanders. That done, the parties were separated. Once apart, police began to establish who everyone was and what their roles were in the incident.

The process of separating and identifying witnesses was called "initial contact." During this process, he would create a "crime roster," which was a list of everyone at the scene. Next he sorted out the facts, which he referred to as the "Reader's Digest version of the investigation." Once he had the basic story, he would pass that information on to a responding detective, who could then fill in the details. The detective's investigation was far more detail- and history-oriented. They separated witnesses so they could be interviewed separately without influencing each other.

The officer remembered two women at the scene named Janet and Jilica. They were "at the south end of the scene," near another vehicle. When Simpkins first saw the women, they were standing with another officer. Simpkins said that the two women were separated; but when he was asked how far apart they actually were, he said, "Maybe a couple of yards." Simpkins admitted that at a couple of yards apart, the two women could easily converse. The key was that they could not talk to one another discreetly at that distance. A police officer could hear what was said. The chance of secret messages between the two was further hindered by the surrounding chaos. In that dry cacophony, whispers evaporated.

During cross-examination, Officer Simpkins said he was aware at the scene that the incident was the result of a "long-term dispute going on between the girls."

Had he seen any blood inside the van?

Yes, on the driver's seat, on the floor in front of that seat, and on the interior paneling.

Jay Hebert wanted to know more about the "Mexican boyfriend" statement.

Janet, the officer said, had made it clear that Sarah had put her phone on speaker so that everyone in the van would be able to hear what Rachel was saying and know what was going on.

Wasn't it true that Jilica told him that she had been shown a text message by Sarah, and that the text was from Rachel and said that she was going to wait by Sarah's house and stab her?

Simpkins said that was true.

At that time, Jilica had not said anything about Rachel's voice on speaker or the "Mexican boyfriend" statement.

* * *

The prosecution called PPPD sergeant Tina Trehy, with Lisset Hanewicz questioning. Trehy said she was in charge of the day shift's patrol section.

Trehy came from a family of police. Her dad, David Cline, was a police detective in Cleveland, Ohio. Her uncle Andrew Zatik was a PPPD veteran. Her husband, James, retired from the PPPD, and took a job with the Florida Department of Insurance Fraud.

Trehy ran the police records bureau; and because of her artistic skill, she was the PPPD sketch artist, drawing perps based on witness's descriptions. She began her career in law enforcement as a police dispatcher and "meter maid" in St. Petersburg. When she joined the PPPD in 1988, she was the third-ever female patrol officer.

Sergeant Trehy had arrived at the scene of Sarah Ludemann's stabbing just a few minutes before one o'clock in the morning, on April 15, 2009. There were several vehicles in the street, among them police cruisers. People were all over the place; teenagers and adults milling about, all very upset. Screaming, crying. She got out of her car and noticed the van in the middle of the street. Next to it, a young girl was lying on the ground.

Trehy's voice shook with emotion as she described how two officers from her shift were attending to the girl in the road. The ambulance and fire department had not yet arrived. She was subsequently informed that the girl had been stabbed.

Hanewicz asked if there came a time that night when the witness came in contact with Rachel Wade. Trehy said she had, and was about to identify her as the defendant when Jay Hebert interrupted and stipulated that the defendant was Rachel Wade, noting that the identity of the defendant was not an issue in this case.

Trehy testified that while at the scene she was in contact with Rachel Wade for approximately forty-five minutes— although it could have been an hour or longer. She was not keeping close track of time. The thing about the defendant's behavior that caught Trehy's attention was her calmness—her "lack of concern" regarding everything that was going on.

Hebert objected, noting that the witness, unless she could read minds, was speculating.

Judge Joseph Bulone sustained the objection and instructed the witness that she could testify to the defendant's demeanor, but not to her thoughts.

So ASA Hanewicz helped the witness show rather than tell. Rachel had not cried or appeared upset. She had not inquired as to the victim's condition. All she wanted was a cigarette.

"No further questions," the fiery prosecutor said.

Hebert saw nothing to gain by cross-examining this witness, so Trehy was allowed to step down.

"The state calls Detective Kenneth Blessing," Dicus announced. The call went outside the courtroom for Detective Blessing, but there was no response. Wesley Dicus furiously typed on a laptop, and Lisset Hanewicz stomped out of the room to see what the problem was. She returned in less than a minute and informed the judge that Detective Blessing was not ready to testify and that the state would instead call PPPD detective Michael Lynch.

Detective Lynch, in a black suit, strode briskly into the courtroom, took the oath, and had a seat.

"On April 15, 2009, were you designated the lead detective on this case?" Hanewicz asked.

"I was. Yes, ma'am."

"As the lead detective, could you explain to the jury briefly what your responsibilities are?"

Lynch explained that during the active investigation, it was his responsibility to follow up on any leads in the case, to interview witnesses and suspects, and to gather any evidence or potential evidence that might exist. He was first contacted regarding the stabbing at approximately 1:00 A.M. on April 15. At that time, he was summoned to the house where Javier Laboy resided in Pinellas Park.

When he arrived at Javier's home, PPPD patrol and forensic units were already there. The first officer with whom Lynch spoke after his arrival was Simpkins, who briefed him as to what he had learned during initial contact interviews. That info was very helpful, especially when Lynch later interviewed the eyewitnesses and suspect more thoroughly.

Rachel Wade was sitting on a bench near the front of the Laboy house. Sarah Ludemann had already been transported to the hospital. The witnesses to the stabbing—Camacho, Smith, Laboy, and Grimes—were still there. As Simpkins briefed him, Detective Lynch was toward the north end of the crime scene; Javier and Dustin were up near the residence; Janet and Jilica were at the opposite end of the crime scene, the south end. Witnesses were primarily separated to get independent statements as much as possible. The secondary reason was the potential adversarial nature of the eyewitnesses: two with the victim, two with the suspect. The knife had still not been located. A canine unit was called in to perform an article search, which was unsuccessful.

Lynch stepped down from the witness stand to testify regarding crime scene photos in a manner that the jury could see. He testified regarding the location of the vehicles in the street.

Yes, he observed blood at the scene, both on the van's driver's-side interior and also a small amount on items of clothing that were on the outside of the van, also on the driver's side. There was neither blood in front of the vehicle, nor on the ground outside the van's passenger-side door. Lynch returned to the witness stand.

Lynch was still at the scene when he learned the investigation had become a homicide investigation. When finished at the crime scene, Lynch went to the hospital, spoke with Sarah's family, advised them that he was working on the case, and observed the victim's remains. (He described the wounds.)

He subsequently conducted an interview with Rachel Wade at the police station and, at that time, observed the injuries she had sustained during the incident. The inside of her lower lip was cut, and there were scratches and scrapes along her back. During that first twenty-four hours, Lynch interviewed all four witnesses to the incident, as well as Joshua Camacho.

He did not interview Ashley Lovelady that night because at that time her name was not known to him. When he did learn who she was, he didn't consider her a key witness as to what had caused Sarah Ludemann's death. In fact, he didn't get around to interviewing Ashley until months after the incident. He could not recall the exact date. Ashley was not completely honest when she was first interviewed. Lynch had expressed his concern that she was not being forthcoming with him, and he urged her to get back in touch with him if she decided to tell the whole truth. It didn't take long for Ashley's conscience to be her guide. She called him back the very next day and expressed her desire to set the record straight.

Among the items discovered at the scene of the incident that night was Sarah Ludemann's cell phone. Rachel Wade's cell phone was "collected that night" as well. The history of each phone was checked, and it was discovered that Sarah had placed a call to Rachel at twelve thirty-three that same night/early morning. Lynch later learned about the voice mails left in Sarah's phone by Rachel. The state then played the recordings.

The first message that the jury heard was the "Why don't you act your age, Sarah?" voice mail, recorded on July 29, 2008. Sitting at the defense table, Rachel seemed more disturbed at hearing her own manic and profane tirade than she had been by anything else she'd heard during her trial. She dabbed at tears as an automated voice noted that the recording had been made at 3:36 A.M. on July 29, 2008, and had lasted for twenty-two seconds.

The August 29, 2008, message was played—the one in which Rachel complained about Sarah putting a new picture of herself and Joshua on her Myspace account. Two moments in the recording seemed to pluck an emotional chord in the defendant: first when she heard herself say "I am going to fucking murder you," and again when she called the victim "fat." The automated voice came on and said this message, thirty-four seconds long, had been recorded on a Friday at 4:33 P.M. By the end of the recording, Rachel was sobbing, perhaps with self-pity as she must have realized how the recordings sounded to the jurors. Her own words—her own stupid words—made her seem so *guilty*.

At one minute and fourteen seconds, the third voice mail played for the jury was the longest of the three—the one Rachel made during the evening of August 31, 2008, the one that started, "It's so funny that you want to talk shit. . . ."

By the time it was finished, Rachel was threatening to be Sarah's "teacher," who was going to "teach her to grow up . . . quick." Both Rachel and her mother were sobbing. Rachel's father, holding and comforting his wife, had a vacant look of despair in his eyes.

"I am going to show you psycho!" the jury heard Rachel say.

The jury then heard the fourth message, the shortest of

the group at ten seconds. It was sent less than an hour after the previous one. It began by taunting, "Why don't you come outside now, Sarah?" The defendant could not have sounded more guilty of harassment, and, now, of stalking.

The fifth message played—thirty-four seconds long—was the one recorded during the early evening of November 12, 2008, the one in which Rachel compared Sarah's eating habits to those of her dog. During that call, Rachel bragged about having her own car, while Sarah had to walk places. Rachel said the exercise might do Sarah good. "Maybe it'll thin you out a little bit," she said.

That concluded the CD, and Hanewicz resumed her questioning.

"Detective, that night, was the knife eventually located?"

Lynch said it was. It was found on the roof of the house next to, just north of, the Laboy house.

"Who arrested the defendant?"

"I did—and I charged her with second-degree murder."

"No further questions," Hanewicz said.

Jay Hebert began his cross-examination slowly. He had Lynch reiterate that he was the case's lead investigator, and that it was a tragic situation. During his investigation, he became familiar with the youthful "drama" with which the tragedy unfolded.

Hebert said they had heard tapes of the defendant threatening the victim, but wasn't it also true that there had been threats from Sarah toward Rachel as well?

Lynch said that the interviews he'd conducted during the course of his investigation would lead him to agree with that, yes.

Hebert said, "In fact, you interviewed Rachel Wade.

You went through a detailed, intensive videotaped interview with Rachel Wade, more than an hour in duration?"

Lynch said it was true. He had interviewed Rachel at PPPD headquarters. The interview was videotaped.

Hebert wondered if during that interview, Rachel discussed the catalytic drama of the buildup. Lynch agreed that there was "some discussion" regarding "what may have led to" the incident.

Hebert inquired if Lynch had been the officer who picked up Janet Camacho and Jilica Smith as they began to walk home. Lynch said he wasn't, but he was aware that the pair had been picked up. Lynch said he would not characterize their actions as "walking home," but they were on the extreme south end of the area and were picked up.

Hebert now held the board with the photos from the scene of the incident mounted on it, the same board Lynch had testified about during the prosecution's direct examination.

Wasn't it true that Rachel's car, the red Saturn, was more or less legally parked at the side of the road? Lynch said that he would have preferred seeing the vehicle pointing north, but agreed that it was closer to being parked legally than the van was. Lynch agreed with Hebert that the van, as it was parked, represented a traffic hazard.

Some spectators felt this line of questioning smacked of desperation. It had long been established that the van was in the middle of the street.

Lynch agreed that since the incident and initial investigation took place during the hours after midnight, it was "very dark." Hebert showed Lynch two photos of the street outside Javier's house, both taken during the hours after the incident, one with the flash, one without. The darker photo showed a scene illuminated only by a streetlight near the end of the block. The detail visible in the flash photo was far greater than in the other, and Lynch agreed that the photo without the flash was a better representation of what the scene actually looked like that night.

Hebert had Lynch agree that because of the location of the blood, Sarah had most likely climbed back into the van after she was stabbed.

"Based on your investigation, did you ever receive any information that Sarah was stabbed inside the van?"

"No, I never received any information like that."

When did Lynch first hear the name Ashley Lovelady? The name "Ashley" had been mentioned that night, no last name, and only as a person who had been seen or observed earlier that night.

Who gave the detective the information regarding Ashley? Lynch thought it was Janet Camacho. Lynch did, at a later date, interview Ashley. She lied at first about her essential role in the tragedy, but she came clean the next day.

One of Hebert's most important tasks, he understood, was chipping away at the strong connection the jury felt between the voice message threats and the stabbing. Yes, it was true that the first voice mail they had listened to was recorded nine months before "anything happened." Hebert noted the date of each phone call and the vast span of time between that call and the night of the stabbing. The most recent of the phone messages, the one recorded in November, not only demonstrated a different demeanor, but that was still five to six months before the incident. Were there any recorded phone calls that Lynch knew of inside of five months from the date of the incident? There were not.

Then, out of the blue: "And the person who told you where the knife was, was Rachel Wade?"

"Objection, Your Honor!" Hanewicz said angrily.

"Sustained," Judge Bulone quickly ruled.

The subject of who had informed police of the knife's location had not been broached during direct examination and therefore was off-limits for cross. Besides, the truth was that Rachel had merely said the knife was "next door" and hadn't mentioned that it was on the roof.

"You found the knife, right?" Hebert asked the witness.

The detective understood the "you" to be collective and said they had. They found the knife because someone told them where it was. The jury, for certain, now knew who had told police where the knife was. Hanewicz was irritated by Hebert's courtroom trickery. Sometimes the jury didn't need to hear an answer. Sometimes, Hebert knew, hearing the question was enough.

Hebert was through; Hanewicz had no questions on redirect; Lynch was allowed to step down.

"Has the state located Detective Blessing?" Judge Bulone asked.

"Yes, Judge. He's outside," Dicus said. "The state calls Detective Kenneth Blessing."

Blessing, who had been named the PPPD Officer of the Year in 1992, was a slender blond-haired man with a mustache. He wore a black suit with a black-and-gray-striped tie that dangled down past his belt. Blessing told the jury that he had been a PPPD employee for twenty-two years. Before being promoted to detective fourteen or fifteen years before, he was a patrol officer.

Wesley Dicus asked Blessing to run down the police training he'd received over the years. The witness replied that he'd attended the police academy, and subsequently took a forty-hour course at "detective school" before his promotion. Before investigating this incident, he'd been involved in "five or six" homicides. At the time of this incident, he was not on duty. He was home sleeping when he received the call. It was common practice for off-duty detectives to be called at home when there was a murder or a stabbing for the simple reason that PPPD detectives only worked during the daytime. Dicus asked at what time Blessing received the call for this case. Blessing referred to his written report and then responded that it had been about one-thirty in the morning. He arrived at the scene fifteen minutes later, so he was on the scene within a "half hour, forty-five minutes" after the stabbing. The first thing he did upon arriving was seek out the lieutenant-on-site for a briefing as to what had occurred. Blessing then waited until Detective Lynch arrived on the scene, as well as Mark R. Berger, who was the criminal investigation sergeant. When everyone was there, they decided who would do what.

"What were your responsibilities going to be?" Dicus inquired.

"I ended up interviewing one of the witnesses, and I stood by at the scene for anything else they wanted me to do."

"Which witness did you interview?"

"Janet Camacho."

He originally had been assigned to interview both Janet and Jilica, but Jilica Smith, as it turned out, was interviewed by another officer. The interview with Janet took place in Blessing's car. Jilica was interviewed by the other detective in his vehicle.

Dicus asked where Janet and Jilica were when he contacted them for an interview. Blessing replied that the pair was standing in the vicinity of Fifty-second Street and Park Lake Drive. Police had closed off the street on either side of the incident with police tape. Dicus asked if Janet and Jilica were inside or outside the crime scene. He replied that they were slightly outside the crime scene, just on the other side of the tape. Dicus asked if Janet had already been interviewed by one of the first responders by the time she got into his patrol car. Blessing didn't know, although he allowed that she "may have."

"During your interview with Janet Camacho, did she

make reference to a phone call to Sarah Ludemann from Rachel Wade in which Rachel Wade threatened to stab Sarah and her Mexican boyfriend?"

"Yes."

Dicus asked what time the interview with Janet took place and Blessing read from his report that it began at 2:10 A.M. It was soon after the incident, Dicus noted, at a time when the details of events should have been fresh in the minds of the witnesses.

"After your interview with Ms. Camacho, what did you do?"

"I stayed at the scene. I worked with Detective Lynch for a while. I also took the two witnesses [Janet and Jilica] home to their residence. That was at two-forty."

"Did you perform a show-up?"

"Yes."

"Why don't you tell the jury what a show-up is."

"A show-up is when we have a crime and we have a witness to it. We take the witness to the person they say did it, and we ask if this person was indeed the one they'd seen commit the crime."

Dicus asked with which witnesses did he do a show-up. Blessing, who apparently had no independent recollection of the night's activities, again referred to his written report, and took a long time before he answered that he'd performed a show-up with both Janet Camacho and Jilica Smith. Those took place at 2:30 A.M.

"Who did you take them to see?" Dicus asked.

Blessing again ran a finger down his written report searching for the answer, a process that had Dicus growing antsy.

"Was it Rachel Wade?" the prosecutor asked impatiently.

"Yes," Blessing replied, although he was still reading. And yes, both witnesses positively identified Rachel Wade as the person they saw commit the stabbing. A sergeant informed Blessing that the knife was on the roof of the house next door, the house to the left of Javier's house. It became Blessing's job to find a ladder—he borrowed one from the sheriff's forensic unit on the scene—and climbed up on the neighbor's roof. With flashlight in hand, he searched—but he did not see the knife at first. He eventually found the weapon on the side of the roof farthest from Javier's house. The blade was bent and bloody.

Dicus showed the witness and the jury a crime scene photo taken of the knife on the roof. Blessing agreed that the photo accurately depicted the location and condition of the knife as it was found. The prosecutor then produced the actual knife, inside a cardboard box. The witness identified it as the one he'd found, and noted that its condition, bent and bloody, was unchanged.

Blessing was allowed to step down from the witness stand so he could personally show the knife, still in its box, to the jurors. The knife was tied to the base of the box and the lid lifted up. The knife had been mounted so that the bent blade pointed upward.

Rachel Wade, emotionless only moments before, now demonstrated signs of distress. Her brow furrowed and her mouth hung open. She gulped and blinked hard, twice, before shutting her eyes completely.

Jay Hebert said his cross-examination would be brief. Kenneth Blessing admitted that compared to other witnesses in this case, he'd been a late arrival at the scene. He had no firsthand knowledge of anything that had occurred before he showed up at 1:45 A.M.

Hebert asked if it was true that when Blessing interviewed Janet Camacho, she claimed that the "Mexican boyfriend" threat came not via Sarah's phone but Joshua

Camacho's phone. Blessing admitted that this was true. She said it was on speakerphone, but that it was on Joshua's phone.

"Ms. Camacho and Ms. Smith were interviewed in squad cars?"

"No, I have a Ford Escape, so I interviewed [Camacho] in that. And the other detective (Lynch) interviewed the other girl (Smith) in his detective car."

The defense attorney asked where the two male witnesses, Javier Laboy and Dustin Grimes, were when he arrived. Blessing said all of the witnesses were more or less in the same area toward the south end of the crime scene, not far from the corner of Fifty-second Street and Park Lake Drive.

"When you interviewed Janet, did she tell you that she'd seen Rachel Wade throw something?"

"No."

"Isn't it true that Janet thought that Javier or Dustin had taken the knife away from Rachel? Isn't that what she told you?"

"Yes."

"Isn't it true that the information you received that enabled you to find the knife was provided by Rachel Wade?"

"Objection, Your Honor," Dicus said.

"Sustained," Judge Bulone replied.

"Your Honor, the state calls Dr. Jon Russell Thogmartin."

The District 6 medical examiner, who wore a green suit, took the stand. Wesley Dicus asked him to explain for the jury what a forensic pathologist did. He said that he dealt with medical examiner/coroner/jurisdictional–type issues.

Using anatomic and clinical pathology, he diagnosed "what killed people" in certain types of deaths.

Anatomic pathology, Dr. Thogmartin explained cheerfully, had to do with diagnosing solid human tissue disorders. "If you have breast cancer, prostate cancer, lung cancer, it is a solid human tissue diagnosis." Clinical pathology dealt with the "liquid human tissue stuff," such as leukemia, blood chemistry disorders, and things like that. "So you have solid and liquid," he summed up with a smile.

As part of his forensic pathology training, he had learned how to determine cause of death in cases of sudden and violent mishap, which included both criminal—gunshot wounds, stab wounds—but also trauma resulting from a car accident. Part of his training dealt not only with finding causes of death in criminal cases but how to testify clearly and distinctly about his findings before a jury in a court of law. He had the authority to investigate certain types of death, usually trauma, usually completely unexpected deaths.

As part of his duties, he performed autopsies "to try to figure out why they're dead." Everything was photographed. Organs were weighed. Wounds were measured. When the procedure was through, a death certificate was prepared; then the medical examiner proclaimed the cause and manner of death.

Dicus asked if he had experience testifying in court. The doctor said he did but couldn't say for certain how many times. "Maybe a hundred. I don't know, possibly more," he said with a small shake of his head. He hadn't just testified in the Sixth Circuit, either, but all around Florida.

Dr. Thogmartin became serious as the subject shifted to the autopsy of Sarah Ludemann.

"At this time," Dicus said, "I am going to be showing photos of the autopsy, so to preserve the victim's privacy I am going to angle them away from the spectator section of the courtroom. So if jurors need to move to be able to see, I suggest they do so."

"They may move if they want," Judge Bulone added.

Dr. Thogmartin was allowed to step down from the witness stand so he could testify directly to the jury as to what the photos showed. Sarah Ludemann, he said, had been a healthy girl. The only things wrong with the victim were the two stab wounds. There were other relatively minor scratches, but the puncture wounds were what stood out, in particular the large one on her left breast.

Dicus showed the witness a close-up photo of stab wound number one and asked him to describe it. Dr. Thogmartin said it was a little bit less than an inch long and approximately four millimeters wide. It was a shallow wound, had done little damage, and was caused by a single-edged blade inserted with the sharp edge up.

Sarah Ludemann's mother began to react to the testimony. She closed her eyes and tossed her head somewhat violently from side to side. She gathered herself, kept her head still, and slowly opened her eyes.

Dr. Thogmartin testified that the wound was too shallow to determine the angle, and that it was a poke rather than a slash.

Dicus showed Dr. Thogmartin the bloody knife.

"To a degree of medical certainty, could a knife of this size and shape cause that injury?" Dicus asked.

"I could not say for certain that this is the knife that caused this injury. On the other hand, I could not rule this knife out, either. This is certainly a knife that could have caused this injury, yes," the witness replied.

Dicus wasn't happy with the doubt inferred by the medical examiner's response, so he followed up with, "Is the shape of this knife consistent with one that could have caused the wound?"

"Sure," Dr. Thogmartin said. "Many different knives could have caused this injury, but I can't rule this one out."

Dicus flashed the witness a look that seemed to say, *Why couldn't you just stop at "sure"?*

"Were this the knife that was used to inflict this injury, to a degree of medical probability, could you determine if this knife would have caused a stabbing injury or a slashing injury?"

The medical examiner didn't answer the question. Instead, he described the nature of the wound again: a poke, not a slash, very shallow.

The prosecutor dropped the point, asking, "Was wound number one the wound that killed Sarah Ludemann?"

"Not in any way, no," the witness replied.

Dicus showed Dr. Thogmartin a photo of the second wound, and asked how large it was. The witness said the wound was gaping; but once the edges of the wound were pushed back together, it was similar in size to the other wound—eight by four centimeters—just *much* deeper. "About two and a half inches deep." He then described the path that the wound took through Sarah's body—through a rib, a lung, and the heart. Fatal.

Rachel Wade began to cry. She carefully wiped under her eyes with a tissue so as to soak up the tears without smearing her eye makeup.

"Approximately how much blood were you able to find pooled into her chest cavity from this injury?"

Rachel Wade gave up with the tissue and allowed the tears to cascade down her cheeks.

The ME said, "A lot. Three hundred milliliters of blood in her pericardial sac, and two liters in her chest cavity. There would have been some external bleeding as well, but the great majority of bleeding was internal."

Dicus asked if when looking at wound number two, could Dr. Thogmartin say what sort of weapon caused this wound?

The medical examiner wasn't certain how to answer. "If you are asking me to forget everything I know about the case and go by just my examination of the body alone, I would first look inside of the wound to see if the weapon left any part of itself behind. If it were caused by a piece of glass, for example, there might be glass that had broken off inside. But there was nothing in the wound. If you are asking me to guess, ignoring everything else, I would say that this is a knife wound."

He added that unlike with the first wound, he couldn't tell if the second wound was caused by a single- or double-edged weapon. Wound number one had had one squared-off edge because the blade had gone directly in and out. Wound number two had two sharp edges.

Why?

"Due to the fact that the victim has a breast here that is relatively mobile, maybe the blade goes in at an unusual angle. There's movement. There's movement both from the person who's doing the stabbing and by the person who is getting the knife put into them, and so there is either movement of the knife causing an enlargement of the wound, or there is a movement of the person relative to the knife, causing an enlargement of the wound." There was no way to tell for certain why.

"Is the fact that the wound goes through skin, fat, muscle, bone, and into the heart consistent with a slashing-type wound or a wound in a defensive-type posture?"

"All I can say is that the knife went into her. This would be consistent with the knife being put into her or the person being put on the knife, one of the two. Unless it is a razor [or a] razor-sharp knife, it is going to take some effort to put it in. The more dull the knife, the more effort it takes to put it in."

As an analogy, Dr. Thogmartin noted that it took a lot more strength to stab someone with a spoon than with a razor-sharp knife. The amount of pressure needed to stab a young woman this deeply was not measurable, the witness said, because it depended so much on the variable of the weapon that was used.

"In general, if we assume that the knife you showed me was the weapon, it would be like a steak knife trying to go through a steak. That's generally what we're talking about."

Bottom line: Dr. Thogmartin testified that he had certified the cause of death as a stab to the chest, and the manner as homicide.

Rachel Wade, still crying, now had her lower lip protruding like a pouting little girl. Her forehead was puckered with tension, her cheeks shiny with tears, and her eyes red and swollen.

The most important aspect of the second wound was that it had torn the heart, causing a one-centimeter puncture. The orientation of the knife for the second wound was a mystery. The sharp edge was up for the first wound, but he couldn't tell with the second wound. The assumption had to be that both wounds were caused with the sharp edge of the knife up. The *boomboom* nature of the stabbing didn't allow Rachel Wade time to turn the knife around in her hand.

The prosecutor asked Dr. Thogmartin for the second time how tall Sarah Ludemann was, and he said, "Five-nine." He sounded impressed.

Dicus's next question began, "Theoretically, if a shorter person using this knife"—Dicus showed the witness the knife in the box—"approached Sarah Ludemann and had a face-to-face confrontation with her, and with the knife in her hand, punched her with a downward motion, would these injuries be consistent with this hypothetical?"

Dr. Thogmartin said it would be close. In that scenario, he said, the stabbing motion would have to be close to horizontal, and not so much downward as the prosecutor had suggested. The downward motion would have only been necessary if the victim was already on her back. Plus the angle at which the knife entered the victim would have been altered by the victim's position. If she bent forward a little bit, that would change the angle. If she twisted a little, that would change the angle.

"People don't stand in an anatomically perfect posture when they are having a confrontation," he concluded. "They bend and twist."

Cross-examining, Hebert asked: "As a part of your postmortem investigation, were any lab tests done in this case?"

"Yes."

"And you tested for different substances that were in her system, correct?"

"Yeah, we are required to do that under Florida administrative code."

"But you did not test for marijuana in her system, did you, sir?"

"No, we don't routinely test for marijuana unless they are the driver of a motor vehicle, or the operator of a machine."

"That's all I have, Judge. Thank you," Hebert said.

"Any redirect?" Judge Bulone asked.

"Briefly, Your Honor," Dicus said, rising to his feet. "Dr. Thogmartin, you didn't test for marijuana, but you did test for alcohol, correct?"

"Yes."

"Did she have any alcohol in her system?"

"No." The medical examiner added that when it came to intoxicants, "she had nothing. Nothing at all."

Dr. Thogmartin was excused.

"What says the state?" Judge Bulone asked.

"Your Honor, at this time the state rests," Hanewicz said.

Judge Bulone noted that some legal issues needed to be discussed, with the jury out of the room, so he would give the jurors an extra-long lunch break. With the jury gone, the subject turned to Joshua.

"As far as Mr. Camacho is concerned," Judge Bulone said, "it is my understanding that you wanted him to corroborate the fact that the defendant knew he had a gun—so, obviously, you're not going to be able to do that before she takes the stand."

The gun wasn't relevant until Rachel testified that she was in fear of Sarah Ludemann; and that because Joshua had a gun, Sarah might end up with it.

Hebert said that he acknowledged the judge's point, but he added that Joshua Camacho could testify to far more than just the gun, and much of what he had to say was relevant before Rachel took the stand. Hebert said, "Perhaps what I will do is call him before Miss Wade and then subject him to recall, after Miss Wade, to ask him about the gun."

Judge Bulone said that would be fine. Hebert then introduced to the court Rachel's other attorney, Jonathon Wesley Douglas, who presented the judgment of acquittal argument, moving for an immediate acquittal on the grounds that the state had failed to meet its burden of proof.

Motion denied.

Judge Bulone pointed out that there were some decisions that were up to the lawyers, but the decision as to whether or not the defendant should testify was hers and hers alone. Obviously, he added, she should listen to her lawyer's advice regarding the possible advantages and disadvantages of being a witness, but she should not let them make the decision for her. The judge then addressed the defendant directly and asked her if she understood everything he'd just said.

"Yes, sir," she said in a tiny voice.

The judge asked if she needed more time to consider whether or not she wanted to testify. She said she did not.

Hebert asked if Rachel decided to take the stand, would she be allowed to testify that she was the one who told the cops where the knife was?

The judge said she would.

Following the lunch break, Judge Joseph Bulone administered an abbreviated version of the oath to the defendant, and then he asked her a series of questions regarding her intentions to participate in her own defense.

No, she was not under the influence of any drugs or alcohol. Yes, she understood what was going on. Yes, her mind was clear. Yes, she was satisfied with the help and advice of her lawyers. No, she didn't need more time to discuss things with them. Yes, she had reached a decision as to whether or not she wanted to testify.

"Yes, I will testify," she said firmly. She felt this was in her best interest. No one was forcing her to make that decision, and she was making the decision of her own free will. Judge Bulone explained that if, at any time, she changed her mind, all she had to do was say so to her lawyers. She said she understood.

The jury was brought in and the judge gave permission for Jay Hebert to make his opening statement.

* * *

Defense attorney Hebert stood and asked the jurors to recall being children, playing with puzzles. In order to complete the puzzle, he reminded jurors, it was necessary to look at all of the pieces. And that was the defense's intention here, to allow the jurors to see all of the evidence, to hear from all of the witnesses, to see the entire picture. He wanted them to see the big picture so they would be able to make a fair-and-just decision. The defense's case was not meant, in any way, to diminish everyone's appreciation of the tragedy that had occurred to these two families—to the Ludemann family, whose pain was unfathomable, and to the Wade family, whose pain was very difficult to deal with. But that wasn't what this case was about.

"This case is about self-defense," Hebert said. He explained that people have the right to stand their ground and defend themselves. "They have no duty to retreat."

Hebert said that in order to look at self-defense, the jurors would need to look at the whole picture, to hear all of the eyewitnesses—including those whom, for whatever reason, the state had chosen not to call.

The first would be Javier Laboy, a friend of the defendant's who had once dated her. He was a confidant to Rachel Wade and understood the *drama* that led up to the tragedy. It all revolved around Joshua Camacho. It included Sarah, Erin, and Rachel. It involved Facebook, Myspace, and phone calls.

Throughout his opening statement, and on occasion during the defense case, Hebert would refer to the date of the stabbing as "November fourteenth." Names and dates were unusually problematic for the lawyers on both sides. Later in his opening statement, Hebert referred to "Ashley Laboy."

Javier would testify that he received a phone call from Rachel Wade that night and he would describe her demeanor.

Javier suggested that Rachel come over to his house. They could hang out and get something to eat and, as Hebert put it, "defuse the situation." And all of this was important because, in order for the jurors truly to understand what occurred that tragic night, they had to fully understand his client's state of mind.

"What was she thinking? What was she feeling? What was going on in her world?" These were questions Hebert wanted the jurors to ask themselves.

Javier Laboy would confront the testimony of Ashley Lovelady. He was there when Ashley drove by that night, and he saw how she was speeding and how she swerved at Rachel, terrifying his client, heightening her awareness that there was a group of kids out to get her.

Javier would testify that things happened quickly, that he wanted to get Rachel out of there because this was a percolating situation, ready to explode.

But he didn't make it to his house because he was almost to his front door when his attention was drawn to Sarah's van, which barreled around the corner, drifted like a street racer, and screeched to a halt in the middle of the street.

"All hell was about to break loose," Hebert noted.

If the van hadn't stopped so abruptly, Javier would say, it would have struck Rachel or Rachel's car. The van stopped four feet away from Rachel's car in the pitch-black darkness. To demonstrate his point, Hebert aggressively walked toward the jury box, stopping when he was about four feet away.

And then Javier was going to say that contrary to the testimony of Jilica Smith and Janet Camacho, *all three girls piled out of the van simultaneously.* Javier would say that Sarah had come to Rachel, and Rachel had no choice but to defend herself. As difficult as it was to say, Sarah Ludemann was the aggressor, the one to throw the first punch, the one who grabbed Rachel Wade by the hair. When that fight was over, and Sarah went back and sat in the van, Janet Camacho attacked Rachel in an immediate continuation of the first fight.

After Javier, the defense was going to call Joshua Camacho, whom he referred to as "the playa." Joshua, the defense anticipated, would testify that he was not dating Sarah at the time of the stabbing. In fact, he would admit that he was planning on spending the night that night with Rachel. He would say that he wasn't dating any of the girls—Sarah, Rachel, Erin—they were all friends with benefits. Joshua knew all about the "banter and the drama." He would admit that Erin was the "baby mama" of his child. But Joshua would also be able to provide important details regarding what was going on at Janet's house earlier in the evening. He would testify that there was much calling and texting going on, back and forth. He would testify that—again, contrary to the testimony of Jilica and Janet—everyone was smoking marijuana that night. And not just a small amount, either: seven blunts.

Joshua would also expose another one of Janet Camacho's lies, Hebert said, when he testified that there were no kids at Janet's house that night. Janet said the kids were home. Her brother disagreed. He would say it was just them having a party.

Hebert promised that he wasn't going to let Joshua Camacho off easy, and he was going to grill him about his role in this case, that he was the focus of the drama and eventually the violence.

Reminding the jury once again that the defense had no burden whatsoever to prove anything, Hebert announced that the last witness he planned to call was Rachel Wade herself. "This is her day in court," Hebert announced.

At the prosecution table, Lisset Hanewicz slumped back in her seat and made a show of rolling her eyes as Hebert said this. In the spectator section, there were many scornful expressions. While Charlie Ludemann's face remained inscrutable, Gay couldn't hide her disdain.

Rachel was going to talk about the reasons why she felt it was necessary to arm herself on the night of the tragic incident, such as the threats that Sarah made to her, threats that went unrecorded on any cell phones.

"'I will beat your f'n ass,'" Hebert quoted Sarah as saying. "'Stay the "eff" away from my man. Watch your f'n back. I will hurt you. You've got something coming to you, just wait. I will find you. If I were you, I'd watch my back because I know where you live.'"

Hebert said it was unfortunate that his client didn't save any of those messages.

Rachel was going to testify about Joshua's gun. She was in fear of that gun. Joshua had pointed that gun at her when they were alone together, and he used that gun to prevent her from leaving on one occasion. She feared Janet Camacho; she feared Sarah Ludemann; she had no idea where that gun was that night. She feared that gun might come into play.

Unfortunately for his client, there was no official record of Joshua's gun threat. The police were not called, and Joshua wasn't going to admit it. Joshua said Sarah knew about the gun, but that Rachel did not.

So the jurors would have to listen to Rachel. She would tell the truth about that gun. She not only knew about it, but she had been threatened with it. She was in fear of it—*that* night—as the drama came to a head.

"All of those issues go to Rachel's state of mind, that heightened alert that was going on," Hebert said. "She will tell you how she felt that night, that she was in a panic at her house because Sarah's van drove by her apartment and she heard a voice."

Hebert made it seem like the most reasonable thing in

the world. She felt as if she was about to be ambushed, so she went to a kitchen drawer and grabbed a knife. Then she called her friend Javier and went to his house.

"She took the knife for her protection," he said. "You've seen the knife. It is a very common kitchen knife. She will tell you that her hope was that she would show the knife and it would never need to be used." Her game plan was sound. The threat of the knife, the sight of the knife, would frighten those who were out to get her. The knife would defuse the violence. Rachel's attackers would turn around and go away.

Rachel's plan, however, didn't work out. She hadn't counted on being startled by the suddenness of the attack. The van raced around the corner, screeched to a halt, and all three girls piled out and came at her.

As he described the fight itself, Hebert moved from behind his lectern so he was standing very close to the jury box. The fight began quickly, and quickly it was over. Five seconds, tops.

Rachel couldn't see what she was doing during the fight because her hair was being pulled and her head was down. She was punched two or three times in the head by Sarah, so she flailed her hands to defend herself.

"She doesn't even remember. She doesn't even remember stabbing Sarah," Hebert said. "It wasn't until she saw the blood that she freaked out. She saw the blood on the knife, and then, instantaneously, Janet was upon her."

The sight of the blood was what made Rachel quit fighting. She didn't fight back as Janet beat her down. And she didn't know that Sarah was seriously hurt, or that Sarah had died. She did not know until police told her hours later.

Rachel would explain the voice mails she sent to Sarah. Hebert knew how the jury felt when they heard them. "They're just awful," he said. But he asked the jurors to place those recordings in context. Rachel was speaking that way because she was responding to threats that had come at her, and that was the way teenagers talked. There was a generational difference in what was acceptable speech. What might seem to them to be the words of a monster was—to the younger generation—just a girl talking smack.

"Make no mistake. You have to look at the whole puzzle before you can see the picture, and we ask you to look at that picture, and to wait until the very end before you make your decision," Hebert said.

There were two families in the courtroom that would never be the same because of what had happened. If they could turn back the hands of time, they would, of course. But they couldn't. His goal was that justice be carried out, and justice meant in this case that Rachel was acting in self-defense. She was not guilty of second-degree murder.

Hebert thanked the jurors for their attention and sat down.

Judge Bulone said, "Call your first witness."

Hebert said, "The defense calls Javier Laboy."

The young man who took the oath and sat down wore a maroon shirt and black tie, no jacket. Javier Laboy introduced himself to the jury and explained he was a bookkeeper for a car dealership. Jay Hebert began by asking the witness to define his relationship with the defendant. He said they "used to date," that they dated between four and six months, remained friends after they broke up, and then "lost contact." They were not dating at the time of the incident.

Yes, he knew Joshua Camacho. They'd gone to Pinellas Park High School together. He and Joshua, in fact, had "a few problems for a few years." He knew Janet Camacho slightly. He'd only met her once or twice. He'd known Erin

Slothower since middle school, and they had dated for a time. He didn't know Sarah Ludemann at all, but he had been aware of the Rachel/Sarah feud. During the evening of April 14, 2009, he'd been at his mom's home. At some point, he'd received a call from Rachel Wade.

"What was Miss Wade's demeanor when she made that call?" Hebert asked.

The witness turned toward the jury and spoke with solemn sincerity: "She was upset and terrified."

"As a result of that phone call, what did you encourage Miss Wade to do?" Hebert asked.

"I encouraged her to come over to my mom's house."

"It had been four or five months since you had had regular contact with Miss Wade?"

"Yes." Long enough for his house to be "off the radar" of anyone who was looking for her. He told no one she was coming over or that she was there.

At some point, Dustin Grimes, a friend of his, also came over. When Rachel arrived, she was in tears, shaking, scared, unable to keep herself together. She said she'd been threatened and felt his house provided her safe haven. They didn't go inside. They sat out front, just hanging out. They tried to calm her down, made plans to go to Starbucks, to have fun, forget about everything else that was going on. But she didn't calm down. She was on her cell phone, rattled, crying, arguing, pacing back and forth, shaking.

In the gallery, the Ludemanns watched, doing nothing to hide their skepticism. Every once in a while, Charlie would shake his head from side to side, not persuaded.

"At some point in time, did something happen that drew your attention to the street?" Hebert asked.

"Yes, we were talking to Rachel. She was on the phone arguing. Dustin and I figured if she never gets off the phone, we're never going to leave. So, as I was walking up

o her to take the phone, we saw a car coming down the
street. At first it was creeping, really slowly, and then, all
of a sudden, it sped up and swerved toward us. I reached
up and pulled Rachel out of the way. We were right behind
Rachel's car, and it was a good thing. If the car hadn't been
there, me pulling her out of the way wouldn't have done
any good. The car would have hit all of us."

"That car was traveling at a great rate of speed when it
got to you."

"Correct." And yes, he was certain the car *swerved—
toward* them. The car came within four or five feet of them.
The incident altered Rachel's demeanor: "She was in
shock." The incident "escalated" the situation. "I thought we
should get out of there. I told them, 'I'm getting my keys.
We're leaving now.'" He headed back toward his house.
Things happened quickly. He made it almost to the front of
his house when something drew his attention back to the
street: tires screeching, coming around the corner, a van.

Again, in the audience, Charlie Ludemann sat all the
way back in his pew and shook his head in disbelief.

"How was that van driving when it came around the
corner?"

"Like a street racer, drifting around the corner." It might
have been up on two wheels. If the van had been going any
faster, it could have tipped. At the time, Rachel was leaning on the hood of her car, "kind of in the middle."

"It was just a couple of minutes after the car swerved
that the van arrived?"

"Yes."

Hebert set up an easel and the witness was allowed to
step down from the stand to ID and testify regarding
photos. As Jay Hebert was setting up, Lisset Hanewicz got
up from behind the prosecution table and circled Hebert
and the easel once. She eyed the defense attorney suspi-
ciously. She let the jury know through her actions that

she wasn't going to allow any funny business, although what funny business she had in mind was unclear. Hebert proceeded as if he didn't notice her.

The first photo was an aerial shot of Javier Laboy's neighborhood, upon which he identified his mother's house. Laboy then showed which direction the swerving car had come from, and around which corner the van had drifted.

Javier pointed out the location of Rachel's car. Hebert showed the witness two photos of the crime scene, one that was taken with the flash and one without. He asked which one best depicted the way things looked on the night of the incident, which occurred around midnight. Javier said the photo without the flash was most accurate. Because of the position of the streetlight, it was darkest-looking in the direction from which the van came tearing around the corner.

Javier said he and Dustin were up on the lawn in front of his mother's house when the van arrived, not in a position to stop either Sarah or Rachel. "When we saw the van, we ran, but it was too late by the time we got there. The van came to a very quick stop."

All three girls got out almost at the same time. Sarah came around straight for Rachel. Sarah grabbed Rachel by the hair and started punching. Using his own arms to pantomime the action, Javier indicated that Sarah grabbed with her right and punched with her left.

"Rachel began to flail up with her arms."

Again he mimicked the action, and his limp-wristed impression of Rachel's flailing appeared defensive and harmless. Nowhere in his motions was there anything that resembled the stabbing of a knife twice into Sarah's chest.

"Meanwhile, Dustin and me ran up. The other two girls were standing to the side."

"When Sarah got out of the vehicle, who was the aggressor?"

"Sarah."

"Who was the first one to throw a punch?"

"Sarah."

"How many punches did you see Sarah throw?"

"She threw a lot, but I think she landed two or three."

"Punches to the head?"

"Yes."

"Did you know if Sarah had a weapon?"

"I didn't."

Immediately following the five-second confrontation, Rachel took two steps back. Sarah got back into her car and Janet began hitting Rachel in the back of her head with her shoe. Yes, *immediately*. Between the altercations, no more than half a second had passed. They were "continuous events."

Like Sarah before her, Janet Camacho was the clear aggressor. Javier saw no knife, not during the Rachel/Sarah fight or the Rachel/Janet fight. He didn't, at that point, know Sarah had been seriously injured. No one did. There did come a time when he realized it, but that wasn't until after Janet had already started beating down Rachel.

"And, if you will, please be very specific. Please show me where the confrontation took place."

On the photo, Laboy pointed to a spot between the vehicles, about midway between the van's headlights. Since, according to his testimony, Rachel had been leaning against the front of her car when the van pulled up, it was clear that Sarah had to travel farther than Rachel to reach the spot.

Janet had been furious, cursing, first in English, then in Spanish. She was hitting Rachel with her shoe the whole time. At no time did Javier see Jilica Smith pulling Janet back.

"Did you see Rachel's shirt get torn off?"

"Her shirt got torn later."

"There was a second fight with Janet a little bit later?"

"Yes, there was."

"There was an interval when the fighting stopped?"

"Yes, the fighting stopped when we realized that Sarah had been hurt. After two, three seconds it started up again."

"When it started up again, who was the aggressor?"

"Janet."

Hebert asked the witness to describe what had happened.

"When we realized that Sarah was hurt, Janet went to check. Then me and Dustin went to check. Janet ran back, so I never made it to her. I took my shirt off, and when I turned around, I saw Rachel on the floor and Janet was dragging her across my mom's lawn by her hair."

"Rachel had been hit, struck, beaten down?"

"I guess so. I'm not sure. It was chaos."

"Don't guess. The only thing you saw was the hair pulling and the dragging across the lawn?"

"Yes."

He never saw Rachel laughing or smirking. She just had a blank look on her face.

At some point in time, the police arrived. Javier and Dustin were separated by the police, put on opposite sides of the street, and were instructed not to talk to each other, not to touch their phones, and to wait for further instructions.

"Since this incident happened, you have visited Rachel Wade?"

Javier said he had. He'd talked to her on the phone and sent her letters. Everything he'd said on the stand was the truth. He was not there to lie on Rachel Wade's behalf.

"You are merely telling the jury what you saw on April fifteenth?"

"I am."

"No further questions."

* * *

On cross-examination, Lisset Hanewicz smiled as she said to Javier Laboy, "Good afternoon."

"Hi, how ya doin'?" Javier replied.

That would be it for the niceties.

Javier testified that he had dated the defendant from some time in November 2008 until maybe the first couple weeks of January 2009, and then for a couple of months, but that Javier and Rachel were not boyfriend and girlfriend at the time of the incident. Then they had a relationship once again after the fatal Ludemann encounter.

"You were planning to marry her, correct?"

"Correct."

"Are you still planning to marry her?"

"No."

"You were planning to have kids, correct?"

"Correct."

"You had the names of the kids picked out?"

Hebert interrupted and asked for a sidebar.

While the attorneys gathered near Judge Bulone's bench, Javier looked down, and his chest heaved with a deep sigh.

When the sidebar concluded, Hanewicz asked Javier if he remembered giving a deposition on October 21, 2009, during the time when he and the defendant were boyfriend and girlfriend. Javier said he remembered.

"And you were asked a question at that deposition about your relationship with Rachel. Isn't that true?"

"Yes." Javier already looked beaten down by the prosecutor's questions.

"You were there. I was there. And you took an oath that day, just as you did today, and that day you denied having a relationship with her, correct?"

"Correct."

"So why should we believe that you don't have a relationship with her anymore?"

"We stopped talking, broke things off a couple of months ago. Now I'm in a new relationship, and we plan, after this is all over, on moving away from here."

"You made this decision after a hearing at which I confronted you with the same issue, correct?"

"Correct."

Javier had now admitted twice to lying about his relationship with Rachel during the preliminary hearing. That was enough for Hanewicz, so she moved on to her next point.

"Let's talk a little bit about what happened that evening. On direct you talked about how you did not see a knife. But you did see the knife before the fight, correct?"

"No."

"You never saw the knife, and told Rachel to put the knife away?"

"She told me about it. I didn't see it," Javier said, wiping his palm across his brow and then placing it over his mouth. He grimaced, as if his stomach hurt.

"You knew she had a knife?"

"I knew she had a knife."

"But you never saw it at any time that evening?"

"Not until the police found it."

"And at the hearing, you said the same thing, that you never saw the knife, right?"

"Yes."

"Have you listened to the tape of your 911 call?"

"No."

"Would it surprise you that you talk about the knife you saw in her hand during the 911 call?"

"Yes."

"Okay, well let's play it."

After a brief pause for the audio equipment to be set up, the court listened to Javier's 911 call, the one in which he said, "We have someone on the floor who has been stabbed. We need an ambulance. Please help."

Further on in the tape, the dispatcher asked the caller where the knife was. He replied, "It's in her hand. You better hurry up and get here quick."

Despite the fact that the point the prosecutor was trying to make was specific—had or had not the witness seen the knife—the *entire* tape was played. So the jury also got to hear Javier say, "They tried to jump her" and "She pulled out her pocketknife trying to defend herself."

At one point during the playing of the tape, the defendant coolly examined her nails. At another she used a tissue to wipe away invisible tears.

When the tape finished, Hanewicz started in again: "You just testified that you never saw a knife. You heard that tape. You did see a knife, didn't you?"

Javier replied, "They asked me what happened. Dustin told me she had the knife, so I told them she had the knife."

"'She pulled out a pocketknife! She pulled out a pocketknife!'" Hanewicz held up the murder weapon. "Does that look like a pocketknife to you?"

"That's what I heard."

"That's what you heard? That's not what you told her!"

Hanewicz was yelling, and her questions, if you could call them questions, were losing their focus. For example, she ignored the obvious conclusion that if the witness gave a faulty description of the knife, it was a further indication that he'd never seen it. Hebert objected to this "question" on the grounds that it was argumentative and Judge Bulone sustained.

Hanewicz used that break in her rhythm to her advantage and freshly attacked the witness's credibility.

"You are here because you have feelings for Rachel and you don't want to see her get in trouble, right? You are lying for her."

"I am *not* lying for her," the witness replied firmly.

"You're not lying for her? You admitted that you lied about your relationship with her. You lied about the knife. . . ." Hanewicz paused, but the witness just stared at her. "Is there an answer?" she asked.

"Could you repeat the question?"

"Didn't you just lie about the knife?"

"No. You asked me if I saw the knife. I never saw the knife. Dustin told me she still had the knife."

Frustrated that she had not won this point, Hanewicz began yelling her next question before Javier could finish his answer, so she was shouting over him.

Judge Bulone decided he'd had enough.

"All right. Let's just calm down," the judge said in a soothing tone. "Let's ask nice, calm questions and nice, calm answers."

Hanewicz was quieter, but she wasn't happy about it. And, instead of moving on to a point she might win, she continued to beat the dead horse, just more softly: "You heard on the 911 call that you said the knife was in her hand. Yes?"

The witness stared at her.

"You want me to play it again?" the prosecutor asked.

"No, I was just waiting for more of a question," Javier said.

"Is that a yes?"

"Yes, that is what I said."

Despite the fact that the jury had twice heard Javier give his explanation for why he mentioned the knife during the 911 call—even though he hadn't actually seen it—and the reason why he called it a pocketknife, when it was actually a kitchen knife, Hanewicz's next question was "How can we believe anything you say? You lied!"

"Objection."

"Sustained."

Finally the prosecutor got the idea. She'd lost. So she quickly tried to change the subject, although it wasn't clear what the new subject was. Hanewicz asked, "You said that she took a step back?"

This presumably referred to Rachel stepping back, but who could be certain? It was also uncertain when "she" stepped back, or when the witness was supposed to have said "she" stepped back.

Javier gave the prosecutor a big break when he simply replied, "Yes."

"Did you tell that to the detective?"

"I honestly don't remember."

Again frustrated, Hanewicz resorted to a hypothetical question: "Is that something you would have told the detective when you met with the detective that night, that she took a step back?"

Javier said he didn't remember. It had been a hectic night and he had no clue what he told the detective.

Hanewicz put the "step back" line of questioning behind her. She finally moved to a subject where she had a shot at scoring points.

"Isn't it true that you testified earlier that Janet was still in the van when the incident happened between Sarah and Rachel?"

"Yes."

"And when they separated, that was the point when Janet got out of the van?"

"No, she got out before that. I'm going to try to explain it, to make it more clear. Sarah came up from the side and grabbed Rachel by the hair. As soon as she grabbed the hair, the other two girls came out, and as soon as Rachel and Sarah separated, Janet came in contact with Rachel."

"Do you remember your deposition on October 27, 2009?"

"Somewhat, yes."

"Somewhat? All right. I am going to show you page twenty-nine of the deposition and see if this refreshes your memory. Start reading from line eight through fourteen. . . . Does that refresh your memory?"

"Yes."

"The question was where was Janet at that point in time, and you said she was still in the passenger side of the vehicle, right?"

"Yes."

"Then you went on to say she got out after they began to separate a bit. That was when she got out."

"Yes, after they separated a bit, after she started hitting her, after they started flailing around."

On redirect Jay Hebert freshly established that the witness and defendant were not currently dating; the witness was in a relationship, but not with the defendant; and from the time of the deposition until the present, Rachel Wade had been in custody. The implication was that a relationship with a woman who was in jail was a lot like no relationship at all.

As Rachel listened, she leaned her head on her hand, her eyelids heavy.

"You have not been physically with Rachel, face-to-face, since April 14, 2009, have you?"

"Correct."

Hebert asked Javier to explain for the jury what he was trying to say earlier about the tape of the 911 call.

"Everything was so crazy. The operator was asking me questions. I was asking Dustin, and anybody else who was listening, questions, trying to answer the operator's questions. Dustin told me she still had the knife in her hand, and that was what I told the operator."

"Did you ever see the knife?"

"I did not. I thought it was a pocketknife until the detectives pulled it off the roof."

Javier emphasized that he was not lying to the operator. It was obvious when he called that Sarah had been stabbed, and he was describing to the operator what was going on in real time. Up until he heard the tape, moments before, however, he had not remembered telling the operator that Rachel was defending herself. Everything he'd said was the truth, and he wouldn't lie to get Rachel out of trouble.

"Defense calls Joshua Camacho to the stand."

Several jurors perked up. This was the guy all the girls loved. This was the guy at the center of all the fuss, the center of this violent and tragic solar system.

If those jurors were anticipating a tall and handsome fellow, the man of every girl's dreams, they were sadly disappointed. Joshua was not very big; he was kind of scrawny. Though he had what might be called a "pretty boy" face, he didn't immediately strike anyone as God's gift. He was sharply dressed, though, in black and white—white shirt, black vest, and tie—and wore a defiant expression on his face.

"Mr. Camacho, are you working now?" Jay Hebert inquired.

"No." Javier had a surprisingly deep voice—gravelly, as if he'd just gargled with rocks.

"Where do you reside, sir?"

Joshua tilted his head to indicate that he either hadn't heard the question or hadn't understood it.

"Where do you *live*?" Hebert quickly added.

Joshua said he'd been living with his parents for the past few months. During that time, he hadn't left Florida.

Yes, he knew Rachel Wade, since elementary school. Yes, they had dated.

Yes, he had dated Sarah.

Yes, he'd had a child with a woman named Erin Slothower.

No, he was not dating Sarah on April 14, 2009. Yes, he was sure.

"How would you describe your relationship with Sarah Ludemann on that date?"

"Friends with benefits."

It was the defense attorney's turn to tilt his head. "I'm sorry. I didn't hear that," Hebert said.

Joshua repeated the phrase, this time just a smidgen louder.

"Could you explain what you mean by that?"

"Not dating," the witness explained impatiently. "They could see whoever they wanted to see."

Back to the one-word answers:

Had he ever been friends with benefits with Erin Slothower? No.

At some point in time, were he and Rachel Wade friends with benefits? Yes.

"You asked your girlfriends to fight for you, didn't you, sir?"

"No, I did not." He had never even talked about them fighting each other. Anyone who said he had was lying.

Hebert asked Joshua what his phone number had been at the time of the incident. Joshua said he didn't remember. Wasn't it true that Sarah had Joshua's phone when she was stabbed?

Not true, Joshua replied.

"Were you aware of all the drama that was going on between Rachel and Sarah?"

"That night?"

"For the entire previous six months."

"Yes."

"Tell me about that."

"They would go back and forth on Myspace or calling."

"What were they calling about?"

"Arguing."

"What were they arguing about?"

"About who was I going to be with."

The witness continued to insist that he had never encouraged those girls to fight. At the time of the incident, he wasn't dating *any* of them.

"You were playing the field, or you were having friends with benefits?"

"Friends with benefits," Joshua replied. His voice held a hint of pride. No, he had no idea how that made those girls feel. He didn't think they were upset with him. Just each other.

"They didn't send you texts asking, 'Why would you do this to me?'"

"No."

"'If you love me, why are you doing these things to me?' You don't remember any of these texts?"

"No."

Hebert's voice had been soothingly calm up until this point, but now there sounded an edge of frustration in it—perhaps annoyance: "You don't remember stacks and stacks of texts and phone calls and drama, all about you and this relationship?"

"No."

Hebert left the lectern and walked over to the defense

table, where he whispered something to a colleague, then returned.

"Getting back to that last question I asked you, your testimony today is that you don't remember any texts whatsoever from the girls about the problem or the drama, or anything like that? You don't remember anything like that?"

"No."

"Let me ask you this. Do you remember anything about phone calls from any of these girls?"

"No."

"Sarah called you and said she was upset by Rachel? Rachel called and said she was upset about Sarah? Anything like that?"

"No."

Hebert gave up, moving on. "Let's talk about that night. You do remember that night, right?"

"A little bit."

"A little bit," Hebert echoed. He leaned across the top of the lectern and rested his head on his hand. "Were ya drinkin'?"

"Yes."

Hebert stood up straight again. "And where were you drinking?"

Joshua said he was at his sister's house. Just he and Janet and Sarah were there. He drank vodka. Maybe a "cup or two."

"Do you remember, maybe, five shots?"

"I don't remember."

"Do you remember having your deposition taken in this matter?"

Judge Bulone interrupted the examination to remind Hebert that since he was the one who called the witness, he could not use previous statements to impeach Joshua. He could, however, use the earlier statement to refresh the witness's memory.

"That is what I intend to do, Your Honor," the defense attorney replied.

"Proceed," the judge said.

Hebert handed a transcript of the deposition to Joshua and told him which section to read silently. When the witness was finished, Hebert asked, "Does that refresh your memory as to what you had to drink that night?"

"No, sir. I don't remember."

He didn't remember being asked how much vodka he had drunk. He didn't remember saying he had five shots. In fact, he didn't remember giving a deposition.

"You don't remember what you were drinking that night?" Hebert asked.

"I said vodka. I don't remember how much," the witness replied, now himself impatient.

Yes, he was smoking marijuana that night. Sarah was smoking, too. They smoked together.

No, he didn't talk to Rachel that night. No, he didn't tell Rachel he wanted to spend the night with her. No, he didn't tell Rachel he wanted to have sex with her and sleep with her that night.

Charlie Ludemann had his glasses on his forehead and his eyes closed; his left hand gripped tightly at the handle of his metal cane. At his right, Gay was smiling, perhaps at what a piece of work Joshua was, perhaps at the notion that Rachel's defense wasn't getting what it wanted out of the "pretty boy" witness.

"Did you observe Janet smoking marijuana?" Hebert asked.

"I don't remember," Joshua replied. "Me and Sarah smoked it."

Hebert asked permission to approach the witness. He handed Joshua a page from his deposition transcript and asked the witness to read to himself a selected passage.

"Does that refresh your memory?"

"No, it does not."

Hebert took the transcript back and read aloud. Asked who was smoking, Joshua had said, in addition to himself and Sarah, his sister and a guy named Rob were also smoking.

Did Joshua recall saying that? He did not.

Yes, there were just the four of them in the house that night. Janet's kids had been home during the day, but not that night.

"After you found out about this incident, you threatened to kill Rachel Wade, didn't you?"

"Yes."

Hebert said, "That's all I have, Judge."

"Thank you," Judge Bulone replied. "Cross-examination?"

Lisett Hanewicz went right to work.

No, he wasn't there when the incident happened between Rachel and Sarah.

No, he didn't even know what was going on.

Yes, he made that threat after he learned what happened to Sarah.

No further questions.

Hebert said that he had no redirect, but he wanted the witness to remain on standby, as he might want to recall him to the stand later in the day. Judge Bulone instructed Joshua to remain either in the witness room or right outside the courtroom until he was recalled.

Some spectators wondered what Hebert had hoped to accomplish by calling Joshua Camacho. Was the witness supposed to corroborate parts of Rachel's story? If so, he did not do a great job. He couldn't remember any of the drama. He couldn't even remember his own deposition.

If the defense wanted Joshua to back up Rachel's assertion that the insulting and threatening messages had gone both ways, Joshua was completely unhelpful—and Hebert couldn't even establish the threats went both ways through phone records because, according to Hebert, Rachel used a "fly-by-night" phone company, which didn't keep records.

For her testimony, Rachel Wade wore a white shirt with a large collar over a black shirt and black pants. When she was called by the prosecution, she couldn't just get up and move to the front of the room. Because of her prisoner status, she had to wait patiently for an armed escort to the witness stand.

She took the oath with her right pinky crooked outward. She said "I do" in a tiny voice.

The full courtroom was silent, all spectators hanging on Rachel's every word. It would have been easy to miss something. Rachel spoke quickly and softly; attentiveness was required.

In many murder cases, the defendant does not testify on his or her own behalf. But in this case, Rachel Wade's testimony was necessary. She was claiming self-defense and needed to describe the circumstances of Sarah Ludemann's death.

"Good afternoon, ma'am," Judge Bulone said to the witness.

"Good afternoon, Your Honor," Rachel replied, still sounding meek and very couldn't-hurt-a-fly.

"Make sure your answers are good and loud so that everyone can hear," Judge Bulone said.

"Yes, Your Honor," she replied, turning her head briefly toward the bench, then returning to face forward, poised for her lawyer's first question.

Hebert told her to turn toward the jury, state her name, and spell her last name. She obeyed.

"Good afternoon, Miss Wade," Hebert said, and she returned the greeting. "You, of course, know why you are here?"

"Yes."

"You are here because you want to tell the jury your side to the story?"

"Yes."

Jay Hebert established that his client was twenty years old, nineteen at the time of the incident. She was born in Largo, grew up in Pinellas Park, and went to Pinellas Park High School. She'd studied on her own and received her GED in 2008. She was also working as a kennel assistant at a pet facility and at Applebee's. She had one sibling, an older brother who was twenty-four. Her mother and father were still alive.

She met Joshua Camacho in first or second grade. They'd gone through elementary school, middle and high school together. They began dating in 2008. She had gotten her own apartment, and he moved in with her. During their cohabitation, there had been issues regarding Joshua's relationships with other women.

Rachel said, "I found out that he previously dated a girl named Erin Slothower and he had a child with her. And he dated a girl named Sarah Ludemann. And when me and him started to date, I began to get harassing phone calls, threats, made to me."

"You had drama, not just from Sarah, but from Erin as well?"

"Yes."

"But you stayed with Joshua?"

"Yes, I did."

"Are you familiar with the term 'friends with benefits'?"

"Yes."

"What does that term mean to you as you sit here today in your generation?"

"It means that you aren't dating exclusively and you can see other people."

"It means you can have sex with other people without cheating on anybody?"

"Yes."

"Were you aware that that was part of Joshua's philosophy?"

"At the beginning of our relationship, no. But when he continued to see and see the other girls, yes."

"Did he cheat on you with Erin?"

"Yes, he did."

"Did he cheat on Erin with you when he was dating Erin?"

"I'm not positive that they were dating, but not that I'm aware of, not while we were together."

"Did he cheat on Sarah with you when he was with Sarah?"

"They were seeing each other. As far as I was concerned, they weren't dating."

There was clearly a distinction in Rachel's mind between "seeing" and "dating." Both included sex, but "dating" came with expectations—or perhaps only pretensions—of monogamy.

"That was because he told you they weren't dating so he could see you?" Hebert asked.

"Yes."

Rachel testified that on the night of the incident, it was Joshua's plan to come over, have sex, and spend the night with her.

Yes, she knew his sister Janet. No, she didn't find Janet pleasant. Rachel explained, "There were a couple of times when I went over there to the house, where he stayed with her sometimes, and spent the night, babysat her kids. But after a couple of times of that, she came over to my house and she told me I was a bad influence on him and she didn't want me to see him anymore. And if I did, she was going to come after me."

"Can you tell me some of the specific threats that Janet made to you?"

"She said that she was going to kick my ass, and she actually came to my door of my apartment, where I lived alone, and tried to break my door down. Other than that, she threatened me, not physically, but verbally over the phone."

"What sort of verbal threats?"

"Just that she was going to come after me and to stay the 'eff' away from her brother," Rachel said, censoring herself.

"Let's talk about the threats that might have been made toward you by Sarah Ludemann. These threats were ongoing?"

"Yes."

"And they went on for months at a time?"

"Yes."

"Obviously, you've been sitting here in court and you've listened to threats you made on tape. Can you tell me some of the threats that were made toward you by Sarah?"

"She said she was going to kick my ass, same thing. She knew where I lived, that I should stay away from her man, and that I shouldn't put pictures up on my Myspace because she had found out where I lived because of that, and she *would* come to my house."

"Did she ever threaten to beat your fuckin' ass?" Hebert did not censor himself.

She had, more than once, probably more than ten times, and that went on throughout the buildup to this situation. The threats she dished out were similar in tone to those she received, same kind of language. That was the way she and Sarah talked. When she talked to Sarah, it was *never* pleasant.

"Tell me about the Myspace. Tell the jury about the Myspace."

"When I was dating Joshua, on Myspace I did like a lot of couples do and posted a lot of pictures of us. I bought a dog for him and we took pictures of the dog. I would get frequent comments from her for putting up the pictures and [that] I was an idiot for putting up the pictures because she was dating him." Rachel felt *harassed*.

Hebert let out a long sigh, as if he were hesitant to introduce an unpleasant topic: "Now, during the time you were dating Joshua, did you ever see a gun?"

At the prosecution table, Lisset Hanewicz sat up a little bit straighter when she heard that question. She immediately began to scribble notes on her yellow legal pad.

The defendant answered the question in the affirmative.

"Could you tell the jury about that?"

Rachel explained that, personally, she did not like guns. "I had a friend who got shot once," she said. "And Joshua brought the gun into my house, and I didn't even care for a BB gun, and he brought a gun in a backpack one night when he came to spend the night, and I told him to get out of my house with it. And when I did, he said he had been joking about, you know, how he didn't care, and waving it around, and pointed it at me and told me that I would never leave him because we were actually having a conversation about how he was seeing other girls." Her words came out rapid-fire, like a babbling brook of consciousness.

Yes, he pointed the gun at her. She took it seriously and was afraid.

No, she'd never seen the gun at Janet's house.

"You didn't break up with him when he pointed the gun at you, did you?"

"Actually," the defendant responded, "at the time we

weren't seeing each other exclusively. We were just kind of back and forth."

Hebert asked his client to explain the five voice mails that they'd heard earlier. She'd said some pretty awful things. What had she been thinking?

Rachel replied that she'd been upset; she'd been receiving harassing phone calls. "Sarah said she was going to kick my ass and I just retaliated out of anger. She'd harassed me. She'd come by my house, and I was upset when I said it. Truthfully, I was scared."

"Had you ever had a physical confrontation with Sarah—with Sarah and a group of her friends?"

Rachel told the Taco Bell/Silly String story: how she and Courtney Richards were chased by a car with six girls in it, how they were forced off the road, jumped, and how Richards's external mirror was smashed.

"Were you harassed at your place of work at Applebee's?"

"Yes, Sarah and her friends would come in, as well as Erin and her friends, and they would bump into me. I was a waitress. They'd spill beer on my customers or they'd complain about me to my manager and make things up. They would bother me while I was in the process of trying to serve my customers. We had karaoke night and they would go up and sing songs. 'Girl Fight,' I think, was one of the songs, and it was just a constant ongoing problem at my place of work."

It was *so* stressful. All of those incidents, the fear of being attacked, were on Rachel's mind that April 14, but she did not set out that day to kill anyone. She first became concerned that day when she was in her apartment and received private phone calls from an unknown caller. She finally answered one, thinking maybe it could have been Joshua. But it was Sarah, who said something about being outside Rachel's house.

At first, Rachel wasn't sure if Sarah was bluffing; but

after she hung up, she heard a car beeping outside. She heard screaming females. This was before Rachel went to Javier's house, the same night that Joshua said he wanted to come over and spend the night, a fact that couldn't have pleased Sarah if she'd known. As a result of the phone call and screams from outside—which Hebert referred to as the "mayhem"—Rachel debated over what to do. She called a couple of her friends. One was sick and the other was "with someone," so she called Javier Laboy, who offered her sanctuary. She didn't call her parents. She didn't call the police. She lived alone and she just wanted to get away from her apartment. So, upset, crying, and scared, she called Javier. She told him she didn't know what was going on, but they were outside her house. She asked if she could come over, and he said sure.

"At that moment, you were in fear of the situation with Sarah and Janet and everyone else that might be involved?"

"Yes."

"What did you do before you left your house?"

"I grabbed a knife." It was a kitchen knife that had been on the kitchen counter. She put it in her purse.

Rachel testified that she felt a need to arm herself because she'd never been in an altercation like that before. She figured if they approached her and she had the knife, they would either be satisfied that "I was scared, or they would just leave because they would be scared." The knife was for protection because she was "in fear," because she *didn't* want to fight. She told no one where she was going. Only Javier knew, a guy she had dated about three and a half months earlier. She wanted her location to be a secret. She wanted to go somewhere where she was unlikely to be found, and she didn't think anyone would look for her at Javier's.

"You arrived at Javier's house and there was calling going on and texting?"

"Yes. Calling. No texting."

Hebert prompted his client to admit that she called Joshua, and Joshua still wanted to come over and spend the night with her.

"He mentioned that, yes."

"Did you notice that Josh was starting to sound a little bit more intoxicated?"

"Yeah. I didn't know what he was doing. I couldn't really tell what he was doing, but yes. It got to where I couldn't read him. He was slurring a bit."

"So you pull up at Javier's house. Is Javier there?"

"Yes."

"His friend Dustin—did he arrive at some point in time?"

"Yes."

Rachel, Javier, and Dustin were out in front of the house. Perhaps there was a juror or two who thought just then that Rachel was not acting like a girl who was hiding. She was acting more like someone in need of backup. Hebert did not ask her why she didn't go inside. Instead, he showed her a photo taken the night of the incident, and she identified the red car as hers.

"At some point in time, a car drives by. Do you remember that?"

She did. She'd been standing near the back end of her car, speaking to Javier and Dustin. She looked up and a car was driving normally down the street. Then it swerved. She didn't recognize the car. It wasn't a car she'd seen before. She did recognize that there was a single female in it. The car swerved so that it drove only a couple of feet away from her. Javier had to pull her out of the way. Rachel went from feeling safe to unsafe in a flash. She couldn't hide. They were *hunting her down*. After the swerving car, she went in her car and took the knife out of her purse. A few minutes later, a van came around the corner.

"Please tell the jury where you were sitting."

"Toward the middle of the hood of my car," the defendant said.

Again, some jurors thought, *Not hiding*.

The van flew around the corner, no stopping, and headed toward her. It stopped about five feet from her. It would've hit her, chopped her in two, if it hadn't quick-stopped. Yes, she was afraid. She was "in fear," as Jay Hebert liked to say.

She'd seen that green van before, and she was able to recognize the two girls in the front. Sarah was driving and Janet was in the passenger seat. There was a third girl, sitting in the backseat, whom Rachel didn't know, but she later learned was Jilica Smith.

"Sarah got out of the car first and walked around to the front of the car. Janet and the other girl also got out of the car and started to walk toward me. Janet got out of the passenger side and Jilica walked around the back of the van and approached my right side. Sarah immediately engaged me in a fight. She grabbed me by my hair. I slid off the front of the car, and I was just on the edge of it. I was just about two steps in front of my car and she grabbed me by the top of the head and had me slightly bent forward, and she hit me about three times."

"Who came at who?"

"Sarah came at me."

"She attacked you?"

"Yes."

Hebert showed defense exhibit number two to Rachel. It was a photo taken by police that night of Rachel's car, taken from the front. Hebert asked her where the fight occurred, and Rachel pointed to a spot on the street about three feet in front of her car and just on the passenger side of center. The fight happened quickly, she explained, and she was knocked down.

"When you got up, you had the knife?"

"I had to grab it because it was on the hood of my car, yes."

Hebert unashamedly led his witness, putting the words he wanted to hear in his client's mouth: "You had the knife out. You were showing the knife, hoping it would scare her . . . warn her?"

"Yes."

Janet and Jilica saw the knife. Sarah saw the knife. Rachel didn't even grab the knife until she'd been hit three times in the head. Sarah was still hitting her after she grabbed the knife, and Rachel swung her arms back in retaliation—to defend herself. She didn't know if Sarah had a weapon. She didn't know if Janet was armed. Either one of them might have had a knife or a bat or a gun. Even if they weren't armed, they could have beaten Rachel to death with their fists. So Rachel defended herself.

"When did you know that you had stabbed Sarah Ludemann?"

"When I heard Jilicia," Rachel said, mispronouncing the name to sound like "Jilisha."

"When I heard her scream and I looked down and I saw blood, I knew. I didn't know who had been stabbed or where. I have no recollection of actually doing it. I heard Jilicia scream that Sarah had been stabbed, but Sarah had already walked away and she was no longer in front of me to physically see that."

"Did you personally see blood and know something had happened?"

"Yes."

"And that whole contact with Sarah lasted about how long?"

"Couple seconds."

"Did you ever mean to stab her, to kill her, to murder her?"

"No."

"Almost immediately after your fight with Sarah, you were attacked by Janet?"

"Yes."

"About how long was there between your fight with Sarah and your fight with Janet?"

"About a second."

"Had anybody mentioned that Sarah had been hurt?"

"Yes."

"Was that after you fought with Janet?"

"No, Janet attacked me at the same point in time that Jilicia was yelling."

"So you were getting beaten down by . . ."

"Janet."

Hebert noted that Rachel was afraid of Janet Camacho, didn't know what Janet was going to do, didn't know if Janet had a weapon, but she didn't try to stab Janet.

"Why was that?" he asked.

Struggling to get the words out, Rachel sputtered, "Because I'd already seen the blood on the knife and I never had any intention of using it. I didn't want to hurt anybody." So she let Janet beat her up. Not once, but twice.

"How would you describe your emotions when you saw the blood and the whole scene?" Hebert quickly decided that the question was too open-ended. He wanted absolutely to govern which words Rachel used in her testimony, so he added, "Were you in a state of shock?"

She was. She'd had no idea what had happened. She just knew somebody was stabbed. She knew it was Sarah, but she couldn't see her. And she threw the knife on the roof. After that, she was just "being quiet." When the police came, she went over and sat on the bench. She'd seen cops get out of their cars with guns drawn.

"And did you cooperate with their investigation?"

"Yes."

At the state's table, Hanewicz wrote something on her notepad in large letters.

In the audience, Charlie and Gay Ludemann glared at Rachel. He had a deep frown; she had a bemused smile—the *audacity* of this girl to be such a bald-faced liar.

On the other side of the courtroom, Rachel's father sat with his arm around his wife's shoulders, literally holding her up. Rachel's mom, wiping away tears, was seemingly without bones, careening through a never-ending tunnel of despair.

Rachel said that at no time that night did she feel she had any choice but to defend herself. She had no idea what might have happened to her if she hadn't brought the knife. She might have been seriously injured or suffered great bodily harm.

Hebert's questions ignored the fact that Rachel had been beaten up, anyway, twice in fact—attacks that left her barely marked.

Hyperbole now painted the defense attorney's urgent queries: "The blows that you inflicted, those blows were done in self-defense after you were struggling several times with the aggressor, Sarah Ludemann?"

Several times? The whole fight lasted five seconds! Still, Rachel replied in the affirmative. This exchange was filed in the jury BS file—right next to Rachel's claim that she'd been punched twice before she grabbed for the knife.

Hebert wanted to talk size. Rachel stood five-four; and at the time of the incident, she weighed somewhere in the vicinity of 110 or 115 pounds. Sarah was much bigger. Taller. Heavier. Stronger. When Sarah hit Rachel, she hit her in the head.

Hebert asked, "Do you remember if Joshua ever instructed you to carry a knife for protection?"

"Yes, he did. While he was living with me, he did, but especially after he moved out and I was living in a new apartment," Rachel replied. "He used to tell me to keep a knife on me, when he wasn't around, for protection."

Janet had testified that Rachel smirked after stabbing Sarah. Rachel denied that.

"Did Joshua tell his girlfriends, including you, that 'if you love me, you will fight for me'?"

"Yes. That was his philosophy. He didn't want us to go against him. He wanted us to fight against each other, and not be mad at him for what he was doing."

"No further questions, Your Honor," Hebert said, his tone indicating that if the jury didn't recognize the truth after hearing that, they never would.

"Ms. Hanewicz, cross-examination?" Judge Bulone asked.

Over at the prosecutors' table, Lisset Hanewicz was slightly coiled, a body of potential energy. It was go time, and the prosecutor was ready to pounce.

"Good afternoon," Hanewicz said icily.

"Good afternoon," Rachel said, trying to gather herself, gird her loins for the onslaught she knew was coming.

Hanewicz's tone shifted immediately. She was all at once sarcastic and incredulous, but mostly accusing. She pointed a finger of guilt at Rachel with each and every question.

"You said during direct examination that you cooperated with the investigation."

"Yes."

Wasn't her cooperation lying? Hadn't she lied to the detective that night? She gave a detailed statement and left out the fact that she'd had a knife. How was that cooperating? The detective had to confront her about the fact that she'd had a knife. Rachel had been forced to admit she lied. How was that cooperating?

"I never said that I didn't have a knife. I—I just never mentioned it."

"You never *mentioned* it! It was like a small detail that you completely forgot, right?"

"I didn't forget."

"You said you don't remember the point when you stabbed her."

"I don't physically remember stabbing her," the defendant insisted.

"You remember everything else!" Hanewicz said, trying to show the other side of Rachel's personality. The prosecutor wanted the jury to see and hear the girl who'd left those messages on Sarah's phone machine. She waited for a response but got none, just a steady gaze and a couple of sniffles, so she continued.

"You remember everything before. You remember all of the threats. You remember everything after, right?"

"Yes."

"You just don't remember . . . *that*."

"Yes."

"Then how can you remember if you acted in self-defense?"

"I just remember swinging my arms. I don't remember stabbing her."

"You had the knife in your hand, right?"

"Yes."

"Isn't that con-*veeeeeen*-ient," the prosecutor said. "So let me get this straight. You lied to the police officer. You never told the police officer that you couldn't remember stabbing her. Isn't that true?"

Rachel's sniffling stopped. She looked at her nails. "Yes," she said.

"That was just an additional fact that you brought out later, correct?"

"Yes."

"You never told the police officer about anyone threatening you with a firearm, correct? In fact, today during your testimony is the first time that you ever mentioned it, correct?"

"I've never been asked about it before."

"Do you remember having a hearing in open court? It wasn't that long ago, in late March, and you took an oath, the same oath you took here today, and you talked about the same issues you talked about today. You talked about the fear and all of the things that scared you, the threats and everything, right?"

"Yes."

"But you never mentioned a firearm."

"It was Joshua, and not Sarah, that threatened me with that."

Jay Hebert asked for a sidebar, which broke Hanewicz's rhythm. Sarah's father was taking notes. When the sidebar ended, Hanewicz moved on to a new topic.

"How were you holding the knife, Sarah? I mean, Rachel . . . sorry."

Rachel said she was holding it outward. "To the side, but out, with the blade pointing out."

Hanewicz asked if she'd ever held it so the blade was back, and the witness said she had not. Did she remember giving testimony in a courtroom on March 30 of this year? Rachel did. Hanewicz had the defendant silently read a transcript of the March 30 hearing. Her recollection refreshed, Rachel admitted, at that time, she'd said that the knife was "facing behind her."

Hanewicz asked, "The only one you intended on stabbing that night was Sarah, right?"

Rachel replied she had no intention of stabbing anyone.

Hanewicz brought up the "stab you and your Mexican boyfriend" comment, and Rachel was adamant: "I did *not* say that."

Hanewicz wanted to get it straight. Rachel had the knife, and she went at Sarah with it, but she didn't think anything would happen? Rachel repeated that she didn't plan on stabbing Sarah. She hadn't thought Sarah would approach her—because she had the knife.

Rachel's testimony had disagreed with all of the eye-witnesses in one glaring way. She said that Sarah had hit her twice while she was still within arm's reach of the hood of her car, and that she hadn't grabbed the knife until she was already under attack. No one else had seen it that way, and Rachel hadn't told it that way during previous statements, facts the prosecutor wanted to make sure the jurors understood.

"You say you were at the hood of your car, right?"

"About a foot in front of the hood of my car, yes."

There was also a conflict in Rachel's argument that Hanewicz wanted emphasized: She didn't think Sarah would follow through on her physical threats, and yet she felt physically threatened enough to bring the knife. It had to be one way or the other, not both.

Did she remember telling the detective that Sarah had threatened to kill her in the past, but she didn't think that Sarah really meant it?

Rachel did recall that.

"So that night, you didn't think Sarah was going to hurt you?"

Again she said she did—but she understood the conflict in her logic, and she wasn't quite sure what to do about it.

"You told the detective that you didn't think she really meant anything by what she said."

"She had never actually come through with her threats

until then. She had never come to where I was or actually showed up."

Hebert looked for an opening to intervene as the prosecutor scored points; but as long as Hanewicz maintained proper cross-examination, there was nothing he could do.

"She had come to your house. Isn't that correct?"

"Yes, but face-to-face we had never had any contact. Before, she'd always been outside my apartment, where she couldn't directly approach me."

Hanewicz had another tough question: If Rachel was supposed to be hiding, why was she out in front of the house, indeed, by the street, leaning on the hood of her car? In fact, the prosecutor didn't even ask it as a question. She accused: "You were hanging out there *waiting* with Dustin and Javier!"

Rachel apparently didn't catch the key verb and quickly affirmed this was true. (She had admitted to waiting for Sarah with—as Hanewicz quickly pointed out—a knife.)

Wasn't it true that Rachel went there because she thought Javier would protect her? Rachel agreed. But, Hanewicz pointed out, no protection had been offered. Javier hadn't even tried to get Janet off her. All he did was yell. Some protection.

The prosecutor again directly accused the witness: Rachel had gone directly to Sarah and stabbed her. She hadn't given anyone a chance to protect her. She'd made up her mind!

Rachel denied it.

The accusatory tone was unrelenting. Rachel said that Joshua encouraged her to fight for him; yet that night she told the detective that Joshua wanted the drama to stop. Rachel admitted that Joshua had instructed her to go home.

"You were upset because Joshua was with Sarah!"

Rachel interjected, "I'd known that for a while."

"You wanted to be with him, but he didn't want to be with you."

Rachel disagreed.

Hanewicz continued her theory: "He said he was going to come over. You drove to Joshua and Sarah's location to see what was going on."

"No."

Dustin saw her!

Rachel said Dustin was lying.

"You heard the voice mail. You said you were going to *murder* Sarah!"

"Yes," Rachel said with a sob.

"You said Sarah had told you the same thing, but you are the only one who actually followed through on her promise. Isn't that true?"

"Yes," Rachel said, with fresh tears flowing.

With this response from his client, an answer that could only be construed as an admission, it was Jay Hebert's turn to sit up a little straighter and scribble a quick note in his yellow legal pad.

Hanewicz continued her grueling cross-examination. She made Rachel admit that she had no way of knowing if Sarah was going to have a weapon that night. For all she knew, Sarah merely wanted to talk smack to her. Rachel admitted that she had not considered an actual face-to-face meeting likely.

"No one ever really approaches people anymore," the defendant babbled. "They just talk to them."

"No?" the prosecutor queried.

"No!"

"So everybody just goes out there and stabs people in the heart. Is that what you're saying?"

"No."

"You knew that you had stabbed her a minute after it happened, correct?"

Rachel spit out phrases between sniffles: "Yes. Couple of minutes. Maybe a minute."

Rachel admitted she had heard Jilica screaming, "You stabbed her!" She admitted that she'd sat on the bench and watched police search for the knife, watched canine teams search, without telling anyone she'd thrown it on the roof.

"You call that cooperation?" Hanewicz asked. "That was how you cooperated? Because, when they told you she was dead, you finally admitted where you had thrown the knife away."

Rachel was silent.

"Huh?" the prosecutor said, well aware that the witness hadn't said anything.

"No," Rachel finally said, although it was difficult to determine exactly what she was denying. Mostly, she was disagreeing with Hanewicz's attacking tone.

"Why did you throw the knife on the neighbor's roof?"

With that question, the dam broke. Words came spilling out of Rachel's mouth.

Jay Hebert couldn't govern her words now.

The defendant said, "Because I didn't know what happened, and I didn't want anybody else to get ahold of it, and I didn't want anything to be done, and I didn't want anybody to be hurt that night."

"You didn't know what happened? You said that you saw blood!"

"I saw blood, but I didn't physically see her stabbed, and I didn't know how severe the situation was."

Some jurors must have wondered: How could she sit and watch the grieving, the urgency of the paramedics, hear the siren of the departing ambulance, without suspecting the situation was severe?

"You say you didn't know she was stabbed until after Jilica yelled that she was stabbed?" Hanewicz asked.

"I didn't know where she was stabbed or how severe it

was," Rachel said. Then she played the "young blonde" card big-time and dramatically added, "I . . . was . . . *scared*."

Rachel elongated the final word, and Hanewicz clipped it with her follow-up: "I thought you didn't know what happened."

"I didn't know *exactly* what happened, no. I don't remember doing it, and I did not see her. She walked directly away from me, and I didn't see her anymore after that."

"You had the knife. You knew she was stabbed, and you wanted to get rid of it."

"I didn't want anyone else to get ahold of it because Janet instantly attacked me after that."

"Oh, so you were worried that Janet was going to take the knife away from you?"

"That—or that I would retaliate on Janet also, and I didn't want anybody to get hurt. I had already seen blood."

"You didn't want to retaliate against Janet?"

"I didn't want to retaliate at all. I didn't think I would have to, if they saw a knife."

"You say that it was self-defense because you got jumped, but the *only person* you stabbed was Sarah."

"That's because I got attacked."

"You did not want to act in self-defense with Janet?"

"I didn't know how badly Sarah was hurt, and I didn't physically want anyone to get hurt."

"If you knew that Sarah was hurt, but you didn't know how badly, how was that operating in your mind when you were fighting with Janet?"

"I saw blood." She'd never even "encountered" a fight before, she explained. She didn't think they would actually physically attack her if they saw the knife.

"So the epiphany of what happened is when you saw the blood?"

"Yes. During the fight with Janet, I got rid of the knife," Rachel said.

"*During* the fight with Janet?"

"Yes."

"No! You had to go someplace and give it a good heave, right?"

"Janet was chasing me around the yard."

Eager to get that image out of the jury's head, Hanewicz asked her next question quickly: Wasn't it true that Rachel didn't stab Janet because she didn't hate Janet?

Rachel said it was not true. She had not intended on using the knife on a specific person. She had planned to show it in case someone attacked her, and Sarah happened to be the one who attacked her.

The prosecutor was confused. Hadn't Janet attacked her? Hadn't Janet gotten the best of her? Yet, she hadn't used the knife on Janet. Rachel agreed that was true.

Hanewicz paused, moving on to a new topic, and the moment of quiet was softly punctuated by Rachel's rhythmic sniffles. The prosecutor, calmer now, slowing the pace a bit, asked if it was true that Rachel and Javier Laboy had wedding plans?

Rachel said it was—and yes, those plans were made after Sarah's death.

Hanewicz made Rachel repeat that she did not deny making those phone calls to Sarah.

"You say you don't like drama, but you were on the phone talking to Joshua and you knew he was with her."

"With her? No, I did not."

"At some point, you did, and you were still having these conversations," Hanewicz fired back. When Rachel acknowledged that was true, the prosecutor asked, "Why were you even bothering?"

"Because I still had *feelings* for him."

"You hated Sarah."

"I didn't hate Sarah. I didn't know her to hate her."

"So you leave those kind of voice mails to friends?"

"No."

"Because those voice mails you left, they're not friendly."

Screaming now, the prosecutor quoted Rachel from the taped messages she'd left Sarah, including the swearwords. "And for that, you were going to murder her? For putting a photo on Myspace, you were going to murder her?"

In sharp contrast to Lisset Hanewicz's booming and accusatory tone, Rachel Wade's response was reduced to an indistinct whimper. "She was harassing me. . . ."

"You killed Sarah because you were done with her. In fact, when you walked away from Sarah that night, that was what you said, right? You said, 'I'm done.'"

Rachel argued that those words had been taken out of context: "I told Janet that I didn't want to fight," she said.

"You said that you were done. Isn't that true?"

"I didn't want any of it to happen, in the first place. I was done before it ever even happened."

"Now you're done because you are in trouble."

"I never went after them. They came after me. I told her to leave me alone beforehand."

"You never approached anyone on the street. Is that your testimony?"

"I never *went* to them. I never harassed her or went to where she was."

"You are denying that you went to Sarah's location?"

"Yes, I never went to Joshua's house that night."

Another pause. Rachel took a deep breath and released a sigh—perhaps thinking that she'd weathered the storm.

But her sense of relief was short-lived as Hanewicz again quoted from the phone messages: the "watch your window" quote.

"You would never harass them, right?" the prosecutor asked.

Rachel claimed not to have gone over there, but—because of the voice mails—she couldn't deny verbal threats of stalking.

Hanewicz wanted a comparison: Who was the defendant more afraid of—Sarah or Janet?

Rachel admitted it was Janet, because she'd had "more encounters" with Janet. Rachel was scared of Janet because she'd threatened her in the past. And yet, Hanewicz emphasized, Rachel showed *no interest* in fighting Janet.

"You had no emotion after you learned that you had stabbed Sarah."

"Yes, I did! I just didn't show it, because I didn't know what to do."

"You are crying here today."

"And I cried when I found out what really happened to her also."

"But you didn't know what to do that night?"

"My whole life, every time I've had any type of conflict, I always tried to avoid it my hardest. I had never actually fought anybody."

"But this time you decided to get a knife."

"I avoided it for about eight months."

"Right!" Hanewicz said, an aha moment for the tenacious prosecutor. "You avoided it for eight months and you were *done*!"

"They came to me, and finally I couldn't go anywhere."

"No further questions," Hanewicz said, smelling victory.

* * *

Jay Hebert leaped spryly to his feet, eager to mend the tears made in his case by Hanewicz's ripping cross-examination.

"A few minutes ago, you were asked if you 'followed through' on your threat 'I'm going to murder you,' and you said yes. So that we're crystal clear, did you ever intend to murder or hurt anyone that night?"

Rachel said no. She had never intended to murder Sarah. Those voice mails were many months before the incident. She hadn't been the only one who sent voice mails. She'd received them from Sarah as well.

"One final question. They came to you that night, didn't they?"

"Yes."

The defense attorney sat down.

Hanewicz had no recross, so Judge Bulone said to the defendant, "You may step down."

Before Rachel reached her seat behind the defense table, Jay Hebert said, "The defense calls Joshua Camacho."

Camacho returned to the witness stand. Hebert reminded him that he was still under oath. Then he asked him flat out: "You own a gun?"

Joshua said he didn't own a gun, didn't have access to a gun, was not familiar with any guns in his house, and hadn't pointed a gun at Rachel Wade. He never went to her apartment, the apartment they shared, took a gun from his backpack and pointed that gun at Rachel Wade.

Joshua did admit to owning a gun on April 15 of the previous year; and though he denied ever discussing that gun with Rachel, he admitted showing the gun to Sarah.

Hebert asked again if Joshua had asked the girls to fight for him, and the witness again denied it.

Hanewicz objected: already asked and answered.

Judge Bulone sustained.

Joshua said he didn't know where he got the gun, but this answer was stricken from the record when Hanewicz objected and the judge ruled it irrelevant.

"Did you get rid of that gun after April fifteenth of last year?"

"No."

"Do you still have the gun?"

"No."

"Then where is the gun?"

"It's . . . I don't have it no more."

Hebert asked his last question: "And you never threatened Rachel?"

"No."

The state had no cross-examination, so Joshua Camacho was allowed to step down.

After a brief conference with his second chair, the defense team rested. It was not a dramatic high point. There must have been jurors who wondered about the relevance of Joshua having a gun.

It had been a long day; it was 5:22 P.M. The judge asked the prosecution if they were going to be presenting any rebuttal witnesses.

"Just one," Hanewicz said.

Judge Bulone called a ten-minute recess.

Detective Michael Lynch was reminded by a bailiff that he remained under oath. Judge Joseph Bulone gave the witness a cheerful "Welcome back."

Lynch testified that yes, Javier Laboy was among the witnesses he had interviewed. The interview, a full interview, took place at the police station only hours after the incident. Although, during the interview, they went over Javier's memory of the incident in some detail, Javier, at no time, mentioned that Rachel Wade "took two steps back" when the confrontation with Sarah took place. Rather, Javier had described a "mutual combat fight" that took place in the street between the two vehicles.

Lynch also interviewed Rachel that night, and she, at no time, mentioned that there had been a knife or that someone was stabbed. In fact, Rachel claimed she didn't know that Sarah was stabbed. Rachel's original story of her own movements was drastically different from the scenario she testified to in court. She initially said that she'd been leaning on Dustin's car when the van pulled up, by the driveway. Lynch had to confront Rachel with portions of her story that were strongly inconsistent with other eyewitness reports. Others had seen her with the knife; they'd seen the fight. Lynch asked Rachel how it was that she didn't know anything about that. It was only after he confronted her with the evidence that she admitted to having a knife.

During that same interview, Rachel stated that Joshua had told her earlier that night that she needed to stop what she was doing. She said Sarah had threatened her in the past, but she didn't really believe Sarah meant it. At no time did she mention that she was in fear that night that someone might have a gun. At no time during any interview, which Lynch knew of, did the defendant even *mention* a gun. Although she admitted that Sarah's threats had frightened her to some extent—even though she didn't believe Sarah would follow through—she never mentioned being afraid of Janet Camacho.

Judge Bulone admonished the jury not to watch the news and instructed them to be back the following morning for closing arguments.

Chapter 12

Day Three

On the rainy morning of July 23, the trial's final day, Rachel Wade sat demurely at the defense table, wearing a gray short-sleeved jacket over a white collarless shirt.

After giving the jury lengthy instructions, Judge Joseph Bulone said,

"You will now be hearing the closing arguments from both sides. Both sides have been allotted equal time, but the state is allowed to divide its time between argument and rebuttal.

"Mr. Dicus, are you ready?"

"Yes, Your Honor."

"Proceed."

It is a common strategy during closing arguments for the lawyer who goes first to hijack key words and phrases he anticipates will be used by the other, to deflate them and thus diminish the effectiveness of the opponent's argument. This technique, when executed properly, can cause the opposition to rewrite their argument at the last second, to practically ad-lib in front of a jury. That was what Wesley Dicus did here. The defense had called this case a tragedy. In voir dire, every juror had to agree with Jay Hebert in his assessment that this was a tragedy.

A tragedy for Sarah—and a tragedy for Rachel, Hebert liked to say.

"And even in his examinations of the witnesses, he worked that word 'tragedy' in whenever he could," Dicus said. "Well, jury members, *nobody* disputes the tragic nature of what happened on April 15, 2009. It always has been a tragedy, always will be. When Rachel Wade armed herself with a knife for what *at least* was going to be a confrontation, at most a fistfight, yeah, that's pretty tragic."

The prosecutor asked the jury a series of questions:

Was it tragic that when Sarah Ludemann pulled her van up, stopped and got out, that Rachel Wade did not stand her ground, but advanced upon Sarah Ludemann?

Was it tragic that it only took five seconds for Rachel Wade to meet Sarah Ludemann, "punch her," as Dustin Grimes said, with a downward motion, twice in the chest, and then turn around, walk away, and announce, "I'm done"?

Was it tragic to hear Janet Camacho take the stand, a person who testified that Sarah Ludemann was close to her, very attached to her, that they had movie nights together, and that she was a friend of the family?

Was it tragic to hear Janet testify that when Jilica Smith told her that her friend was stabbed, and she walked around the van, she saw Sarah lying on the ground, foaming from the mouth, dying?

Was it tragic to hear how Janet turned back to Rachel Wade and yelled, "You stabbed her! You stabbed her!"

Was it tragic to hear how Rachel Wade almost laughed and said, "I don't care"?

Dicus then answered his own questions: "Well, murder is always a tragedy. That's why there is justice."

He explained that you can't have justice without two things: truth and accountability. And that was where the jurors came in. "You are the *truth seekers*," he said.

He told them that they must examine each piece of evidence. Did it fit into the puzzle easily—or was it misshapen and needed to be crammed in? The pieces that fit were the truth. Those were the ones jurors could "hang their hat on."

The misshapen pieces were not true and should be discarded. Using that process, they would find that the state's case was truth and that they had proven beyond a reasonable doubt that Rachel Wade was guilty of second-degree murder.

"Use common sense," he said. There were several witnesses at this trial who lied. Some had told white lies, self-protective lies, which were not germane to the issues being decided. The question of whether or not Janet Camacho's children were home while there was vodka drinking and weed smoking going on came to mind.

Then there were witnesses who lied about "crucial evidence." Javier Laboy and Rachel Wade had planned to get married and had plans to have kids. That was crucial evidence. That was evidence that Rachel Wade and Javier Laboy had both *lied under oath* during a preliminary hearing.

Dicus said, "When someone takes an oath and is lying in this manner, when they show that they have no respect for the oath they took today, can you ever depend on what they say? Can you rely on what they say? Can you hang your hat on it? No, you can't."

When determining the credibility of a witness's statements, jurors shouldn't look just at the words alone. They should look at the person delivering the statements—

how did the words come out? What was the emotion behind them?

Dicus tried to discredit Javier Laboy's testimony. Laboy testified that he hadn't seen the knife in Rachel's hand—but on the 911 tape, he had said there was a knife in Rachel's hand. Alert jurors may have deflated Dicus's point by remembering Javier's explanation for this: that he hadn't seen the knife, but rather the information about the knife in Rachel's hand was relayed to him as he spoke to the operator.

What else did that 911 tape say? Dicus asked. Javier loved Rachel. That was bias. Javier protected Rachel. You could hear it in his voice. When the operator asked him, "Who stabbed her?" He said, "Uh." He was conflicted. He refused to give Rachel's name.

Javier lied under oath. He was biased toward the defendant and could not be trusted. Rachel lied under oath also. She had been uncooperative during the investigation. She, too, couldn't be trusted.

Dicus moved to the crux of the argument. The defense wanted the jury to believe Sarah Ludemann attacked Rachel, that Rachel Wade was protecting herself. But, he explained, the facts indicated otherwise. If they looked at the testimony of an unbiased witness, they would find the truth. Dustin Grimes said Rachel approached Sarah. His allegiance, if he had any, could only have been to Rachel and to Javier. He didn't know Sarah, Janet, or Jilica from Adam. Yet he told the truth.

The last thing the state needed to prove in order for the jury to convict was that there was an unlawful killing by an act imminently dangerous to another, demonstrating a depraved mind without regard to human life. Did Rachel Wade's actions fulfill that definition? Dicus said they did. She plunged the knife into Sarah's chest, not once but twice, so hard that she bent the blade. Dicus showed the knife to the jury one more time. That blade went through skin, the fatty tissue of Sarah Ludemann's breast, her rib bone, lung, pericardial sac, and ultimately her heart.

The defendant, stoic up until this point, crumbled. She winced, swallowed hard, and her eyes welled with tears.

Dicus said, "Common sense tells you that when you do that to a person, it is reasonably certain to kill or cause great bodily harm. You don't plunge a knife into someone's chest unless you have no care whatsoever about whether that person lives or dies. *That's* indifference to human life! Janet Camacho told you about that when she said, 'Are you serious? You stabbed her?' And Rachel Wade said, 'I don't care.'"

Was the act done of ill will, hatred, spite, or illegal intent? The state, Dicus said, didn't have to prove that she acted with all of them, just one. And to do that, they needed to look no further than the voice mails. The Rachel on those tapes wasn't the same one the jury heard testify. Dicus walked over to a tape player and pressed a button, and the jury again heard the voice mails.

In the courtroom, the defendant's mouth fell open at the sound of her own voice. Her recorded words were rapid-fire, as if they were rehearsed, or maybe she was reading. There were never more than a few words between obscenities.

There was something artificial, something just *off* about the cadence, and the defendant seemed shocked by her voice, her choice of words, as if she were having an out-of-body experience. Could that really be her on the tape? Could this really be her sitting at the defense table, then and there, stuck in the nightmare?

By the last voice mail, the defendant was softly weeping as she heard her recorded voice:

"You don't know when to stop. You haven't learned your lesson yet, and I'm the fuckin' teacher. I'm warning you

now, keep fucking with me, Sarah, and you and Erin both
are dumb psychotic bitches. I'm warning you now, I am
going to show you psycho! So stop fucking with me. You
are fucking with the wrong person, and you're fucking
with the wrong thing that I care about. So keep it up, keep
playing your motherfucking game and I am going to teach
you how to grow up real motherfucking quick."

Dicus stopped the tape. He told the jury that they were allowed to listen to the tape as many times as they wanted
while deliberating. Rachel had said her words weren't serious. But Sarah sure must have thought Rachel was serious.
Why else would she have saved messages for nine months?
Why else would she have played them for her friends?

"For one reason, and one reason only," Dicus said. "If
Rachel Wade 'showed her psycho,' if Rachel Wade made
good on her guarantee to murder her, her friends could tell
the police that *this was evidence* and *justice could be had.*"

You could hear the anger and ill will in her voice, the
hate and spite that grew in Rachel Wade for nine or ten
months, unbridled and unresolved, until April 15, 2009,
when it finally came to a head. And they all knew how it
ended.

"It ended in murder in the second degree," Dicus said.

He discussed "reasonable doubt." The doubt that the defense was trying to cast was self-defense, that Rachel was
justified in the use of deadly force.

Dicus reviewed the facts: Sarah was the first one out
of the car. Sarah alone was stabbed. Was Sarah armed? No.
Rachel *knew* she didn't have a weapon. She *knew* she
didn't have a gun. During cross-examination Rachel said,
"I wasn't worried about a gun with Sarah. I was scared
about a gun with Joshua." It was Sarah and Rachel, one-
on-one, a confrontation that Rachel *walked up to,* walked
ten to twelve feet to create.

"That's not self-defense," the prosecutor concluded. "The only one who used justifiable self-defense in this case was Sarah Ludemann."

Sarah had just gotten out of the van when Rachel was on her. Dicus mimicked the motion for the jury. His right hand was clenched into a fist, as if holding the handle of a knife and cocking his forearm upward, ready to stab downward. Sarah knew she had to stand her ground and fight back. She brought her arms up and tried to punch her attacker in the head. Sarah tried to defend herself, but it was no use. Two quick jabs with the knife—one deadly wound.

Dicus invited the jury to look carefully at all of the evidence. If they did that, there was only one verdict they could possibly come up with: guilty as charged.

The prosecutor sat down, and Jay Hebert stood up.

Hebert began a methodical argument, reviewing the state's case, witness by witness, in the order it was presented. Leading off had been Ashley Lovelady, who—as Sarah's best friend—had clearly come into the courtroom with a heavy heart.

"These are teenaged girls. This was incredibly difficult," Hebert said. "She acknowledged that Joshua was a cheater, that he cheated on Erin, on Rachel, and on Sarah." Joshua liked the term "friends with benefits." Cheaters cheat. If he was in a relationship, he cheated. Ashley understood what was going on in Sarah's life: the Facebook, the Myspace, the texting, the phones, the hate, and the banter.

According to Ashley, and only Ashley, she went to Janet Camacho's house to drop off a cell phone. The problem was that these were kids with inchoate personalities—and this was the way they talked. They hedged. They cut corners. They ignored nuance.

As her defender spoke, Rachel Wade was without expression. She expertly used a fingertip to pluck a loose piece of mascara from a lower lash. Rachel's lips were dry and she held them clenched tightly. At one point, she tried to moisten her lips with the tip of her tongue, but her tongue was dry as well.

Throughout his closing, Jay Hebert used far too many pronouns and too few proper names. "She did this to her" and then "she did that to her"—it reached the point where the jury had to be confused. When Hebert did use proper names, he sometimes got them wrong. "She did that to Sarah. I mean Rachel." Most of the time, he corrected himself, but it added to the jury's strain, trying to understand.

There were problems with Ashley's testimony, but Hebert was inclined to give her a pass—for the most part. Chalk it up to the verbal sloppiness that so often accompanied teenage-itis. It was just a symptom of the way teenagers thought, he said. A little bit scrambled up. Still, there was one facet of Ashley's testimony that he wanted to emphasize because it was "really her only role in this case." That facet involved the moment Ashley said she came in contact with the van.

"She doesn't admit to swerving and trying to hit my client as she drove by, but at some point she knew that my client was at Javier's house. And if you'll remember when I asked Rachel and I asked Javier, 'Did you discuss where you were with anybody else in the world?'"—Hebert raised his palm to the jury and moved it slowly in a large circle, indicating he meant the entire world—"'Did you tell anybody that you were going to a safe house?' They said no."

So there was only one way that Ashley knew where Rachel was. She must have driven past Javier's house. The jury had heard Dustin Grimes's testimony that Ashley swerved and that she was speeding. They had Javier's testimony that he had to pull Rachel out of the way so she wouldn't be struck by the speeding vehicle.

There was disagreement about when Ashley told the occupants of the van where Rachel was, and about which direction the vehicles were pointing when the info was relayed, but everyone agreed Ashley did tell Sarah where Rachel was. Ashley didn't want to admit it at first. She didn't want to be blamed. But she told the truth eventually. Reaction to Ashley's info was instantaneous and extreme. Sarah was angry, in a rage. She slammed her foot on the accelerator and left rubber.

Hebert noted there were four eyewitnesses, four plus Rachel herself. The state called only three.

Was Jilica Smith credible? Jilica didn't admit to smoking or drinking. Jilica said Janet and Sarah were in Janet's house when the red-car-with-a-blonde stopped at the corner. Janet testified she was outside and approached the car. Chased it off. Kids partied, Hebert said with a shrug. Fact of life. They had faulty memories, imprecise communication skills. He poked at the air with a stiff forefinger, more of a jab than a stab. "That. Is. The. Way. Teenaged. Girls. Talk. She's not telling the truth. It didn't happen," he said.

If they couldn't believe which direction the cars were pointed or who was talking to whom, then how could they believe the story about "your Mexican boyfriend" comment? Were we supposed to believe Jilica's version of that story? She'd mentioned it here in court, but had skipped that part during her initial police interview. Jilica said as soon as the minivan encountered Ashley Lovelady that "all hell broke loose."

"Her words, not my words," Hebert said, and then he repeated them: "All hell broke loose."

Janet said they cruised by Sarah's house to see if Rachel was there before being instructed to go to Javier Laboy's. Jilica didn't mention that part.

Hebert asked the jury to look at the logic of the thinking that was going on in that van. If Sarah was truly in fear of Rachel, because of threats made on voice mails months before, if she really feared that Rachel might murder her, why did she get in the car and pass her own home, and "hunt her down"?

Hebert's voice grew louder. He karate chopped the air with his left hand. The answer was in Jilica's next statement. She was pretty sure something bad was going to happen. Sarah wanted to fight.

"Ladies and gentlemen of the jury, they . . . came . . . to . . . her. You have to look at this situation. How charged it was, how fluid it was," Hebert said.

At the defense table, Rachel dabbed at her right eye with the balled-up tissue she'd been clenching in her fist.

"It was *bam, bam, bam, bam, bam, bam,*" Hebert said, slapping the top of his lectern. "And it was electric, and it was festering, and it was exploding."

Jilica had testified that there was "no stopping" Sarah. The minivan was no longer headed to McDonald's. Getting out was not an option. With Sarah behind the wheel, they raced to get there. Sarah knew where Rachel was.

Hebert summed up: "Sarah was going to get Rachel. Sarah was going there, going there to *beat her down . . .* and Janet had her back." Jilica knew Sarah was in a rage. Janet was mad also. Those few seconds, as they headed for Javier's—it was one charged car ride. Jilica described the driving. When the minivan stopped in front of Javier's house, it wasn't a normal stop.

It was dark. Sarah came around the corner hard, slammed on the brakes to keep from hitting Rachel and her car. Hebert had the jury look a second time at the two crime scene photos, one taken with a flash, the other without. The dark picture was the more accurate rendering. In the direction Rachel Wade was standing, the only light was behind her.

"That light casts a lot of light on this end of the car. The area where the light doesn't shine is very dark."

Jilica didn't see who threw the first blow or how many blows were thrown. Did the jury recall Jilica's 911 call?

"'I don't know how she was stabbed,'" the defense attorney quoted. "'I . . . don't . . . know . . . how . . . she . . . was . . . stabbed.'"

Jilica was completely unhelpful when it came to determining if Rachel had acted in self-defense. She simply didn't know. But there was an interesting twist in Jilica's testimony: She said she was on the side of the van with Janet and was holding Janet back. All of the other eyewitnesses—Dustin, Janet, Javier—agreed that didn't happen. If the jury looked at the eyewitness testimony side by side, the only thing that matched up perfectly was when they knew Sarah was hurt, and that had been when Jilica screamed.

Hebert moved on to the next prosecution witness, Janet Camacho. As was true of Joshua, Janet was very vague when asked if Joshua and Sarah were dating. Janet said her children were home. Josh said they were drinking vodka and smoking marijuana, and the children weren't home.

"If you believe Janet," Hebert said. "She left her kids with Joshua, I suppose, while she and the rest of them went to McDonald's." Janet knew about the drama, the triangle. Janet admitted that she hadn't been around much when Rachel was with Joshua. She wasn't a big Rachel fan. The jury had heard about the animosity, the threats by Janet, Rachel's fear of Janet.

Janet's mind wasn't on Rachel that night, not at first.

"Janet was with a boy named Jeremy," Hebert said. "She didn't know his last name, and she didn't have his cell phone number. And she said, 'I wasn't smoking pot.'"

Nobody was smoking pot; nobody was drinking; there was no party—although Joshua said they burned copious amounts of weed. Janet also told a part of the story that no one else remembered, even though they were there. She said Rachel parked at the end of the street. Jeremy flashed his lights. Rachel flashed back. Janet walked that car down; but before she got to it, Rachel left.

"None of those statements are corroborated," Hebert said. They were not consistent with the other evidence; and for Janet, they were "self-serving." Another inconsistency: Janet didn't know anything about Ashley showing up at the house to deliver the cell phones. Only Ashley remembered that part.

Hebert asked the jury to look at the sequence of events regarding the alleged "Mexican boyfriend" phone call—a call Hebert believed never occurred. Janet said it took place before they ever found Ashley—not consistent with any of the other testimony.

She said that once Sarah got the phone call they put it on the speakerphone. And despite that—even if you believed that happened—they still went looking for Rachel. Janet remembered Sarah being on the phone saying, "Where you at? Where you at?" Bottom line: Sarah was looking for Rachel.

"Nobody called the police. Nobody went home. Janet had Sarah's back," Hebert said.

Jilica acknowledged that Sarah was angry, in a rage. The car drove up fast. It stopped four or five feet from Rachel's car. And what did Janet have to say about the prosecution's burden to prove that Rachel Wade did not act in self-defense?

Just like Jilica before her: nothing. Janet said she saw the knife, but she did not see the tussle. She didn't know who threw the first punch. She didn't know who grabbed whose hair. Her view was obstructed. She fought Rachel before she knew Sarah was hurt.

Value to the prosecution: zero.

Jurors were again asked to look at it from Rachel's POV. Three girls flew out of a car; one girl engaged her. In a continuous event, a second girl engaged her. Jilica did not hold Janet back.

Janet offered a couple of "really poignant quotes" near the end of her testimony. "If I'm there, Rachel's not going to fight," she said. Janet said Rachel "didn't want to deal with me."

Next topic: Dustin Grimes.

Dustin said Rachel was crying and a little angry. She was looking for a diversion, an escape from the street trouble she was in. He said Ashley's car flew by and almost ran Rachel over. Admittedly, Dustin's timeline was a little inconsistent. He said that it was minutes between the time Ashley drove by and when the van pulled up. Dustin heard Rachel say she was going to kill Sarah, but he didn't take it seriously. He thought she was talking smack.

Dustin was able to contextualize Rachel's words. They were consistent with the way teenaged girls talked. Dustin testified that Rachel had the knife for protection, and that all three of the girls flew out of the van at the same time. This was not a one-on-one fight. It was three on one. Sarah moved first and moved fast. Sarah had Rachel by the hair and he saw three punches.

Hebert wondered how much time it took for a person under attack to determine whether or not they needed to defend themselves.

"I submit to you that you take the knife out of that situation and those three girls beat the crap out of my client," Hebert said. "They brought the fight to her."

Dustin said that when he looked up, he didn't know that Sarah was stabbed. The fight was continuous—there was no pause between Rachel and Sarah's fight, and the fight between Janet and Rachel.

"That's it," Hebert said, palms upward. "Those are the three witnesses that the state is relying on to convict my client of second-degree murder." It was the state's burden of proof, after all. Had the jury heard *any* evidence that Rachel Wade had not acted in self-defense? Jilica didn't even know Sarah was stabbed. Dustin said that Sarah was the aggressor—and that's the government's case.

The eyewitness the state didn't call, of course, was Javier Laboy. Javier's testimony was even less helpful when it came to proving murder. As Dustin had, Javier said Sarah came after Rachel. Rachel stood her ground and defended herself. Rachel had a right to be there. She wasn't trespassing. She had an absolute right to be there.

"They brought the fight to her," Hebert said, and he moved on to the testimony from law enforcement that the jury had heard.

Officer Benjamin Simpkins "didn't offer much." He testified regarding Jilica's initial statement, the one in which she said nothing about the "Mexican boyfriend" phone call. Back then, Jilica said she saw a text message from Rachel.

Sergeant Tina Trehy testified as to Rachel's demeanor. She said Rachel was calm. Hebert had asked, "Calm as, say, in shock?" Trehy said yes.

Rachel didn't know Sarah was dead, Hebert pointed out. She was in shock, stoic.

"You can draw any conclusions you want when an eighteen-year-old is in this type of situation, how they should react," Hebert said.

After Trehy, the state put lead investigator Michael Lynch on the stand. He offered the state's key pieces of evidence—in their mind, anyway—the audiotapes. The prosecution could not hammer those voice mails into the jurors' heads repeatedly enough. But, Hebert suggested, jurors were going to have to make a "judgment call" when it came to those recordings. There was such a long period of time between those recordings and the incident in the street. There was no connection at all between the two.

"Do you think that, for one second, that when Rachel Wade was talking big, talking smack, that she thought she was going to have to come to court one day and say, 'I didn't mean to murder her'?"

Rachel had remained relatively composed until this point in Hebert's closing. Her face crumbled and the tears flowed freely.

Sometimes Hebert referred to the prosecution as "the government," realizing that this term made Wesley Dicus and Lisset Hanewicz seem less trustworthy.

The government's last witness was the medical examiner. Hebert knew how tough that had been on the jury—the details, the photos. The government wanted the jury to feel emotional, all the better to distract them from the physical evidence.

"Try not to be drawn in by the prosecutor's passionate plea for this awful, awful event," he said.

Hebert summarized the defense case. What was interesting about Javier Laboy's testimony was that the state did not ask him very many questions about the event. They just wanted to hammer him: about marrying Rachel Wade, about dating and having a relationship with Rachel Wade while she'd been locked up, and corresponding and calling, talking about running away together, and what they were going to name their kids.

And that was all irrelevant. All of that happened after Javier made his first statement; all of that happened after Javier called 911. Javier said he didn't see the knife. Dustin Grimes told him Rachel had the knife as Javier spoke to the operator. The prosecution had tried to make a major issue of it, but the jury heard Javier. He'd explained that beautifully. That 911 call was important, but for a different reason. He told the operator that Rachel had "gotten jumped" and that she was "defending herself." That was a quote!

"That's the best evidence we have here in this case," Hebert said. The state's attempt to impeach Javier backfired badly for them on that issue. "Well, you get to use your judgment as to whether or not Javier was being truthful."

Javier said the minivan was like a "street racer" when it pulled up; Sarah was the aggressor, and they met between cars. "Javier said that Sarah struck first," Hebert said, "that Sarah struck three, four blows to the head, that Sarah grabbed her by the hair. She charged Rachel."

Yet, the state's cross-examination focused on things that happened six months later. Hebert shrugged.

The "Javier loves Rachel" angle was overblown. Rachel and Javier might have thought they were in a relationship months after the incident; but if the jury used their common sense, they'd realize it was ridiculous. They were just being silly kids.

"It's kind of hard to be in a relationship when someone is locked up," Hebert said.

* * *

The next witness, Hebert said with distaste, was Joshua Camacho. He wasn't on the stand for long, but his testimony was important. Joshua played a "pivotal role" in the case. The state hadn't wanted to call him. Hebert didn't know why. It had been up to the defense to get Joshua's testimony to the jury.

Hebert had little tolerance for Joshua: "I'm not sure what he really had to say. I'm not sure what he really had to offer."

There was a new expression on Rachel Wade's face, maybe anger.

"Joshua had a small harem of friends with benefits. He was a playa. He lied. He lied about the gun. He lied about Rachel knowing about the gun. He lied about pointing a gun at Rachel's head. Joshua Camacho had washed his hands and feet of all of these girls," Hebert said.

For a blink or two, Rachel looked about to call out in protest; then she returned to her default countenance of groggy resignation.

"You got a flavor of what Joshua Camacho is all about," Hebert said, as if there were a bad taste in his mouth. "I don't think I have to tell you any more about him."

Hebert gestured toward his client with an open palm, as if he were introducing her to the jury for the first time. The last witness the defense called was Rachel. "Members of the jury, it is your job to evaluate the testimony of all of the witnesses. I would submit to you that Rachel Wade testified truthfully."

She had testified like a twenty-year-old girl—he didn't say "woman"—who was going through the most horrific experience imaginable.

"Look into her eyes," he suggested. Rachel had never

meant for any of this to happen. She had described the night's events. She was at her house, heard Sarah pull up in the van, wanted to get out of there, and grabbed a kitchen knife from her drawer and put it in her purse.

The defendant again dabbed tears with her crumpled tissue. A box of facial tissues sat on the defense table in front of her, but she didn't get a new one. She was content with worrying the one she had.

Hebert told the jury how Rachel made one phone call at that point, but it wasn't to anyone pertinent to the trouble she was in. It was to someone she hadn't had contact with in months.

She didn't tell anybody where she was. She was crying and upset. And she was tired of the drama, too. The fight hadn't occurred at McDonald's or Subway or Taco Bell or Sarah's house or Janet's house.

"The fight was brought to her."

The state, in its closing argument, asserted that the jury shouldn't believe Rachel because she lied about her relationship with Javier. Hebert suggested that they give that nonsense the weight it was worth, which was not much, and focus on the relevant.

The state was reaching for straws. "Let's keep our eye on the ball," Hebert urged. The first car swerved, almost hitting her. The van pulled up. Three girls piled out. Sarah, bigger, heavier, came at her, the aggressor. She threw the first punch, and grabbed Rachel's hair.

At what point did a citizen have to figure out what is in the mind of an assailant? When? They didn't know what those three girls were capable of.

Jilica said she was just along for the ride that night.

Maybe so, but did Rachel know that? Did Rachel know Jilica wasn't part of the posse? Absolutely not!

If Rachel didn't have that knife, the posse would've beaten the crap out of her, beaten her down. Would they have killed her? They could all speculate. Would they have seriously injured her? More speculation.

Hebert held up a forefinger. "It only takes one blow. How many times have we heard about cases where a person gets knocked down to the ground, where a purse snatcher knocks an older person to the ground, she hits her head on the curb and she dies? How many times have we heard of one-punch fights where someone gets hit in the wrong place and they die? Or they have serious bodily injury. Or they have brain injury. Rachel doesn't have to figure out what. She only has to figure out if she has the right to defend herself."

Hebert introduced a "sensitive subject" to the jury: the juvenile mind. What was it like to be a teenager? Everyone went through it. Some lessons were learned the hard way, and with experience came wisdom. But teenagers universally lacked wisdom. They operated on emotions. They said and did things without thinking. The jury could sit there and say, "Oh God, if only Sarah had gone home." What were those girls thinking? Simple. They *weren't* thinking.

Another difficulty in understanding the kids' actions was generational. Young people today lived in a world of satellite technology and instant feedback. When they texted each other, they wanted an immediate response. Cross that immediacy with the emotion of the teenaged mind, you get "dangerous impulsiveness."

Rachel had reason to believe she was in danger of death or great bodily harm; therefore she had a right to arm and defend herself. She was not guilty.

* * *

At that moment, an alarm went off in the courthouse.

"Is that the fire alarm, Your Honor?" Hebert asked.

"No, that happens every Friday at noon," Judge Bulone replied.

Many spectators laughed. Rachel Wade's face remained frozen.

Hebert continued. He told the jury about reasonable doubt. There was no precise definition. He couldn't explain what it was. You had to *feel* it.

"I would challenge the state to point out how they disproved our self-defense case. Their eyewitnesses did not address this issue," Hebert said.

He couldn't tell the jury what reasonable doubt was, but he could certainly tell them what it wasn't. Suddenly speaking in a rapid-fire cadence, Hebert said that reasonable doubt was not a speculative doubt. It wasn't imaginary or forced. If they felt such a doubt, they "must find the defendant not guilty."

Contrary to the defense attorney playbook, Hebert sometimes referred to Rachel as "the defendant" or "my client." A lot of defenders only refer to their clients by their first name, to maximize perception of their humanity.

Hebert stopped his oration for a moment and went into action. He placed three white cardboard cutouts about four or five feet in front of the jury box. The cutouts were life-sized, measured to precisely represent the three girls who confronted Rachel. The perfectly round heads were without features, maximizing the dehumanization of the victim and prosecution witnesses.

The six jurors and two alternates watched without expression.

Hebert set the three figures up, side by side, as he repeated his mantra: "They came to her. They came to her." He

old the jurors that they were in the same position his client
ad been in that night, facing three attackers, four to five feet
way. The difference was that in real life it was dark and the
hree girls were in rapid motion, coming at Rachel Wade.
Iebert submitted that all three attackers saw Rachel's
nife. If Jilica and Janet saw the knife, Sarah must have, too.

"There is no doubt that this is a tragic situation. Do not
et a second tragedy occur here today," he said. They should
pply the facts to the law, and see that justice was carried
out. "Rachel Wade had a right to defend herself. Nothing
we say or do can ever bring Sarah back, but you, *you* can
ake the evidence and the facts and see to it that justice is
carried out. She had the right to be there and to defend
herself, and we ask that you find her not guilty, as the evidence and *the law* requires. Thank you for your attention."

Jay Hebert solemnly removed the cardboard silhouettes.
Rachel Wade wept.

"Thank you, Mr. Hebert," Judge Bulone said. "Rebuttal?"

Lisset Hanewicz stood and told the jury that she would
be addressing some of the things the defense had just said
in their closing argument. "The theme was 'they came
to her.' Because someone decides to confront someone
else—verbal confrontation, let's say it would have been a
fistfight, a catfight—that does not mean that you can bring
a knife to the fight."

Hanewicz noted that Hebert had a lot to say about the
testimony of Ashley Lovelady and Joshua Camacho, interesting because they weren't even there when Sarah
Ludemann was stabbed to death. When the defense attorney said that if Ashley Lovelady hadn't said anything, we
wouldn't be here, he was playing a game with the jury. He
was trying to shift blame off his client. When Hebert called
Joshua "a cheater," it was just a diversion. The prosecutor

scoffed at the notion that the defense attorney spoke about Sarah's vehicle as if it was a deadly weapon. The fact was Sarah did not run over anybody with her van. She hit the brakes and stopped.

Regarding Jilica's 911 call, she might have said that she didn't see the stabbing, but she saw Rachel with the knife before and after the stabbing; so understanding that Rachel had done the stabbing wasn't much of a leap. Contrast that to Rachel's testimony. Rachel said she didn't even remember the stabbing. If that was true, how did she even know if she acted in self-defense? A three-on-one encounter, and in Rachel's mind it was a beat down.

"She called it her safe house, two guys and a knife. How was *that* three on one?" Hanewicz said. "Deadly force would only have been justified if Rachel was in fear of imminent death. *Imminent death*. Or great bodily harm. *Reasonably* believed. That was the standard."

Hanewicz introduced a new topic. She quoted the defendant: "'I didn't mean to murder her.'" Rachel had said that on various occasions, and now the prosecutor repeated the sentence two more times.

Rachel's intent to kill was not required with a second-degree murder charge. She doesn't have to intend to murder her. All Rachel had to do was demonstrate a depraved mind, without regard for human life. Did she do it with ill will, or hatred, or spite, or with evil intent? Hanewicz said it was pretty clear she did.

Why hadn't the prosecution called Javier Laboy? Hebert had made an issue of it. The reason was Javier's own lies had destroyed his credibility. The jury "couldn't believe a word" he said. That was why.

Rachel had appeared to drift off into her own world as Hanewicz spoke. But she snapped out of it when Hanewicz questioned Javier's credibility and glared at the prosecutor.

Hanewicz sounded incredulous as she noted how the defense had deemphasized Rachel and Javier's relationship. A witness to the murder was now engaged, after the murder, to the defendant. That was more than relevant. Hebert had made a fuss over the discrepancy in which direction the cars were facing when Ashley told Sarah where Rachel was. *That* was irrelevant.

She had the jury wearing its common-sense cap, so she dispensed some issues she wanted considered:

After Rachel twice plunged the knife into Sarah, why did she walk away like she didn't care? What did Rachel say, according to Jilica and Janet's testimony? "I'm done." No one had to pull her away. She walked away on her own, acting as if she didn't have a care in the world.

"And why? Because she'd accomplished her objective," Hanewicz said.

Jilica and Janet were not the only two to comment on Rachel's demeanor. The police had done so as well. Sergeant Trehy couldn't believe Rachel's lack of emotion. Rachel wasn't in shock. She wasn't numb. She was satisfied with what she'd done. It showed malice.

Another fact: Rachel lied. She told the detective the whole story, but she left out the knife. One of Hanewicz's first questions of Rachel had been: did she lie to the detective? She said no. Hanewicz was astonished. Another lie. Under oath!

How was Rachel holding the knife? Rachel gave three versions of that story. At first she said she was holding the knife at her side. Later she said that she was holding the knife in front of her. On a third occasion, she said she was holding the knife so that the blade was away from Sarah. If you counted the story in which she didn't mention the knife at all, she'd given four different versions of events.

Once, Rachel said she was just hitting her and somehow

she stabbed her. In another version, she said she didn't re member the stabbing. Then there was the version that ha emerged for the first time the day before, that she was i fear of a gun—a gun that might have been brought to th fight by Sarah because Joshua had a gun and she knev about it. Bringing the gun into it—clearly Hebert's idea— was the last desperate attempt to convince everyone tha she was acting in self-defense.

Hanewicz addressed the stabbing itself. That was som puncture wound. The worst some cops had ever seen. I showed anger. Rage. Rachel stabbed toward Sarah's chest It wasn't one stab. It was two. Rachel said that Sarah wa punching her and she was flailing her arms. That scenari didn't jibe with the facts, however. Sarah wasn't slashed She was *stabbed*.

The defense had asked what would have happened i Rachel had not brought a knife to the fight. Now the pros ecution invited the jury to do the same thing. Maybe i there had been no knife, there wouldn't have been a figh at all. Maybe, without the knife, it was just a verbal argu ment. More "talking smack." Maybe there would have been a fight, which would have ended—as did the grea majority of fights—without either side receiving a seriou injury. Each might have landed a couple of blows, and then friends would have gotten in there to break it up.

"We know one thing for sure," Hanewicz said. "If Rachel had not brought a knife that night, Sarah would be alive, and we would not be here. Thank you."

Judge Bulone said, "Thank you, Ms. Hanewicz." He told the jurors that in a few moments, a bailiff would escort them to the jury room and they would begin deliberation. First thing, they were to elect a foreperson to lead the de liberation as a chairperson leads a meeting. Six jurors would decide the verdict. He specifically told them who the alternates were. He thanked the alternates and assured them that their time had not been wasted. The service they'd performed for the justice system was every bit as important as that of the jurors who got to deliberate. They were insurance against a mistrial, and mistrials cost taxpayers big-time bucks.

If the jurors had any questions during deliberation, they were to write them down and give them to the bailiff. If possible, the court would answer them. All they had to do was knock on the jury room door. There would be a bailiff posted outside that door at all times. The same was true when they reached a verdict. If deliberations took time—and it was okay if they did—and the jurors had to be sent home for the night, it was important for them to remember that they were only to deliberate while in the jury room.

"Any questions?" Judge Bulone asked. No hands were raised.

The jurors filed out of the courtroom.

Moments later, Rachel Wade was escorted out by a guard.

The trial had been unusual more for what it didn't include than what it included. The jurors had been given almost no information about the victim. The state had not bothered to introduce biographical info regarding Sarah Ludemann to demonstrate the young life full of promise that had been lost, and the only photos the jury saw of the victim were those taken during the autopsy.

Chapter 13

VERDICT

The jury was less than a half hour into deliberation, and Jay Hebert was doing interviews with the media, explaining that the most difficult thing about this case, as far as he was concerned, was the age of his client. Rachel, he said, was "flat-out scared." He'd given her a hug there at the end and he had felt her trembling. Still, he believed that she retained hope and was pleased and satisfied with the defense she'd received. Rachel was "devastated" by Sarah's death and there was nothing she wanted more than to be able to turn back time so she could walk away from all of this, and Sarah would still be alive.

If Rachel was acquitted, she was going to go someplace and make a fresh start of her life. Although, he noted, the courtroom was filled with her friends and family, so she had a lot to stay for as well. "There are a lot of people who care about that little girl," Hebert said. She'd had more than thirty supporters in the courtroom for each day of the trial.

Asked if he was worried the jury might turn on him because his self-defense scenario cast guilt upon the victim,

Hebert fell back upon his "this is a terrible tragedy" theme. No good guys, no bad guys. Just kids being kids, and now one of them was dead. It was simply his job to humbly get Rachel's story out so the jury could make a fair decision.

During deliberation no one moved too far from the courtroom. Though the courtroom was empty and locked, youthful spectators remained in the wings for fear they would miss the verdict. According to courtroom reporter Beth Karas, a correspondent for the *In Session* TV program, the hallway outside the courtroom "sounded like a high-school cafeteria."

After a little longer than two and a half hours of deliberation, the jury reached a verdict. The courtroom was unlocked and the public gallery promptly filled. Rachel's friends and family were on one side; Sarah's supporters on the other.

Judge Joseph Bulone said, "Has the jury reached a verdict?"

The bailiff replied, "They have, Your Honor."

The judge addressed the packed room, noting that spectators varied from the curiosity seekers to the emotionally involved. He urged everyone to maintain their composure. "I have not witnessed any inappropriate behavior at all by any of the spectators in this courtroom. And we need to keep it that way," he said. "Okay, let's go ahead and bring the jury in."

The panel solemnly filed in.

Judge Bulone asked the jury's foreperson, who was male, to confirm that a verdict had been reached. Then the jury instructed him to hand the jury form to the bailiff, who, in turn, handed the sheet of paper to the clerk.

The judge said: "If the defense will please rise—and will Madame Clerk please publish the verdict."

Rachel Wade and her lawyers, one on either side, rose to their feet. Jay Hebert stood close but did not lift an arm around his client to offer support.

Madame Clerk read the case number and said, "*State of Florida* versus *Rachel Wade,* murder in the second degree, we the jury find the defendant *guilty* of second-degree murder as charged, so say we all on this date July 23, 2010."

The judge's warnings about audible reactions to the verdict had accomplished nothing—at least not on the defense side. Many of Rachel's friends immediately burst into tears, but Rachel herself crumbled slowly. Perhaps she thought she'd misheard at first. She bowed her head and sobbed. Hebert still did not put his arm around her, but he did pat her on the back a couple of times. She eventually sat down and put her hand over her mouth.

Rachel's mother buried her face in her husband's chest, and he held her as she convulsed with grief. Rachel had been a problem for them as a teenager, the reason she had gotten her own apartment at such a young age, but none of that pain compared with this.

There were no tears on Sarah Ludemann's side, but the celebration was muted.

"Your job is not through," Judge Bulone told the jury. They had a choice: be escorted immediately to the parking lot and drive home, or return to the courtroom and talk to anyone they liked.

The media was going to be in this room as well. If they wanted to speak to them, they could. They didn't have to. They had the right to be silent or talk. Their choice. Each would receive a Certificate of Appreciation. Judge Bulone urged them all to have a good weekend.

"Try to stay dry. I think it's raining pretty hard right now," Judge Bulone said.

Rivulets of tears rolled down Rachel Wade's cheeks, faster than she could wipe them away. Still, she wasn't crying as hard as her mother, who continued to shudder, face buried in Barry's chest.

The judge scheduled the sentencing for 1:30 P.M. on September 3. That concluded the day's courtroom activities. Only then did Jay Hebert put an arm around his client's shoulders and whisper something in her ear.

The moment of comfort was short-lived. An officer escorted Rachel Wade from the courtroom. She remained in the custody of the Pinellas County Jail, which was right behind the courthouse.

Although the minimum sentence for second-degree murder in Florida was twenty and a half years, Judge Bulone could lessen that stretch if he found three mitigating factors in place: Rachel felt remorse, this was an isolated incident, and she had no criminal history.

The court already knew Rachel's previous most serious offense was shoplifting. The first two, however, were judgment calls.

Chapter 14

Aftermath

Within minutes of the verdict, Jay Hebert was in front of microphones again: "I am somewhat shocked. Especially as quick as this verdict was. I didn't think it would be a second-degree murder charge. I respect it, but that wasn't what I expected."

Although the prosecution had asked Sarah's parents not to make a statement to the press until after the sentencing, Charlie and Gay Ludemann did speak briefly.

"It's a tragedy for both sides," Charlie said. "That's all I have to say."

Gay added, "My husband said it. Justice has been served."

Rachel Wade's friends remained after others had left. The press was not allowed to photograph them, and they were escorted out of the courthouse through a separate exit.

Sarah's friends found small solace in the fact that Sarah herself provided the evidence that led to her killer's conviction: the voice mails of a nasty Rachel Wade making threats.

Rachel's defense was based on the premise that she was afraid of Sarah Ludemann, but that was hard to believe after listening to the aggressive and bullying tone she used on those voice mails.

How different the case might have been if those voice mails had been erased.

Rachel's case might also have been boosted, at least a little, if portions of written police reports stemming from earlier incidents had been allowed into evidence, but they constituted hearsay, Judge Bulone ruled. Read those police reports in front of the jury and there was a much better chance of a compromise verdict, manslaughter. They might have established that Sarah was harassing Rachel.

But the mitigating nature of those documents was limited. Sarah never mentioned weapons. The worst incident, the one involving a Taco Bell parking lot, included Sarah's friend attacking the car of Rachel's roommate with Silly String. One could easily imagine Lisset Hanewicz making fun of a girl who brought a knife to a fight because she was afraid of Silly String.

Another factor had to be that if one police report was allowed into evidence, they all would have to come in. Hebert didn't want the jury hearing that his client had "threatened to slit [Erin Slothower's] throat," or that both Slothower and Ludemann were afraid of Wade.

The prosecution, on the other hand, would not want the jury to hear that Joshua Camacho told police that "Ludemann was just trying to antagonize Wade into a fight."

Although it was true that insults and threats were hurled in both directions, the pattern seemed to be that Wade's threats were always more violent, intense, and vicious.

* * *

On the Monday after the verdict, Jay Hebert said everyone in his camp was still in shock. He'd seen Rachel that morning and "all of this" was just starting to sink in. Rachel Wade was under psychiatric observation over the weekend, but not because of any specific thing she did or said, but because of an abundance of caution by the sheriff's office and the jail.

Hebert said, "They felt it was in her best interests to be monitored. She has since been returned to her own cell. I think she is doing remarkably well under the circumstances."

He criticized the composition of the jury. They were a mixed group: a couple of teachers, a couple in the marina business. His complaint was not so much with the jury as with the jury pool from which they were plucked. No young people—those who would be most apt to understand this case's language and nuances, most apt to understand what his client was going through. Methods of youthful communication, high-tech stuff, were a key point in the case. A youthful jury might have better understood how young people "talk smack."

Hebert said he "mock trialed" the case with both older and younger jurors, and the reactions to Rachel Wade's voice mails were very different. "We talk like this," the younger mock jurors had said. Hebert thought the underrepresentation of young adults in Pinellas County jury pools should be corrected.

Then Hebert sounded defensive. If he was being blamed for allowing a jury that was thinking "guilty from the get-go," the public needed to know how difficult the process could be. During the brief time lawyers got to spend with prospective jurors, they had to learn and gauge their priorities, their life experiences, and their predilections.

Hebert's critics were unmoved. A jury of "peers" need not be comprised of citizens demographically similar to the defendant. It need be comprised only of people who are eligible to serve on a jury. There was no guarantee, despite Hebert's frustration, that a jury solely comprised of nineteen-year-old females would have delivered a different verdict.

Also on Monday, Rachel's father, Barry Wade, spoke out. He said that his daughter was holding up as well as could be expected, and that she had been "very, very surprised" by the verdict. The family had tried to prepare themselves for the worst and hope for the best. He himself had been surprised. He knew some of the evidence (the voice mails, for instance) would be difficult to overcome. He thought the jury would choose manslaughter. His daughter was a "very good person," a fact obvious to anyone who knew her. Everybody had "nothing but great things" to say about Rachel. No one thought she could intentionally hurt someone. Unfortunately, she was part of today's generation with the way they communicated and talked back and forth, the e-mailing and the texting and so forth. That was what had caused the situation to escalate—but Rachel was basically a very good person. High-tech communication wasn't the only catalyst, however. A lot of the tragic situation was the creation of Joshua Camacho and the way Rachel felt about him, although Barry was at a loss as to what his daughter saw in Joshua.

Camacho, he noticed, had a certain amount of control over the girls and had them following him and doing what he said. He was like a Svengali, using hypnotism and mind control, or something. Barry believed that Joshua could have easily stopped all of the drama between his "friends with benefits," but that wasn't going to happen. Camacho *fed* off the drama. He told them to fight for him. That was just his mentality. He was never going to tell them to back off because instigating was too much fun. He was right in the middle of it, stirring things up.

"He *played* the girls," Barry said, starting to show emotion. "And they were both wonderful girls."

Barry said that the morning after the incident, Rachel told him the same story she'd told in court: she had brought the knife in hopes it would scare the other girls away.

Unfortunately, the dad added, with today's kids, "nothing scares 'em." There was a time when you would have stayed away from a person with a knife, but it wasn't the case anymore.

He'd spoken with a neighbor who confirmed Rachel's story that Sarah had been harassing his daughter during the hours before the incident.

Also, he wanted it noted that Sarah was not the only one Rachel was afraid of. There really was an issue with Janet Camacho, and Janet had threatened his daughter "many a time." Rachel was very afraid of Janet, and she knew Janet would have Sarah's back.

"Our lives are upside down," Barry Wade said.

Realizing the pain he and his wife were experiencing, he could only imagine how much suffering the Ludemanns had endured.

If he could talk to the Ludemanns—and, of course, he could not—he would ask them to look deep in their hearts and look at Rachel and realize that she was a good person, and that there was the possibility that Rachel had no intention of using the knife that night. The incident exploded in seconds, and the biggest mistake Rachel made was bringing the knife in the first place. That was what he would say; although, obviously, none of that was going to bring their daughter back.

* * *

In most cases, a guilty verdict brought great joy to the police and prosecutors who'd worked it, but lead investigator Michael Lynch didn't enjoy this one.

"There were no winners on either side of the aisle," Detective Lynch said.

One side lost a daughter to violence, and the other side lost a daughter to prison, maybe for life. He said he was pleased at the outcome, but he found no joy in the circumstances.

The detective had been aware of problems between Rachel Wade and Sarah Ludemann long before that violent night. Charlie Ludemann had contacted the detective regarding the threats that Rachel Wade had made toward Charlie's daughter.

Lynch was a father himself, and cases like this made him worry about his own children. High-tech communications made it harder to be a young person. Teenagers were an impulsive and emotional lot. In the old days, putting distance between them cooled off youthful combatants. Today, with a variety of instant forms of communication, what might formerly have been a cooling-off period might be used to enflame a situation and send it spiraling out of control. Thank goodness, in Pinellas Park, there had not been an increase in murders because of instant communications between young people.

This case was still the exception rather than the rule. But the number of harassment and stalking cases in this age group was on the rise in Florida. Hostilities were not only growing because of text messages but also because of photographs that could be easily taken and instantaneously disseminated.

Sure, Sarah had done a better job of preserving Rachel's messages than vice versa, but Lynch was still satisfied that the battle of words, verbal and written, between the two was not a one-way street. Both girls made inflammatory statements. There were Sarah's words of antagonism on Myspace, although he felt the point was moot. Everyone was responsible for her own actions. Rachel was responsible for what she did, no matter what Sarah Ludemann might have done or said to anger her.

"Rachel needed to step back and act as an adult," Lynch said. "We forget that she is an adult, and should have had the self-control to take herself out of the picture."

Lynch added that during his investigation, he never found any evidence that Joshua Camacho wanted the girls to fight over him, either in messages from him to the girls or in girl-to-girl communications. The detective did, however, believe—based on the personalities involved—that Joshua enjoyed the fact that there were girls fighting over him. If the detective had found evidence that one or both of the girls were fighting under Joshua Camacho's instructions, Joshua might have been arrested.

"We certainly would have talked to the state attorney's office about that," Lynch concluded.

Detective Lynch never turned down a teaching moment, and he reminded anyone who might be receiving threats through their cell phone or computer to *save those messages,* and to bring them promptly to the attention of local law enforcement.

"The idea," he said, "was to nip the situation in the bud so that it didn't escalate and spiral out of control, as it did in this case."

Why, in his opinion, were young women of low self-esteem so common? A kind of "pimp and ho" subculture permeated America's youth. It was certainly evident in this case, with a flock of women fighting over one scrawny male, who seemed like a creep to outsiders.

Lynch didn't have a good answer. He could only guess. The social/sexual rules were being determined by young men. That was for certain. It was either give in to the demands or risk being kicked to the curb.

"That was Joshua Camacho in a nutshell," Lynch said. "He would use bits and pieces of those he met, and then he would trash them just as quickly as he found them."

Maybe these girls just wanted to fit in, to feel like they belonged, and perhaps they wanted to have an interesting story to tell when they got back to their friends.

"It's hard for me to believe that there are that many people out there who would allow their daughters to have such low self-esteem," Lynch admitted. He had two young daughters, who were still small, but he was very conscious of keeping their egos inflated. He and his wife tried to build their self-esteem. They hoped that when the girls were older, they would feel that no one was good enough for them. They should demand the best in how they were treated, no matter what.

Plus they were being trained to be polite and respectful of their elders, qualities that seemed lost much of the time today. His intuition told him that most parents wanted their children to be the best, strive for the best, and to insist that others treat them the best.

Taking this case specifically, Sarah's behavior was somewhat understandable. She'd been a big girl, with a weight problem. She had been teased in school; and all of a sudden, she had status because she had a boyfriend. It made a certain sense that she was willing to fight for him.

But where was Rachel coming from? Here was a girl who seemed to have everything going for her. She came from a middle-class home; both parents were still living at home; she was good-looking and popular. She could have had anything she wanted, another boyfriend, any boyfriend she wanted. In many ways, Rachel was not a typical teenager. She had lived on her own for years at that point. Very unusual.

"Heck, we've got officers here at the PPPD that still live with their parents," Lynch said. "Rachel was one of those kids who said, 'I want to be on my own. I can make it on my own.' And she did it. Until that bad night, she had been somewhat successful. She'd earned her GED. She had an apartment. She had a job." Most cases like this involved kids who were products of broken homes. Not this one.

How low was the self-esteem of this crowd's teenaged girls? There was even status in becoming pregnant. Being a baby mama allowed a young girl to lay some claim forever to the father. It was as if the young woman were saying, "Not only have I been there and done that, but the baby is proof!"

"Pinellas Park is not by any stretch of the imagination a community with an epidemic unwed pregnancy problem, but it was common in this group," Detective Lynch said.

That night Jay Hebert went on CNN's *Issues* program and pleaded his case. That brought the ire of criminal profiler Pat Brown, who said Rachel Wade should consider herself lucky that she was not charged with first-degree murder because, based on the facts as Brown understood them, this was a premeditated killing. Wade was a "jealous stalker," in Brown's opinion, as well as a psychopath.

Chapter 15

SENTENCING

Rachel's sentencing hearing was held in the same Largo, Florida, courtroom as her trial, on Friday, September 3, 2010. She wore her dark blue prison uniform. There had been a startling change in her appearance. Her youthful appearance was fading fast. Her makeup-free face had grown puffy since her conviction. She'd developed jowls. Her hair wasn't dyed blond during the year and a half she'd been in jail, and there was just as much dark as light in her hair, which now hung limp to the middle of her back.

The Ludemanns and the Wades were present. All four parents wore black. Both sets of parents gave statements at the hearing; both expressed sympathy for the other. At no time did the Ludemanns and the Wades make eye contact.

Letters written on both sides were read into the record. One of Rachel's teachers, now retired, wrote: *Concerning the Rachel Wade case, I am asking that you consider reducing her sentence. I'm sure Rachel was on the brink of cracking.*

Jo Anne Reuter, Sarah's aunt, wrote: *To say I cannot*

comprehend teenagers today is an understatement. How sad that the interaction between Rachel and Sarah had escalated with no one intervening to stop it.

Barry Wade said, "Two beautiful young girls both made the same decision to get involved with someone who not only didn't love them, but used and demeaned them. These girls were so much alike. Now they have both lost their dreams and their futures."

Charlie Ludemann said, "I'll never get to hold my daughter again, never get to see her get married, never hear her laugh at my dumb jokes. The only way I can hear her voice is when I call her cell and she says, 'Hey, this is Sarah. Leave me a message and I'll call you back.'"

When it was Gay Ludemann's turn to speak, she placed two large photos of Sarah on an easel and turned them to face the judge. "Remember, Judge Bulone, this is my daughter. She lives in a cemetery. I go visit her."

Rachel herself took the witness stand and gave a statement, which she read from a piece of paper without looking up. To the Ludemanns, she said: "'I never wanted our worlds to collide like this, especially over a boy, and a worthless boy at that. I am so sorry to be the one that caused you this pain. I need you to know that I, too, was just a teenaged girl, not a monster or the murderer, as it may seem. Some days I feel like it should have been me.'"

At that moment, Gay Ludemann did feel sorry for Rachel. She thought of how hard it must have been for Rachel to say she was sorry for killing their daughter. "And she wanted us to believe, she truly wanted us to believe that she was sorry," Gay later said.

Gay might have been feeling sympathetic, but Judge Bulone was not.

"The murder was no accident," Bulone said. "It took a lot of force to plunge that knife through skin, through fat and bone, through someone's heart."

He said he had been tempted to give Rachel Wade a life sentence. He didn't believe she was sorry for what had happened that night. He felt that when she put that knife in her purse, she was "almost hoping" she would have an opportunity to use it on Sarah.

"The issue is the defendant tried to conceal the evidence in the case, and actually did a good job of concealing it when she threw the knife onto the roof of a neighbor's house. This court will sentence her to twenty-seven years in the Department of Corrections. The actions of Rachel Wade have caused a lot of pain," Bulone said. "I hope now healing can occur."

Rachel Wade, sobbing, was led from the courtroom. Even with best behavior, she was spending the next twenty years behind bars. By the time she was once again a free woman, more than half of her life would have been spent incarcerated.

Gay Ludemann's moment of sympathy was over. She had hoped that Rachel's sentence would be twice as long. She'd been hoping that she'd be long dead by the time Rachel was released, so she would not be around to see her.

Barry Wade did the math—and was overwhelmed by the cruel chunk of Rachel's life that would be past before she could again be free.

Sitting in the spectator section during the two-hour hearing was *St. Petersburg Times* reporter Lane De-Gregory, who spent much of her time during the sentencing hearing looking for something that was not there. She kept looking for some sort of connection among Rachel Wade, her parents, and her grandparents, who were all in court. With the exception of Rachel's older brother, who never came to the courthouse for his sister's trial, Rachel's whole family was there.

DeGregory kept thinking Rachel was going to turn around and make eye contact with them, or see them and have some sort of emotional reaction. But there was nothing. It didn't seem so much like she was going out of her way to ignore them. It was more like she didn't care enough to make a connection with them.

The journalist didn't know if it was self-preservation or if Rachel was just trying to get through the moment. However, she had just learned that she was going to be put away for all these years, and Rachel still didn't want to turn around and look at them.

"You figure at a time like that she would want to look at her mother, blow her a kiss or something," DeGregory said.

Jay Hebert wasn't sure if there would be an appeal. Such a move was expensive and labor-intensive. The Wades couldn't afford it, although there was a possibility that the court might appoint a public defender to handle the appeal, as they clearly qualified for it. If there was going to be an appeal, the grounds would be that the judge's instructions to the jury were too complicated. The jury did not understand the difference between second-degree murder and manslaughter. The maximum sentence for manslaughter would have been eleven years. Asking for a second trial was risky, however, as there was always the chance that state attorneys would decide to up the ante and charge Rachel with first-degree murder, in which case a conviction might mean life behind bars without the hope of parole.

The Wades left the courthouse without comment.

When only a few stragglers remained in the courtroom,

Charlie Ludemann was overheard saying, "I'm not happy, but what can you do?"

"Where from here?" the Ludemanns were asked.

"To the cemetery," Gay said. "To tell Sarah the news."

On November 19, 2010, the case was featured on the *20/20* TV program, with Ashleigh Banfield reporting. Lisset Hanewicz told Banfield why the voice mails were the key to getting a conviction. People often said, "I'm gonna kill you," when they were upset. But Rachel had said, "I'm gonna *murder* you," and then she went out and did it. It was as if Sarah had kept those voice mails so that the world would know what had happened.

Banfield also interviewed Rachel, whose take on the events that ruined her life remained unchanged. It was Sarah's fault. Everything was Sarah's fault. She didn't hate Sarah. She hated the situation. She didn't understand what made Sarah so mad, why she came at her like that. Sarah was *with* Joshua. Sarah had everything she wanted.

Banfield asked what Joshua had? He seemed like such a *loser*. What gave him such control over his harem?

Rachel said it was the way Joshua made her *feel* when they were alone. "Like he really cared about me," Rachel said. Joshua told her he didn't care about the other girls, and she believed him. "I believe everything that he said to me," Rachel said.

Had he visited her in prison? No.

Written? No.

Did she still love him? No.

Any feelings at all for him? No.

Rachel said she "talked to Sarah" all the time, telling her that she was sorry, how much she hoped they could have been more mature, that they could have sat down and

had a civilized conversation, that they could have just
walked away. They both deserved so much better.

Rachel Wade was a sex addict. Judging from the in-
tensely prurient nature of her jailhouse correspondence, she
probably still is. Her behavior from age fourteen on—a pre-
cocious reliance on sex as a balm for her feelings—was
much like what one might expect from an abuse victim.

What made this situation blossom into tragic violence?
For one thing, according to New Jersey psychological
counselor Kathy Morelli, there is a change in brain chemistry that happens to people when they have sex. A biolog-
ical attachment forms. Brain changes that come from
having orgasms together produced potent emotions, causing normally mild people to resort to violence. Teenagers
weren't adults, so it was a strong yet immature attachment. Passion stirred up primal possessiveness.

Morelli agreed that there was a strong chance that
Rachel had problems at home. Most teen girls did not drop
out of school or run away from home because of an unwanted curfew. This wasn't to say that Barry and Janet
Wade were bad parents, but there might have been a disconnect of some sort in the parent-child relationship. Perhaps there was an underlying and undiagnosed depression
in Rachel or in the family (as this is usually hereditary). The
parental relationship was strained for some reason. It is
clear that Rachel was a difficult child with whom to cope,
and there was a mismatch in temperaments between parents
and child. (Pregnancy during the teenaged years was a
common trigger.) Date rape and promiscuity could also be
part of a constellation of behaviors that included *shoplifting*. It was clear that Rachel had very low self-esteem, beginning for whatever reason (temperamental, underlying
learning disability, underlying depression, a not-so-overt

disconnect with her parents) and then reinforced by poor decision making. Extreme anger usually masked fear, depression, and helplessness.

Joshua Camacho, on the other hand, was narcissistic. He had an inflated sense of self-importance and an exaggerated need for admiration. As was true of many narcissists, he appeared arrogantly self-assured and confident, although this may not have been the actual case. Case watchers could see by observing Joshua's behavior that he reacted poorly when things weren't going his way. He punched Sarah, pulled a gun on Rachel. His work history demonstrated a lack of ambition, perhaps because he feared competitive situations. He might be living his life avoiding the risk of failure.

Narcissists, with their intrinsic lack of regard for other's feelings, preyed on people with dependent personalities. They fed off others and enjoyed being fought over, enjoyed manipulating their sexual partners, and didn't have a well-developed sense of self. They were often abused (at least emotionally), so they got their feelings of efficacy by surrounding themselves with subservient others. Sarah, Rachel, Erin, and no doubt others were all prey for the opportunist narcissist, who was drawn to those with low self-esteem like a shark to blood.

As for the cyber bullying, Morelli believed all parents of teens should have a monitor on their child's smart phones and computers, access to his or her online social network accounts as silent friends, and they should check in to see what was being said in their minor child's world. Parents were woefully uninformed about how to parent in the cyber age and needed a presence online as silent friends. They needed to know where their teen was going in the virtual world, which was a real place, not imaginary. Cyber threats were real threats, and these needed to be reported. Sarah's friends served as the virtual bully gang egging her and Rachel on. In teenaged naivete, the Sarah camp thought it wasn't real, and no violence would occur. But it did.

The fact that the Internet played such a key role in this case was interesting to psychology professionals because the phenomenon was still so new. There was a researched and documented "online disinhibition effect" in the virtual world, a world where people were more apt to express the unedited id, for they felt protected by their online avatar.

Education regarding Internet practices was the best way to bring awareness about this effect. Those with underdeveloped identities (teens, for instance) took on avatars and railed against the world. They thought they were somehow veiled and empowered by their avatars. So adolescents who didn't have fully developed self-identities could easily get lost in their avatars, become intoxicated by their feeling of power, and allow unedited violent feelings to come to the forefront.

That point was again made through tragedy in March 2011 when there was another battle of teen tweets, this time in Brooklyn, New York. It turned out there didn't have to be a boy at the center of Internet violence. Tweeting about money could also be incendiary.

Eighteen-year-old Kayla Henriques was arrested and charged with second-degree murder for the fatal stabbing of twenty-two-year-old Kamisha Richards. The young women were friends. Kamisha gave Kayla $20 for diapers for Kayla's eleven-month-old baby; then Kamisha learned Kayla had spent the money on something else. Three days before the stabbing, the young women began a war of words on an Internet social network site, which escalated without restraint.

Kamisha Richards concluded the word portion of the

war with the phrase: Ima have the last laugh. She went to Kayla Henriques's apartment and demanded her money back. The argument started in the kitchen, and finished in the bedroom, where Richards was stabbed.

Henriques stayed calm, she said, and tried to save her friend. An ambulance was called immediately and she applied pressure to the wound, but it wasn't enough to save Kamisha Richards, who made it into the apartment's hallway before collapsing and dying.

Insults were hurled in public, which meant each girl had to be both angry and embarrassed, a volatile mix even in the most mature egos.

This was more evidence that the Internet could take a little disagreement and turn it into a big one, the social network providing mob mentality.

Maybe so, but Jamie Severino had another explanation. She believed the secret villain in this story was drugs. She felt Rachel was taking them, and they were affecting her decision-making process.

"Why else would she decide to do something stupid like killing somebody?" Jamie asked.

Ah, but Jamie Severino was not Rachel's friend. Lisa Lafrance was, and she insisted that drugs had nothing to do with Rachel's actions.

According to Lisa, Rachel's fear was what made her lash out. Rachel wasn't innocent, her longtime friend said after the trial, but she was being *way* overpunished. It was those nasty voice mails. Rachel's fear caused her to commit the crime, and it was her big mouth that earned her the long stint in prison.

Lisa attended the trial and watched that jury. She could tell they didn't get it. They were all older, and there was only one woman! When those jurors listened to the tapes, they took everything Rachel said *literally*.

A different kind of "wisdom" came from a blog called Chateau Heartiste, and its controversial column "Chicks Dig Jerks" set forth the premise that what girls *want* was *very* different from what they *said* they wanted. His argument was that women were subconsciously seeking the alpha male, and the guy who seemed most in charge was rarely the most likeable fellow.

One symptom of this was that the alpha male often attracted more than one woman; while the beta male struggled for companionship. Being a beta male, it followed, was an ugly virus of being second best, which consumed a man's soul. Extrapolating from this theory, Heartiste believed there was a part of girls' minds—with "all girls" being a constant, identical to one another in his world—that understood that being the alpha man's old lady, though full of prestige, was not always going to be the smoothest ride.

They would gripe and cry and be miserable. "I'm so over him," they would say, and that meant they were never more into him. That's why girls were a mystery to most men. A girl's perception of her own behavior was skewed.

There was a certain caveman sense to the theory, but the trouble in this case was convincing his readership that Joshua Camacho was in any way alpha. Real playas replaced compassion with instinct, he wrote. They knew what girls really wanted, and paid no attention to what girls said.

Alpha males didn't say, "Okay, baby, I want to see you, too."

They said, "Bring the movies."

Joshua had game, intense game: he was the puppet master, pulling strings, making girls cry.

Fathers of daughters should be warned, Heartiste believed. Men worried about predators in the weeds, when the real enemy for a man was his daughter's desire for bad-boy sex.

Rachel gave away her freedom. Sarah lost her life. That was the power Joshua had. Rachel still believed Joshua wanted her, even when Joshua was texting: I don't like you no more. Why are you down this street? Go home.

Long before Sarah lost her life, she lost her grip on a promising future. Veterinary plans replaced by Joshua plans.

So the tawdry world of youthful Pinellas Park in 2009 wasn't anything new. It was a typical community with the most intense misogynists being other females. It was just human nature, played out by grown-up kids trolling in cars—kids whose perceived lack of options spawned a reckless ennui.

Heartiste pointed out that Joshua Camacho's sexuality was his *only* source of power. He lived off the women he dated. He either worked at Chick-fil-A or not at all. No money, no size—Joshua's status in society came from the powerful fact that he had girls fighting over him.

Killing over him.

Epilogue

On September 8, 2010, Rachel Wade was moved to the Lowell Annex, a facility for women prisoners in Ocala, where she was known as Florida Department of Corrections Number R67662, and scheduled for release April 7, 2036, when she was forty-six years old.

There was a "Free Rachel Wade" page on Facebook, dedicated to the proposition that although Rachel was hardly an innocent bystander that night, her life was in danger at the "exact moment" she lashed out. The same social media that stoked the flames of hostility leading to Rachel's incarceration, were now being used in an attempt to set her free.

As of Halloween, 2011, the "Free Rachel Wade" page had 349 "likes."

In 2011, Detective Michael Lynch was a member of the PPPD's Community Redevelopment Policing Unit (CRPU). The unit focused on a blighted two-square-mile area of Pinellas Park's downtown, where there was an epidemic of crime. The idea was to saturate the area with police officers who worked in that area, and in that area only. Lynch conducted follow-up investigations, worked with crime analysis systems, assisted officers with day-to-day operations, and conducted training sessions for businesses and residents. The unit tried to rally businesses and residents to help clean up the community—painting, picking up the garbage, etc. The CRPU also used surplus tax revenues to help out the designated area in other ways, such as a major drainage project.

During that same year, defense attorney Jay Hebert went on a consciousness-raising campaign, lecturing at schools and elsewhere about the potential effects of the Internet social networks on youth crime.

Erin Slothower graduated from Everest University in 2009 with a degree in medical assistance and nursing. The degree enabled her to cut down from two jobs to one. She gained employment as a medical assistant at a dermatology office in St. Petersburg. That meant she could spend more time with her and Joshua's son, who stayed with her parents and her brother when she was working.

She got back with Joshua briefly, but "he wasn't the same." She didn't talk to Joshua anymore, and she was content with her "new life." She used to let herself get caught up in the social drama, but she'd grown up and had no use for that lifestyle any longer.

Erin Slothower would always have a connection to Joshua Camacho in the form of their son. As for that horrible night, and the press attention it brought her, she just wanted to be left alone.

Erin explained, "I mean, I could say a lot, but what good would it do? I just wish I had a do-over button so I could change this terrible outcome. Sarah really did love Joshua. I also know he loved her also, despite everything."

In December 2010, Lisa Lafrance took the bold step of cleaning up her act. As of this writing, she remained clean of painkillers, and was taking it one day at a time.

By 2011, Jamie Severino was out of jail, but her legal woes weren't completely over. Her daughter with Jay Camacho was three years old. Alliana Camacho had been staying in day care for a while; but in 2011, Jamie's mom, who no longer worked, babysat. Jamie was gainfully employed as a customer service representative over the phone. She was allowed to go to school, but she wasn't allowed to operate a motor vehicle. She had to wear an ankle monitor at all times.

According to police, Joshua Camacho left Florida and was living for a time in New York City with relatives. Joshua's mother refused to give Joshua's new contact information, claiming that the media had been distorting the image of her boy.

"Everyone already put his reputation down so bad, told so many lies about my boy. I don't have nothing to say," she said.

As of 2011, Joshua had returned to Florida.

During the summer of 2010, not long after Rachel Wade was convicted of murder, Jay Camacho pleaded guilty of possession of crack cocaine. As he was in violation of probation on charges of stolen goods, he was sentenced to nine months in the Gulf Correctional Institute Annex. He was released on April 21, 2011.

Charlie Ludemann has three tattoos of Sarah on the inside of his right arm: one was made when Sarah was a year old; a second, when she was ten; and a third after her death, at age eighteen.

After his daughter was cremated, Charlie had Sarah's ashes mixed with the tattoo ink so he would carry her around with him forever.

When Charlie drove his cab, he would sometimes stop at the spot where she lost her life. It was there that he felt closest to her.

He asked her why: Why did she go? Why did she leave? Why didn't she listen to him?

He'd tried so hard to protect her.

Over the years, at night, Gay Ludemann tried to soothe the ache in her heart by standing in her backyard and gazing at the sky.

She believed Sarah was a star "as bright as a diamond."

In the dark, she can be heard to say, "Good night, honey. I love you."

In March 2011, Rachel Wade wrote a letter to the author in which she apologized for not getting in touch sooner, explaining that, obviously, she "had a lot going on."

Despite her predicament, Rachel described herself much as she might've before her freedom was taken away: *I'm laid-back, carefree, fun-loving, silly, outgoing, hard-working [and] very family oriented.* She loved music, work, the beach, and animals. Her interests were art, music, and fashion.

I'm very creative, she wrote.

Her flaw was her own trusting nature. She said she always looked for the good in people, even when it wasn't there.

She also smoked *way* too many cigarettes.